4-95
31.00
B+T
VER

Teaching & Learning in the Community College

By
Terry
O'Banion
& Associates

Published by the Community College Press, a division of the American Association of
Community Colleges
One Dupont Circle, N.W.
Suite 410
Washington, D.C. 20036
(202) 728-0200

ISBN 0-87117-266-6

To my Irish Tribe:
Kerry
Erin
Kevin
Colin
Katie
and Meghan

Table of Contents

Part Three: The Outcomes

Preface

"Forget education—Let us talk rather about Teaching and Learning."

Jacques Barzun
Begin Here: The Forgotten Conditions of Teaching and Learning, 1991.

It is somewhat surprising that this book needed to have been written. From all the claims made by its leaders for decades that the community college is a learner-centered teaching college, one would have expected a glut on the market of books on teaching and learning. There are a growing number of books on community college history, mission, faculty, leadership, and special programs, but, except for K. Patricia Cross's *Accent on Learning* (1976) and *Teaching as Leading* by George Baker, John Roueche, and Rosemary Gillett-Karam (1991), there is no general book on what most agree is the heartbeat of the educational enterprise. There is much written about "education" but little about teaching and learning.

The purpose of teaching is to help students make passionate connections to learning. That is the premise on which this book is based and the theme addressed by the authors throughout.

In Part One, four authors frame the context for teaching and learning in the community college. I review the major forces that impact teaching and learning in the community college and make the case for the 1990s as a particularly opportune time for developing this emphasis. In October 1991 I keynoted the annual conference of the National Council for Staff, Program, and Organizational Development. My topic was "The 1990s: The Decade of the Teacher." The response was a sitting ovation, but an ovation nevertheless, and I at least had to stand a second time to acknowledge the response. That experience triggered the action that led to the development of this book, and the notes from that speech formed the basis for the first chapter.

In Chapter 2, John and Suanne Roueche review the important elements that must be present if a positive climate is to be developed to support effective teaching and learning. Noting that leaders must "consciously embed and shape values" that support teaching and learning, they review the key academic policies and practices that undergird a positive institutional climate, and they cite outstanding examples from leading community colleges.

Robert McCabe, in Chapter 3, cites his experience at Miami-Dade Community College in leading the nation's most thorough reform of teaching and learning in a community college. He reviews the difficulties and challenges of undertaking such major reform and outlines the leadership responsibilities of the key stake holders in bringing about such reform.

Following a review of the current context for higher education policy, Kay McClenney provides an overview of the important role that policy plays in developing a climate for teaching and learning. She suggests a "policy audit" that provided the impetus for the development of the last chapter in the book.

In Part Two, the authors provide more explicit insights into how teaching helps students make passionate connections to learning. In Chapter 5, Peter Ewell suggests that the community college needs to develop a "distinctive approach to assessment that must be developed on its own terms." Reviewing the special goals of community colleges, Ewell reviews assessment practices that have proven successful in community colleges and links these practices to improved instruction in the community college.

Drawing upon their research funded by the Ford Foundation, Dick Richardson and Diana Elliott, in Chapter 6, suggest a specially meaningful framework for understanding diversity among community college students. Describing the needs of these diverse students in their own words, the authors report the responses of community college faculty and suggest practices faculty can use to respond more effectively to student diversity.

Tom Angelo, in Chapter 7, discusses the need for and barriers to effective faculty development programs in community colleges. He calls for a shift in focus for these programs by embedding classroom research as a key component for faculty development and thus for the improvement of teaching and learning.

Pat Cross is the acknowledged inventor of classroom assessment and research. In Chapter 8, she takes classroom assessment one step further by pointing out its similarities to Total Quality Management. She believes that the merger of these two innovations "offers an unprecedented opportunity for addressing the quality challenge" that is the most serious challenge to education in the years ahead.

George Vaughan has been calling for the community college instructor to be a scholar for many years. In Chapter 9, he offers a definition of scholarship compatible with the community college mission, suggests ways to eliminate some of the barriers to faculty scholarship, and offers practical suggestions for faculty members who wish to engage in scholarship and publish the results of their work.

Roberta Matthews suggests that "learning communities enhance the quality of campus life, contribute to the development of connections beyond the college, and help prepare students for the challenges of leadership." In Chapter 10, she reviews the development of learning communities, outlining their purposes and structures, and notes the considerable impact that learning communities can have on faculty and on students. She concludes with advice on making learning communities successful, gleaned from a study of pioneers in the field.

In Chapter 11, Don Doucette points out that technology has had only limited impact on teaching and student learning in community colleges thus far, but suggests there is great potential for transforming teaching and learning by applying information technology. He cites a number of excellent examples of how technology is currently increasing both the quality of student outcomes and the productivity of the instructional process, noting the challenges and issues that arise from these applications.

For Chapter 12, Kurt Lauridsen surveyed the coordinators of selected teaching and learning centers across the United States. He presents the most recent information available about funding, organization, administration, purpose, and programs conducted by teaching and learning centers in community colleges.

In Chapter 13, Mardee Jenrette and Vince Napoli provide a succinct overview of the Miami-Dade Community College Teaching/Learning Project, now in its eighth year. There is much to be learned from this most extensive fundamental reform of teaching and learning in the modern community college.

Part Three concludes the book with three chapters that relate to outcomes of helping students make passionate connections to learning. The outcomes are not related to the success of students, but to the success of teachers and institutions that would improve student success.

Dick Alfred, in Chapter 14, reviews the elements of effective teaching, relating these to the students and the institution. He offers six essential changes that organizations need to consider if they are to develop effective teaching practices that will ensure effective student outcomes.

Building upon four concepts valued by community college faculty, Nancy LeCroy, in Chapter 15, "breaks set" to recast a framework for faculty reward and recognition. She relates this framework to the research that is known about reward and recognition but recasts it here for a refreshing approach to this topic.

Building upon McClenney's recommendation that colleges should conduct a "policy audit" and Richardson's observation that the teaching and learning climate is the visible product of an institution's invisible values, I have, in the last chapter, attempted to develop an audit to be used by institutions for reviewing the effectiveness of their teaching and learning practices. Noting that community colleges have characteristics that make them different from four-year colleges and universities in their commitment to teaching and learning, the audit provides an opportunity for community colleges to measure whether or not they are the "nation's premier teaching institutions."

—Terry O'Banion
Mission Viejo, California
February 1994

PART ONE:

The Context

Chapter 1

Teaching and Learning

A Mandate for the Nineties

BY TERRY O'BANION

T he past three decades were re-
markably busy for community colleges as they tackled the mam-
moth job of refurbishing the colleges so hastily organized and
built during the 1960s. Responding to the increasing demand for
access, leaders in the '60s and '70s were primarily interested in
structure—the structure of buildings, the structure of organizations, the structure of curricula and programs, and the structure
of political alliances. Perhaps in the creation and expansion of institutions for hordes of new students, leaders had time only to design and develop these basic structures. In any case, during this
pivotal period of community college history, leaders did not set
high priority on the teaching and learning process that must undergird all other structures if student success is to be the ultimate
achievement of community colleges.

Perhaps the great abundance of faculty members in the '60s
and '70s lulled community college leaders into believing that the

3

teaching and learning process was well tended. The unchallenged assumption was that the community college was the "teaching college," and the lack of research and publications on the part of its faculty was ironically cited as proof.

In these early days of the modern community college, "to care about students" was the only evidence required to prove that the teaching and learning process was in capable hands. It made little difference to the leaders occupied with developing and maintaining structure that most of the faculty members came from the secondary schools with little understanding of the mission and philosophy of the community college; that most of these faculty members had not been schooled in adult development theory or basic theories of learning; that most of these faculty members had little or no experience in working with the diversity of students flocking to these new opportunities for higher education; that these faculty members carried heavy teaching loads while also serving as academic advisers, participating on numerous committees, and sponsoring various student organizations; that indeed, these faculty members took pride in not conducting or publishing research. In the leaders' view, teaching and learning were natural processes adequately tended by an underprepared and overworked faculty.

In retrospect, it is a remarkable feat of courage and commitment on the part of faculties that community colleges have done as well as they have in fostering student success. While the record on helping underprepared students succeed is not so sterling, community colleges have been highly successful in preparing students for employment in vocational and technical fields and equally successful in preparing a small number of students, excluding minorities, for transfer. While this success is important, the outcomes might have bordered on the extraordinary had community college leaders and their faculties paid more attention in earlier years to teaching and learning as the heart of the community college educational enterprise. In fairness to the leaders and faculty members of the past three decades, the success stories would have been different if we had known then what we know now about instructional strategies and the measurement of outcomes.

Now that community college structures are fairly well in place and the community college is acknowledged as a key institution within the higher education framework, leaders can turn their attention to teaching and learning as the primary area for emphasis in the '90s. Indeed, leaders now have a clear mandate to place teaching and learning at the top of the educational agenda in order to repair the neglect of the past and prepare for a new future beginning in the year 2000.

The past five years have witnessed an increasing emphasis on teaching and learning in conferences, articles, books, research reports, and most importantly, educational practice. Parker J. Palmer has noted this developing emphasis: "I spend half my time traveling among colleges and universities. Everywhere I go, I find hunger among faculty to reflect on teaching and learning; a hunger that is unparalleled in the twenty-five years I have been doing this kind of work" (Palmer, Undated).

Numerous developments and forces in the late 1980s and early 1990s have contributed to this new emphasis on teaching and learning. Many of these forces have been external to the educational community, but there has also been a great deal of ferment within education that has given rise to creative innovations from practitioners and substantive policies and standards from professional leaders. A brief review of some of the major forces provides a framework for understanding the current emphasis on teaching and learning and, as illustrated in subsequent chapters in this book, on how faculty members and educational leaders are implementing this mandate in community colleges across the country.

REFORM MOVEMENT FORCES

The activities of the quality reformation that have been driving the educational agenda for almost a decade have helped usher in the more recent emphasis on teaching and learning. Most of the early reports of the reform movement did not emphasize teaching and learning, but the reports and the responses to the reports made education a highly visible national concern and helped prepare the groundwork for an emphasis on teaching and learning.

The 1983 publication of *A Nation at Risk* (National Commission on Excellence in Education, 1983) launched the reform movement in education in this country and has since triggered more than 30 national reports and more than 150 state task force reports. Most of the early reports emphasized the problems of education and made recommendations primarily related to its structure. More recently, some of the reports focused on the teacher teaching and the student learning as areas for major reform.

In 1988 the Commission on the Future of Community Colleges, established by the American Association of Community Colleges, issued the landmark report *Building Communities: A Vision for a New Century*. This document may well be the most important document ever written on the community college. It has certainly been the most widely distributed and read in recent years. Although the report addressed numerous structural issues confronting the community college, it emphasized the community college's commitment to teaching in one of its key statements—"Building communities through dedicated teaching is the vision and inspiration of this report" (p. 8). With statements such as, "The community college should be the nation's premier teaching institution. Quality instruction should be the hallmark of the movement" (p. 25), the *Building Communities* report helped usher in, more than any other document in recent community college literature, the emphasis on teaching and learning.

Even the most research-oriented American universities are examining ways in which they can initiate new projects in teaching and learning. For instance, Ernest Boyer, in *Scholarship Reconsidered: Priorities of the Professoriate* (1990), proposes a redefinition of faculty scholarship to include discovery, integration of knowledge, teaching, and service. Faculty commissions at Stanford, Berkeley, and Harvard quote heavily from this report as they attempt to focus new attention on teaching as an important service of the university equal to that of research. *Scholarship Reconsidered* has outsold every publication ever distributed by the Carnegie Foundation for the Advancement of Teaching, indicating the seriousness with which readers are taking this new emphasis.

More recently the Office of the President of the United States has helped create an environment focusing on education as a national priority. The Bush administration issued *America 2000: An Education Strategy* (1991), a document suggesting that it is time to quit issuing reports and instead initiate a revolution to develop new schools for a new world. While the emphasis in this report is primarily on structure and involvement with business, there is nevertheless an underlying focus on teaching and learning, particularly in the proposal to develop academies in every state to train teachers in core subjects. The authors of the report recognize that "the quality of the teachers and teaching is essential to meeting our goals" (p. 68).

While many educators have reacted with cynicism to the report as well as to former President Bush's claim to be the "education president," at least there is some concern about education from the White House. This initial concern, and the continuing attention given to education under President Clinton, who played a key role in issuing the *America 2000* report, supports the contention that teaching and learning will be key themes for the rest of this decade.

POLITICAL FORCES

In addition to the direct involvement of the White House in educational strategy, other political forces are moving education to the forefront of the nation's agenda. The accountability movement, for example, initiated in states such as Florida, Texas, and New Jersey by direct acts of their legislatures, has mandated increasing interest in teaching and learning. Outcomes assessment, designed to measure what students have actually learned in classes, programs, and colleges, has become the primary focus of the assessment movement. As outcomes assessment becomes more sophisticated, researchers will begin to link learning outcomes to patterns and processes of teaching.

Accreditation is a self-enforced political force in education that has the power to bring about enormous change. In the past, accreditation standards focused on the extent to which an institution fulfilled its stated mission, a flexible approach to provide for the diversity of institutions included in American higher education.

Standards were relevant to structures and programs that reflected mission and were often limited to simple measures such as the number of books in the library.

In the last decade, the regional accrediting associations have become much more assertive in establishing more relevant standards, and they now require institutions to include outcomes assessment as a key part of their programs. Several of the regional accrediting associations emphasize the institution's responsibility for ensuring that diversity among the teaching faculty reflects student diversity. While most higher education institutions, and especially community colleges, have been making progress in measuring student success and diversifying their faculties, the accreditation process is a powerful force for encouraging those directions within a specific timetable.

The unionization of community college faculty has also been a force in bringing teaching and learning to the forefront of the educational agenda. After three decades of steady growth, approximately 60 percent of all public community college campuses have been unionized, according to the National Center for the Study of Collective Bargaining in Higher Education.

While union programs do not usually emphasize processes of teaching and learning, they certainly emphasize the conditions in which teachers teach and, therefore, serve as an important force in underscoring the key role of teaching and learning in the institution. Indirectly, the union movement has contributed to teaching and learning by separating some of the most difficult faculty issues such as salary, benefits, and working conditions from discussions regarding curriculum development and review, teaching processes, and student evaluation. Faculty senates and councils, unencumbered by these more personal issues addressed by unions, can work in concert with institutional administrators to improve teaching and learning.

INNOVATIVE FORCES

In the great growth period of the 1960s, innovation became a hallmark of the community college movement as colleges experimented with a variety of structures and programs reflecting their comprehensive mission. During the '70s and early '80s, community colleges were fine-tuning the innovations of the '60s and beginning to deal with declining resources and other realities that slowed the pace of innovation dramatically. The mid-'80s saw a renaissance of innovation in the community college, perhaps related to the quality reformation throughout the educational system. The reasons for the renaissance of innovation and a review of the variety of innovations that emerged in community colleges in the late '80s are detailed in *Innovation in the Community College* (O'Banion, 1989).

At the vanguard of this most recent renaissance were innovations related to institutional systems that support student success. Capitalizing on the availability of information technology, community colleges designed student information systems to assist in assessing, advising, registering, and monitoring the progress of students. Information technology made it possible for community colleges to track their students and to intervene with prescriptive programs to ensure retention and achievement. These were innovations that supported teaching and learning, and soon faculty members began to experiment with instructional innovations that would complement the success of the student information systems.

Foremost among these innovations was classroom research, a concept first suggested by K. Patricia Cross, as an approach designed to move the quality reformation from institutional structures and programs monitored by committees and administrators directly into the classroom to be implemented and monitored by individual faculty members. Classroom research became classroom assessment, the purpose of which is to provide faculty members with techniques to examine the effectiveness of their teaching during the time that their teaching is taking place. In their book, *Classroom Assessment Techniques: A Handbook for Faculty* (1988), Cross and Angelo describe thirty specific techniques that faculty members can use to check their teaching against learning outcomes they expect or desire.

A nonthreatening and practical approach to improving teaching, classroom assessment is spreading rapidly through education and particularly the community colleges. Hundreds of community

9

colleges now use classroom assessment as a major element in their formal staff development programs, and a number of community colleges have developed faculty support groups that create their own assessment techniques. More than any other recent innovation in education, classroom assessment emphasizes the importance of teaching and learning at the grassroots level.

A number of formal programs exist in which faculty members can share ideas regarding teaching and can learn specific instructional skills. The Great Teachers Seminars and the Instructional Skills Workshops are good examples of these staff development programs offered as national workshops or tailored for individual colleges. The Great Teachers Seminars, conceived several decades ago, were originally reserved for a few "great teachers" who met each summer to share their insights on teaching. This excellent form of staff development has since become commonplace and is available to hundreds of teachers throughout the year. The Instructional Skills Workshops, designed and developed by Canadian educators, is based upon research and consists of structured lessons designed to help faculty members improve their instructional skills. As with the Great Teachers Seminars, there are a number of national workshops that can be tailored for individual colleges.

In each decade, creative faculty members experiment with learning communities. According to Gabelnick et al., "Learning communities create a unique environment of social and intellectual belonging that is important at any college; they are particularly valuable in large institutions and commuter campuses, where close personal contacts and community making are problematic at best.... While stressing the centrality of intellectual endeavors, learning communities provide close personal contact and continuous social support—a clear message that college need not be a lonely enterprise" (1990, p. 64). Although they take many different forms, learning communities characteristically involve from twenty-five to 100 students working with three or four faculty members. Built around common themes, they provide participants with an integrated learning experience in a community environment.

In the late '80s, the state of Washington initiated an effort, based at Evergreen State College in cooperation with Washington community colleges, to restructure the curriculum and revitalize teaching through learning communities. Today, every community college in Washington has a number of learning communities that have proven highly effective in retaining students and improving their achievement, especially in composition courses. In addition to serving students well, the learning communities have proved to be highly stimulating opportunities for faculty renewal.

The Distinguished Research Chair has long been an accepted concept in universities, bringing distinction to the leading research universities that can afford such chairs. In the community college, where the focus is on teaching rather than research, such chairs were once nonexistent. The first Distinguished Teaching Chair in the community college was established in 1973 at Edison Community College, Florida. It was a chair of nursing supported by local hospitals. Several other community colleges have also established individual teaching chairs usually in nursing or other vocational/technical fields. In June 1989, Miami-Dade Community College, Florida, initiated a faculty endowed chair program with a goal of establishing 100 endowed chairs. The Faculty Endowed Chair at Miami-Dade is designed to serve as the capstone of a comprehensive teaching and learning project—the best example in the community college today of how an institution can muster its resources to revitalize and reform teaching and learning. Beginning with a statement on teaching and learning values in 1987, Miami-Dade faculty have now developed a statement of faculty excellence, used to select and orient new faculty, evaluate and promote faculty, and encourage and provide student feedback on teaching. Professional staff development programs support faculty in developing and maintaining excellence in the teaching and learning process. On June 10, 1992, Miami-Dade awarded twenty-five faculty members Faculty Endowed Chairs, the first large-scale implementation of this concept in the nation.

In the last ten years American business has been applying the concepts of Total Quality Management (TQM) to improve services and products in order to compete. Edwards Deming proved

11

the value of these concepts decades earlier in Japan. More recently, American educators began exploring TQM concepts for their applicability in managing American colleges. Initial applications have focused on structures and systems such as registration, payroll, physical plant, and mail distribution. Writing in the *AAHE Bulletin*, Ted Marchese suggests that the goal of TQM in education is to develop an institutional culture that is "quality-driven, customer-oriented, marked by teamwork, and avid about improvement" (1991, p. 4). Fully implemented in an educational institution, TQM promises nothing less than a total restructuring of the institutional culture, the management systems, and the processes for creating change including the improvement of teaching and learning.

In a few institutions, faculty members are beginning to apply TQM concepts to the classroom, and the emphasis on customer-oriented teaching reflects similar values evident in classroom assessment and learning communities. In 1994 TQM appears to be ready for widespread experimentation and application in community colleges. If TQM is widely adopted, it is likely to be incorporated into the classroom in creative ways that will underscore teaching and learning as the key focus for ensuring total quality.

SOCIAL AND DEMOGRAPHIC FORCES

Many social and demographic forces impact the community college, but three in particular—the changing faculty, the changing students, and the expanding mission—have significant implications for teaching and learning.

A great number of community college faculty members are retiring, and many will continue to retire throughout the '90s. The replacement of these faculty members provides college leaders with an opportunity to influence the future of the community college for decades to come.

Many of the retiring faculty were selected in the '60s, when community college leaders were not as sophisticated as they are today about the psychology of learning, the importance of diversity, and the skills needed to teach in a community college.

Community colleges have been assigned the most difficult tasks in all of higher education, requiring the very best possible teachers if they are to succeed in coming decades. Community colleges must give high priority to identifying and selecting these new teachers and organizing staff development programs to serve their needs. As community colleges face these challenges, there will be a renewed interest in teaching and learning.

Although few graduate programs are designed specifically for the preparation of community college instructors, a great deal of reform effort directed at the preparation of public school teachers might influence community college instruction. The Holmes Group is a national organization of deans of colleges of education committed to reforming the way teachers are prepared. The Carnegie Foundation for the Advancement of Teaching is supporting the National Board for Professional Teaching Standards, which hopes to develop national teaching standards to credential outstanding teachers in the United States. If these reform initiatives become successful, teachers who are influenced by them could gravitate to the community college with new skills, better prepared to address the special challenges of teaching there.

Whereas students in four-year colleges and universities tend to be homogeneous along a number of dimensions, such as full-time, young, residential, and prepared for college, community college students are as diverse as American society in general and share special characteristics related to the special nature of community colleges. The majority of community college students attend part-time, hold jobs, are older than their university counterparts, are first-generation college attendees, and are often underprepared for college-level courses. Many are single parents, minorities, physically challenged, senior citizens, or recent immigrants. They tend to come from lower socioeconomic levels than do students in four-year colleges and universities, and they tend to score lower on measures of self-esteem. A great many community college students are unsure about their educational goals and sign up for community college courses because they have nothing better to do.

New instructors facing a class of community college students for the first time often find traditional teaching methods ineffective.

What works for a class of high school students of the same age or a class of university students of similar socioeconomic backgrounds and SAT scores often does not work in a class of community college students with no common denominator except membership in the human race. Given this diversity, it is no wonder the community college is called the "teaching college," and community college teachers are among the most creative innovators in all of higher education. As the nation continues to become more diverse and even learns to celebrate diversity, community colleges will become the primary institutions of higher education that reflect this diversity. In so doing, teaching and learning will become even more visible and more significant as instructors respond to the overwhelming challenge of providing successful educational opportunities for the most diverse group of college students in the history of the world.

While community colleges respond to a changing faculty and an increasing diversity of students, they are also responding to social forces that cause them to expand and realign their mission. Ideally, community colleges are designed and committed to responding to the special needs of their communities. In recent years, community colleges have been broadening their definition of community in serving business and industry and deepening their definition of community by addressing some of the more difficult social problems.

Community colleges are increasingly called upon by business leaders and political leaders to play a major role in preparing the work force of the future. Every national commission that has studied the U.S. economy in recent years has recommended the community college as a key institution in providing work force training for the nation.

As community colleges begin to explore new alliances with business and industry, they will be required to examine new approaches to teaching and learning for the special clients they serve. For the millions they will earn in contracts with business and industry, community colleges will learn new ways of assessing client needs, new ways of delivering instruction, and new ways of evaluating success, their own success as instructors and the success of their clients. These experiences may influence the more traditional college programs. The business and industry institute or program has the potential of becoming an in-house experimental laboratory in teaching and learning for the rest of the college. In this way, teaching and learning may be reviewed by traditional faculty members with fresh perspectives.

For decades, community colleges have been involved in community development through a series of courses, most often noncredit, ranging from leisure time activities to skills upgrading. In addition, community colleges serve their communities as centers of culture and entertainment through a variety of musical, theatrical, and artistic programs. Recently, a number of community colleges have extended this commitment to their communities by tackling difficult social issues.

When Iowa farmers began to lose their farms because of the economic conditions of recent years, Kirkwood Community College in Cedar Rapids responded by organizing family counseling programs, career counseling, and worker retraining programs. When environmental groups in the timber industry clashed over the spotted owl in Oregon, Lane Community College hosted several community forums to bring representatives of the two groups and many other agencies together to work on solutions. Lane faculty helped create a national clearinghouse related to conflicts between environmental groups and industries and organized special retraining programs for laid-off timber workers. At Miami-Dade Community College, the Medical Center Campus has created the Overtown Neighborhood Project and has adopted a neighborhood next to the college in which 50 percent of the residents earn incomes below the poverty level. The college has initiated a number of projects to deal with teenage pregnancy, homelessness, housing, drugs, crime, and education. One major effort is designed to provide child care and residential living for welfare mothers as they attend classes.

These imaginative programs in community development require faculty members to "get out on the street" as they learn new ways of serving their communities. These new challenges in new settings with new kinds of students will require faculty members

15

to experiment with teaching and learning. Faculty will engage these "new customers" carefully, assessing their needs and prescribing learning strategies with a new sensitivity. There will be a premium on flexibility and responsiveness. As they participate in these new experiences, they will be renewed, and they will bring their new knowledge and experiences into the traditional enclaves of the college. Teaching and learning can be transformed in this process to the benefit of all involved.

TECHNOLOGICAL FORCES

Among higher education institutions, community colleges have been avid users of information technology. They have been leaders in applying technology to student information systems, to institutional management systems, and to the instructional process. Unfortunately, these applications have been used, for the most part, only to speed up the old ways of doing business. The community college of today looks very much like the community college of 1963, except that information technology helps faculty and administrators do their work faster and, in some cases, more efficiently. The revolution that was to come in education with the widespread use of information technology is still anticipated.

A number of national leaders have suggested that information technology, if applied in creative ways, could revolutionize the educational process much in the same way as the printing press. Robert C. Heterick, Jr., appointed president of EDUCOM in early 1993, said "Technology is the primary vehicle by which institutions of higher education are going to re-engineer the teaching and learning process" (DeLoughry, 1992a, p. A17).

If the teaching and learning process is to be re-engineered through information technology, there must be breakthrough applications in at least three areas related to increasing productivity (more students learning more without increased numbers of faculty). First, information technology must be used to increase the number of students an individual faculty member can teach. Second, colleges must provide sophisticated, organized learning experiences driven by information technology for large numbers of students that are monitored or supported by a teacher or teacher's aide. Third, colleges must design and provide sophisticated, organized learning experiences driven by information technology for large numbers of students that stand alone without any assistance from teachers or teacher's aides. When colleges are able to negotiate these changes with faculty unions and other groups within the institution, teaching and learning can be truly re-engineered.

The groundwork is currently being prepared for the development and successful implementation of these changes. Through its ten-year project, "The Community College and the Computer," the League for Innovation in the Community College has made a major contribution to preparing community colleges for dramatic changes in their use of information technology. Working with twenty major computer corporations, the League, through its member colleges, has developed and field-tested over twenty-five specific applications of information technology with support of more than $30 million. Six monographs developed by leading community college experts and computer corporation consultants on key topics of information technology have been distributed free to every community college in the United States and Canada. Some of the monographs have been adopted by several states as official guidelines. The League also hosts the only national conference on information technology in the community college, and attendance increases each year. The 1993 conference attracted more than 2,000 participants, the great majority of whom were faculty.

While this League project serves as a national focal point to stimulate interest and share knowledge about information technology, the innovative applications occur on the campuses of community colleges under the direction of creative administrators and faculty. Distance education redefines the parameters of the traditional classroom and challenges faculty to sharpen their communication skills. At Kirkwood Community College a handful of faculty members teach hundreds of students across seven counties through one of the nation's most sophisticated telecommunications networks. Functionally illiterate citizens by the thousands flock to special computer centers staffed by volunteers located throughout Charlotte, North Carolina, to raise their reading and math levels. This Adult Basic Literacy Education program, developed and coordinated by Central Piedmont Community College, has been cited as one of the most effective in the nation. Karen Schwalm at Glendale Community College in Phoenix, Arizona, has been able to reach the "unvoiced or marginalized" community college student in her composition courses through her Electronic Journal. Using pen names to ensure anonymity, the students communicate with each other via computers in ways they never would in regular classes. Using information technology, Glendale Community College has figured out a way to build a sense of community in a class and even throughout the college in an Electronic Forum in which students and faculty link up to share ideas on a variety of planned and unplanned topics.

These applications of information technology, and hundreds like them taking place in community colleges everywhere, are the precursors for even more advanced use of information technology for re-engineering the teaching/learning process. The rate of change will be even more rapid in the next ten years than in the past ten because of this basic foundation and because students attending the community college are increasingly technologically literate. The Nintendo Generation will require colleges and faculties to respond to their needs. As important, the infrastructures are already in place through telephones, televisions, and satellites to make information technology immediately available to every faculty member and student in the country. Community colleges have been leaders in experimenting with these networks, from the national Community College Satellite Network of AACC to the Cuyahoga Community College State Network in Ohio.

There is growing evidence of the pervasiveness of information technology in education and in community colleges. In 1970 the education industry spent $2 billion on computers; in 1990 that figure rose to $8 billion. In 1970 only 1 percent of that amount was spent on instruction, but in 1990, 50 percent of that amount was spent on instruction. Campus purchases of computers in community colleges has increased 50 percent from the 1988–89 to 1989–90 academic years. Today, 16 percent of community college students own computers, and 37.5 percent of community college faculty own computers (DeLoughry, 1992b, p. A17). Even in difficult financial times, community colleges continue to purchase computers for instructional purposes as a reflection of the emphasis on teaching and learning.

THE TIME IS RIGHT FOR CHANGE

The forces briefly noted in this chapter—reform movement forces, political forces, innovative forces, social and demographic forces, and technological forces—support the mandate that community college leaders will have to transform teaching and learning in this decade. The Quality Reformation has called for nothing less than the complete overhaul of education. State legislators are mandating specific changes in that overhaul. The changing nature of the community college faculty in terms of kind and number offers a window of opportunity for change. As creative community colleges realign their missions, creative community college faculties are experimenting with new forms of teaching and learning as never before. Information technology promises new breakthroughs.

There has never been a more propitious moment for the community college to leap forward in its continuing commitment to quality education. The signs are right for a major breakthrough that will place teaching and learning at the heart of the community college enterprise. The chapters in this book are important beacons that help light the way to the transformation of teaching and learning that will become the hallmark of the community college by the year 2000.

REFERENCES

America 2000: An Education Strategy. Washington, D.C.: U.S. Department of Education, 1991.

Boyer, Ernest. *Scholarship Reconsidered: Priorities of the Professoriate*. Princeton, N.J.: Carnegie Foundation for the Advancement of Teaching, 1990.

Commission on the Future of Community Colleges. *Building Communities: A Vision for a New Century.* Washington, D.C.: American Association of Community Colleges, 1988.

Cross, K. Patricia and Thomas A. Angelo. *Classroom Assessment Techniques: A Handbook for Faculty.* Ann Arbor: National Center for Research to Improve Postsecondary Teaching and Learning, 1988.

DeLoughry, Thomas J. "EDUCOM's New Leader Expected to Play a Key Role in Promoting Technology." *The Chronicle of Higher Education*, October 7, 1992a, pp. A17–A18.

_____. "Information Technology." *The Chronicle of Higher Education*, November 4, 1992b, pp. A17–18.

Gabelnick, F., J. MacGregor, R.S. Matthews, and B.L. Smith. *Learning Communities: Creating Connections Among Students, Faculty and Disciplines.* New Directions in Learning, no. 41. San Francisco: Jossey-Bass, 1990.

Marchese, Ted. "TQM Reaches the Academy." *AAHE Bulletin*, 1991, *44* (3), pp. 3–9.

National Commission on Excellence in Education. *A Nation at Risk.* Washington, D.C.: U.S. Department of Education, 1983.

O'Banion, Terry (Ed.). *Innovation in the Community College.* New York: ACE/Macmillan, 1989.

Palmer, Parker J. Personal Communication in a flyer advertising the National Teaching and Learning Forum. Washington, D.C.: National Teaching and Learning Forum, undated.

Terry O'Banion *is executive director of the League for Innovation in the Community College.*

Chapter 2

Creating the Climate for Teaching and Learning

By John E. Roueche and Suanne D. Roueche

No educational organization has ever undertaken a mission as seemingly impossible as that of the open-door community college. Not only do community colleges accept underprepared and nontraditional students, they actually devise marketing and recruitment strategies to attract them to campus and into academic programs. More and more of today's entering students are unprepared for the academic reality of the college experience—they are working too many hours, they have too many family responsibilities, they are not focused on the personal and professional goals necessary to persist in an academic environment, they come without support from family and/or friends, and they are "unclear" on what they wish to do with their lives. This increasing "diversity" creates major difficulties and problems for the community college as a teaching/learning institution and for those faculty and staff who labor mightily to help the institution make good on the promise of the open door.

McGrath and Spear (1991) suggest that this diversity and homogeneity of students has created an impossible situation for faculty who strive to keep standards high and who wish the first two years of the community college to be somewhat parallel to the quality of university curriculum. They suggest that community colleges have "watered down" their programs of study and that the entering nontraditional student has little chance of graduating from the community college, much less of going on for more advanced professional preparation in a four-year college or university. They lament the multiple responsibilities placed on community college faculty that have little to do with student intellectual development. In sum, they suggest that community college faculties are being asked to be all things to all of these diverse student groups and that such demands not only are unreasonable, but also greatly undermine the academic integrity of the community college.

Community colleges have few options regarding their admissions policies. All public institutions have policies established by state law, and they usually translate to an acceptance of any student "who can profit from instruction."

The issue is not about closing the open door and/or putting in an academic "floor" for the open door. The issue facing community colleges is how to accept more and more of these "at-risk" students while keeping academic standards and outcomes at a level of academic respectability. This requires the development of a college climate that supports teaching and learning.

A college's climate is a learned pattern that develops over time, resulting in a commonly held understanding of the accepted way to think, feel, and behave. Climate develops in organizations as "common ground"—those values and beliefs held common by the various constituencies composing the institution, namely, the board of trustees, the campus leadership team, the faculty, the support staff, and those of the community served by the college. In his pioneering work, *Organizational Culture and Leadership*, Schein (1985) views the basic model of climate development as a matter of leaders consciously embedding and shaping values, attitudes, beliefs, and ultimately behaviors in the organization.

In a college setting, what the leadership pays attention to, re-acts to emotionally, models, rewards, sanctions, and values are the most powerful mechanisms for embedding culture and climate. In this chapter, attention is focused on leadership strategies that lead to a positive teaching and learning climate.

COLLEGE VALUES

Major responsibility for accommodating at-risk students while keeping academic standards high must rest with the college president and the governing board that selects the president. Rules, regulations, and policies always speak to and reflect the basic values of any organization, including colleges and family units. It is the role and function of the college leadership team, in collaboration with faculty, to establish value-based academic policies and procedures that address the difficulties placed on the institution by an open-admissions policy. Too often, open admissions has been interpreted by community colleges as unhindered access to any course and/or program of study. This policy is usually interpreted as the students' "right to fail" in its purest sense. Sadly for the students, this particular open-access policy usually leads to a student's failure and/or withdrawal within the first six weeks of the fall semester.

Policies and procedures flow from the deeply held values and beliefs of a college community, creating a distinctive college environment and climate. In its master plan for 2001 ("The Facet Report," St. Petersburg Junior College, 1990), St. Petersburg Junior College (SPJC), Florida, defines the values of its ideal community college as follows:

- Concern for student success permeates all areas of the college
- Excellence in teaching and learning is known and embraced throughout the institution as the primary reason for the college's existence
- An identifiable, shared-value system based on equality of opportunity is the foundation for a sense of community within the college whereby students, faculty, administrators,

23

and staff see themselves and each other as important, respected participants in the educational process
- Students and employees of all ages, races, and ethnic groups feel accepted, cared about, and comfortable learning and working at the college
- Relationships among administrators, faculty, and staff are marked by mutual respect and appreciation for each other's roles and responsibilities, by open communication in an atmosphere of healthy and friendly debate, and by shared power in accomplishing the mission and goals of the college
- Communicated to the community at large and within the institution, there is a clear sense of purpose, direction, and vision arrived at and sustained especially by the leadership of the college president
- College leadership does not dilute the institution's main interests, or what it does best, in attempting to be everything to everybody, yet an atmosphere is maintained that allows innovation and risk taking; that nurtures an entrepreneurial and intrapreneurial spirit; and that permits expeditious response to promising opportunities
- By visionary leadership, vitality in teaching, commitment to mission, and openness to change and the free discussion of ideas, the college generates and sustains a contagious educational excitement
- The institutional personality, grave by nature and mission, includes, however, a dimension of mirth
- The highest educational and ethical standards are expected and adhered to
- Public trust and confidence are pursued and achieved through management, fiscal, and instructional practices that are efficient, productive, and successful
- Accountability is practiced at all levels of responsibility and changes made when necessary

According to the SPJC master plan document, a focus on excellence in teaching and learning is recognized and celebrated throughout the college community and demonstrated in college policies, procedures, staffing patterns, publications, activities, reward programs, and quality of classroom space and laboratories. A definite climate that values even more quality in teaching and learning is an anticipated outcome.

It is one thing to care about and strive for excellence in teaching and learning; it is quite another to achieve the variables involved in creating a teaching situation where community college faculty and staff can actually be successful with entering students. The SPJC master plan identifies early the importance of policies and procedures that create a teaching climate where quality and excellence are possible outcomes.

ACADEMIC POLICIES AND PROCEDURES

The academic policies and procedures developed and implemented by a college speak to deeply held values and beliefs and outline vividly the parameters of institutional climate. A careful analysis of any institution's policies and procedures will lead to a basic understanding of the institution's belief system in place at any point in time. Following are those academic policies and procedures that promote teaching and learning effectiveness in collegiate settings.

Proactive Pre-enrollment

More than a decade ago, Jefferson Community College (JCC), Kentucky, developed a Recruit and Retention and Attrition (RRA) project to address an institutionwide problem: the need to personalize relationships with prospective students who expressed interest in JCC. For the past decade, when students write or call the college, not only are they notified promptly about their admission, but they also receive a letter of welcome and greeting from the division chairperson of their intended major, as well as a letter from the appropriate academic department. This expanded system of personalizing communication with students creates a feeling of welcome, acceptance, and personalized attention. Feedback from JCC students since the project began indicates that the additional attention increased their commitment to completing

25

enrollment and to spending quality time in a collegiate setting. Student persistence to course completion also increased.

Concern for the student who demonstrates interest in JCC is expressed throughout the college. For example, the classified staff have developed strategies for improving student advising by providing even more accurate and proper information, directing troubled and/or confused students to appropriate personnel, and personally referring students in an effort to humanize the experience. Students at JCC are not "sent" to another office; they are personally escorted by faculty and staff. Data from JCC over many years indicate that student retention has been positively affected by these proactive pre-enrollment efforts.

At Paradise Valley Community College in the Maricopa County Community College District, Arizona, support staff play a critical role in proactive and positive pre-enrollment. The college furnishes staff members with official college blazers and name tags during the preadmission and registration period. These employees are visible across the campus from the parking lots to the entrance ways and are stationed throughout the campus buildings. Their self-initiated responsibility is to meet and greet all visitors to campus, creating a warm and hospitable first impression for students during the critical week of advisement and registration. The result is a perceived "caring college community" that makes students feel welcome on their first visit to campus.

Salt Lake Community College, Utah, is also striving to create an "invitational campus" climate, using advanced honor students to help with proactive pre-enrollment and creating positive first impressions. All of these colleges report better engagement of entering freshmen and more positive behavior during the important first weeks of the fall semester.

Orientation and Advisement

Students who enroll in open-door colleges are more in need of proper socialization and enculturation to postsecondary education than any other group of learners. Yet it is the four-year colleges and universities that require (not recommend or suggest) a full week of orientation for all entering students to enhance the likelihood that they will graduate. Universities intend (a deeply held value) for their students not only to graduate, but to savor and relish the quality of their undergraduate days forever. University orientation is an effort to socialize, to enculturate, and to embed the academic values held dear in a university climate.

Orientation is important for community college students; it should not mean a one-day experience where all entering freshmen are greeted by the college president and all other college officials in a large auditorium and/or gymnasium and given bits and pieces of information relative to college life. Beal and Noel (1980) have documented that college orientation programs can improve the retention of freshmen by more than 20 percent—if the orientation experience provides quality time for interaction between an entering freshman and a mentor who has been assigned to the student. First, and ideally, the mentor should be a faculty member who teaches in the student's proposed field of specialization. If an entering freshman leaves orientation having spent quality time with a faculty member and feeling honestly welcomed and valued, the chance of enrolling and persisting increases dramatically. Second, Beal and Noel found that similar improvements in student persistence occurred if an orientation program facilitated the establishment of a student-peer relationship, preferably with a second-year or upper-division student.

Lord Fairfax Community College, Virginia, has developed an excellent handbook for academic advising loaded with critical "keys to success" for all entering students. Lord Fairfax also works hard to prepare the faculty adviser-mentor to understand the professional qualities and attributes necessary to achieve the intended positive socialization of entering students. At Lord Fairfax, a good adviser:

- Is personally and professionally interested in being an adviser
- Listens attentively, attempting to hear all aspects of a student's expressed problems
- Sets aside enough regularly scheduled time to adequately meet the advising needs of students assigned

- Knows college policy and practice in sufficient detail to provide students with accurate, usable information
- Refers students to other sources of information and assistance when referral seems to be the best student-centered response
- Attempts to understand student concerns from a student point of view
- Views long-range planning as well as immediate problem solving as an essential part of effective advising
- Shares advising skills with working colleagues who also are actively involved with advising
- Continually attempts to improve both the style and substance of the advising role
- Willingly and actively participates in adviser training programs (Lord Fairfax Community College, 1991)

The college has also synthesized and consolidated the research on excellent advisement and intervention strategies, and those faculty and staff involved in mentoring and orientation are well equipped and well trained for the assignment before they accept this responsibility.

Orientation programs can produce powerful and positive results and should be in place in every community college. Entry-level orientation programs should be followed by formal orientation courses throughout the freshman year. Here again, most universities offer such courses during the freshman year to further socialize and enculturate beginning students. These university courses are sometimes called "college survival courses," "college success courses," or "the freshman year experience." Community college students need the reinforcement provided by these courses, namely, more attention to personal motivation, time management, the development of study skills, values clarification and career goal exploration, and good planning. The combination of "intake" orientation programs coupled with a year-long one- or two-credit-hour formal orientation course will yield tremendous dividends for community college students.

Adirondack Community College, New York, developed a number of freshman-year orientation options to address its self-described "revolving-door" problem—resulting in high attrition and low achievement. The freshman-year options available to each full-time student focus on the relationship among faculty, staff, and students and provide students with the best chance to succeed in their first semester at the college.

The Freshman Seminar is required for every first-time, full-time, nontransfer student identified as in need of one of the other programs. This one-credit course, taught by the student's faculty adviser, introduces first-time students to campus resources, presents college skills building, and encourages the development of a significant relationship between each student and his/her adviser.

The College Survival Option, for students with weak academic backgrounds, focuses on countering the failures students may have experienced (due to lack of academic skills and/or low self-esteem) by creating a very challenging but supportive college environment. Students enroll in English, math, an elective, and HRD 100 ("College Learning: Theory and Practice"). HRD 100, which is team-taught by the student's counselor and by math and English instructors, focuses on helping students obtain a feeling of academic self-confidence and motivating them to continue seeking academic success.

An Honors Seminar involves two required seminars—HRD 199 (encouraging students to articulate important interdisciplinary issues and questions) and HRD 299-Honors Independent Study (giving students an opportunity to work closely with a faculty mentor)—plus three honors courses from at least two different divisions. To prepare the honors student to transfer to a four-year institution, both writing and research are valued and healthy competition is encouraged.

Developmental Studies is a precollege program designed to help new full-time students acquire college-level skills in reading, writing, and math. This intensive one-semester, noncredit program offers classroom instruction and one-on-one tutoring for high school graduates or GED holders who do not possess the skill level necessary to succeed in college coursework.

As a result of implementing the Freshman Year Experience, more students with broader capabilities have been able to attend

Adirondack Community College and begin a college career in which they can succeed and be challenged. Eighty-seven percent of first-time students in fall 1988 returned to Adirondack Community College the following spring. The retention rate is five percent higher than the typical fall semester from 1981-1987 and continues to remain five to seven percent higher than in previous years (Adirondack Community College, "The Freshman Year Experience," 1991).

Academic-Personal Assessment

Most American colleges and universities strongly favor and practice mandatory assessment of all entering freshmen. In many states (Texas, Florida, New Jersey, and others), entry-level assessment is now required by law to properly identify those students needing compensatory and/or remedial work.

Those colleges that have implemented thorough assessment practices followed by directive placement policies have seen dramatic improvements in student persistence and achievement. Better assessment and placement should not be interpreted as a recommendation to close the open door. To the contrary, students should be assessed at entry to make certain they have the skills, the necessary prerequisites, and the attributes needed to have a reasonable chance of success in college classes, and to refer those students with deficiencies to remedial programs.

Entry-level tests to determine student academic preparation are a self-evident need with an open-door policy, but assessment should always be more intensive than just a cursory examination of a student's ability to read, write, speak, study, and figure! Assessment protocol should also determine the number of hours that a student is working. This information is as critical to the adviser and/or faculty member as a math score might be. For example, a student working more than twenty hours a week should be dissuaded from anything resembling a full academic load. Assessment should also seek to discover if the entering student is attending college with financial assistance and with support and encouragement from family and/or spouse. If an entering student is

working too many hours and has little support and encouragement, the odds of persistence and graduation are dramatically
against the student and the college. These questions of personal
circumstance will result in better advisement and counseling and
direction to college support services.

Midlands Technical College, South Carolina, has developed an
integrated program of testing, admissions, orientation, and advisement now called SOS (Student Orientation for Success). The college has restructured its programs to include student educational
plans, identification of student needs upon entry, and the establishment of an ongoing proactive intervention system, all designed
to help properly advise, place, and counsel entering students.

Midlands administers the ASSET Placement Test in all area
high schools to encourage students to consider college. College
recruiters then return to the high schools to interpret test scores
and to provide enrollment and placement information. In 1991–92,
on-site admission and fee payment services were offered at high
school post-assessment counseling sessions as an added customer
service feature. High school assessment, placement, and entry
services are reasons that 30 percent of all college-bound high
school graduates in the greater Columbia area sought enrollment
at Midlands Technical College.

Major universities never gave up on the practice of entry-level
assessment and placement following the student revolution of the
1960s. These policies derive from a deeply held value system that
helps explain the greater success universities enjoy with their students. Community college leaders must become more serious
about implementing rigorous policies of entry-level academic and
personal assessment.

Mandatory Placement

The word "mandatory" strikes fear into the hearts of r
well-intended community college professionals. There is /
thing bothersome about the notion of telling adults wh⟨
should do in a college environment, but not telling them/
much more harmful to the students in the long run. Just/

an entering student is 25 or 35 years old in no way assures readiness for success in an academic environment. Students who are deficient in the basic academic skills should not be permitted entry to any regular curriculum course until they have mastered the generic academic skills needed for success in college.

Many colleges have rigorous placement in English, reading, and math courses while permitting students to enroll simultaneously in biology, sociology, economics, and accounting (Roueche, Baker, and Roueche, 1984). Consider for a moment the ridiculousness of this "simultaneous enrollment" academic policy. The college has already determined that a student is in need of preparatory work in reading, writing, and math and has "placed" the student properly into developmental English and math courses. At the same time, the student is encouraged to go forward in the regular college curriculum. Before the student can be remediated and/or assisted with academic skill development, she is already in serious academic trouble in regular college courses. And, if the student is not in trouble in these courses, it would suggest that college faculty are doing nothing more than responding to what they believe are lowered standards being thrust upon them, given that they are required to attempt the impossibility of teaching quasiliterate students in regular college courses.

Ending Late Registration

The first week of any academic term is the most critical and important week in the school year for getting students positively involved in the life of a course and generating enthusiasm for success. No academic policy is more counterproductive to positive student retention and learning than late registration. At many community colleges, students may enroll two or three weeks after the beginning of an academic term, creating a true "mission impossible" for instructors.

While many community colleges have changed the period of late registration to the week preceding the first day of class, sadly, most still offer late registration possibilities to students as a means of bolstering enrollment and college budgets. Data indicate that changing late registration to the week before the commencement of the fall semester does not reduce college enrollment, and faculty and students are much better served in the process. College students enroll when the catalog indicates they should, and faculty and students alike benefit from a responsible college policy on late registration.

Mentoring

Community college students need excellent faculty mentors. For those students who are the first in their families to attend college, the community college represents an environment almost as alien as any they could possibly envision. We need to have faculty involved with students personally and professionally in serving as role models, and providing both personal and professional advice to students relative to success in the college's various programs.

Triton College, Illinois, developed a Partners in Education mentoring project (Triton College, 1990) to assist the disadvantaged students enrolled in their student support services programs. Faculty and counselors are invited to apply as mentors and are compensated for their time and effort based on student retention rates and evidence of achievement as measured by final GPA.

Triton mentors understand that students need to see them as their confidantes and "answer persons" at the college. Mentors are expected to meet with student mentees at least twice a month, with the first contact occurring at least one week before the commencement of the fall semester and a second contact during the first or second week. The Partners in Education program was developed to reduce the number of nonproductive student grades (W's and F's) and to improve the retention rates for underprepared students. The project director ascertains the number of meetings held between faculty mentors and mentees, and data indicate that time spent together in mentoring improves both retention and student success. Triton College also sponsors a peer counseling program in which an upper-division student agrees to serve as a "buddy" to one or more entering freshmen. These two programs have improved student success in quick order.

Midland College, Texas, implemented a Survival Skills program for nursing students, which included an orientation for family members and significant others at the beginning of the school year. Peer support included the establishment of big brother/big sister relationships between second-year students and entering freshmen. This program helped reduce attrition in the nursing program and led to dramatic improvements in students' evaluation of their experience at Midland.

At Utah Valley Community College, the Learning Enrichment Center offers a peer tutoring program to all students in all programs and classes. The focal point of the peer tutoring program is one-on-one tutoring in addition to "study group" tutoring. The one-to-one program is designed for classes in which group tutoring would be difficult, i.e., accounting, computers, drafting, and electronics. One-on-one tutoring also assists students with learning disabilities, and such tutoring is available upon student and/or faculty request.

Study group tutoring is offered for a variety of general courses. Generally, students in these classes do not need a great deal of intensive assistance, and the organized study groups typically meet individual needs. Study groups are scheduled at specific times, and attendance is on a voluntary basis. Many students attend every session while others attend only on an as-needed basis—usually before an examination.

Prospective tutors must be recommended by an instructor and must have received a B+ grade or better in the course they wish to tutor. Tutors go to regular lecture classes and announce to students when and where tutoring sessions will be held. The student program has resulted in improved student persistence in all subjects, and approximately 600 students were served in the program in the 1992 spring semester.

De Anza College, California, implemented A STARTING POINT (Minority Transfer Program) for minority students who were the first in their families to attend college. The program focused on assisting students from four minority groups—Black/African American, Latino/Chicano/Mexican American, American Indian, and Filipino—by providing them with the opportunity to become fully involved in the academic, campus, and community life of the college and to ultimately transfer to a baccalaureate-granting institution. Students are required to attend a one-week orientation course and to enroll in a one-year transferable communication sequence that focuses on strengthening verbal and writing skills, and in developing self-confidence. Students are also scheduled for regular counseling interventions and are provided with a wide variety of services including peer mentors, a strong alumni network, and formal orientation for parents in both English and Spanish. Students in the De Anza program maintained an 80 percent retention rate through the first year, compared with the 40 percent rate for nonprogram students.

After five years, more than 150 students participating in De Anza's A STARTING POINT have transferred to baccalaureate institutions. Beyond these numbers, participants have been involved in various experiential educational service programs, and more than 40 have received academic scholarships (De Anza College, 1991).

OTHER CLIMATE FACTORS

It would be impossible in one chapter to discuss in any detail all of the variables that affect the values, culture, and climate of any organization, but especially an open-door community college. As Schein has demonstrated, what leaders value and pay attention to reinforces in powerful ways the cultural determinants of the institution. It is critical for the constituents of a community college to spend time identifying and clarifying commonly held values. In addition, institutions should publish those values, as in the case of St. Petersburg Junior College, and distribute copies to all employees. College convocations should include routine and regular reiterations of the commonly held values that bind team members together for the common college good.

Once an institution has clarity on values, it is equally important to select new faculty and staff members who also share deeply in their individual commitment to those values. Over the past two decades, many institutions have selected faculty members who truly would prefer to be at a more selective institution working with students who do not require much help. It takes a particular kind of professional to value working with students needing aid and assistance. Hiring staff members who understand the mission of the comprehensive community college and greatly value being a part of that organizational team must be "job one" for any college president and/or dean of instruction. Research further indicates that college credentials have little validity in predicting successful teaching competence in open-door settings.

Greenville Technical College, South Carolina, gives top priority to the identification and selection of individuals whose values are congruent with the needs of the institution. Any new faculty member hired must be evaluated and recommended by the program advisory committee, by the combined faculty in the respective department, by the dean of that division, by the academic vice president, and finally by the president. In the process, the faculty member is evaluated for technical expertise as well as for excellence in classroom teaching.

Community colleges should require an actual teaching experience of all teaching finalists before a hiring recommendation is made. Salt Lake Community College, Greenville Technical College, St. Petersburg Junior College, and many other excellent open-door institutions today require this as part of the selection process. These institutions document the importance of seeing a candidate "walk his talk" as a prelude to any hiring. Hiring is truly "job one" in building a college culture with proper priority on teaching and learning effectiveness.

Similarly, an ongoing staff and professional development program is critical in reinforcing those values and attributes of newly hired employees. Fortunately, many excellent community colleges have excellent staff and professional development programs. For example, in its effort to socialize and enculturate new faculty and to reinforce the primacy of teaching and learning, Miami-Dade Community College requires two formal graduate courses of all newly hired faculty members. These graduate courses are offered for credit by the College of Education at the University of Miami, and the learning experiences incorporated into the two graduate courses are mutually determined by Miami-Dade faculty and administrators in concert with the university's professors.

Humber College in Toronto has literally involved hundreds of its employees (both faculty and support staff) in ongoing formal undergraduate and graduate education programs in collaboration with Central Michigan University, and more recently with an on-campus doctoral program from Michigan State University. Humber has brought universities to campus with tailored programs designed to improve the competencies and efficiencies of staff and faculty members who pursue the formal degree opportunities. One can imagine the kind of climate for improved service to students when hundreds of staff and faculty have persisted to complete a tailored program of study reinforcing commonly held values and beliefs.

Many colleges are actively involved in rewarding and recognizing teaching excellence. Cuyahoga Community College, Ohio, recognizes an outstanding faculty member and staff person on each of its three campuses at an annual fall convocation. Richland College, Texas, has an excellent program of faculty celebration and recognition. These and other colleges send teaching award winners to the NISOD Conference on Teaching Excellence, hosted by NISOD and The University of Texas each May in Austin. Many of the deans and presidents of these institutions accompany award-winning faculty members to the national conference to present them with NISOD Excellence Award medallions.

Most excellent colleges today have brought focus and clarity to their mission statements with respect to teaching and learning effectiveness. For example, these institutions have endeavored to define measures of program and institutional effectiveness with such specificity as to be able to evaluate institutional and departmental progress toward the attainment of teaching and learning goals. All accrediting associations are also pushing colleges and universities to such agreed-upon definitions of institutional effectiveness.

Lansing Community College, Michigan, Midlands Technical College, and De Anza College are leaders in articulating program outcomes that address teaching and learning effectiveness.

Midlands Technical College has specified goals and outcome measures in the following six general areas:

- *Accessible, Comprehensive Programs of High Quality.* The first major determinant of the college's effectiveness is a strong academic curriculum. It should provide opportunities for access to the college, while monitoring placement within an individual program based upon a student's projected likelihood of success. It should be comprehensive, with quality instruction and support services that prepare the student to successfully transfer to a senior institution or enter the workplace.
- *Student Satisfaction and Retention.* Students are the college's number one clients and products. Retention of students to goal completion is critical to accomplishing the college's mission.
- *Post-Education Satisfaction and Success.* Employment preparation and transfer success are two dimensions of the college's mission that must be successful for the college to consider itself effective. In-field placement rates of graduates and transfer students' GPAs should reflect the extent to which the college has effectively prepared students for post-education success.
- *Economic Development and Community Involvement.* For Midlands Technical College to be truly a community college, its programs, services, and students must contribute to the community the college serves. The college supports economic development through the appropriate education and training of entry-level workers and the retraining of current employees, based on local business and industry demands. In addition, as a community college, Midlands faculty and staff are encouraged to become actively involved in the community and to host community groups on campus.
- *Sound, Effective Resource Management.* In order to be effective, the college must be fiscally responsible to the citizens and students who provide its resources. This includes adequate and equitable distribution of funds, appropriate use of personnel and facilities, and support of the college by both public and private entities.

- *Dynamic Organizational Involvement and Development.* The faculty and staff who work at Midlands Technical College are its most valuable resources. Their ongoing professional development and enthusiasm for the *Vision of Excellence* measurably affects the college's effectiveness in serving students. The college will provide professional development opportunities, be a proactive supporter of affirmative action, and support equitable salaries for all employees (Midlands Technical College, 1992).

The establishment of a climate for effective teaching and learning begins with the identification of values and attitudes that reinforce the importance of the college mission, emphasizing excellence in teaching and service as much as community colleges have traditionally valued access. It also requires the implementation of strong academic policies and procedures that help students become more responsible and self-directed in their pursuit of academic goals and objectives. Faculty and staff selection is absolutely critical to the achievement of those goals once they are identified, and colleges need to exert more effort in the recognition and celebration of award-winning faculty and staff. Outcome measures of effectiveness must identify those indicators of excellence that document college ability to deliver quality teaching and learning.

REFERENCES

Adirondack Community College. "The Freshman Year Experience." Queensbury, N.Y.: Adirondack Community College, 1991.

Beal, P.E. and Lee Noel. *What Works in Student Retention.* Iowa City: American College Testing Program, 1980.

De Anza College. "A Starting Point: Minority Transfer Program." Cupertino, Calif.: De Anza College, 1991.

Lord Fairfax Community College. "Handbook for Academic Advising." Middletown, Va.: Lord Fairfax Community College, 1991.

McGrath, Dennis and Martin B. Spear. *The Academic Crisis of the Community College.* Albany: SUNY Press, 1991.

Midlands Technical College. "Vision of Excellence." Columbia, S.C.: Midlands Technical College, 1992.

Roueche, John E., George A. Baker, and Suanne D. Roueche. *College Responses to Low-Achieving Students.* Orlando, Fla.: HBJ Media Systems, 1984.

St. Petersburg Junior College. "The Facet Report: Toward 2001." St. Petersburg, Fla.: St. Petersburg Junior College, 1990.

Schein, E.H. *Organizational Culture and Leadership: A Dynamic View.* San Francisco: Jossey-Bass, 1985.

Triton College. "Mentoring as a Component of Student Retention." River Grove, Ill.: Triton College, 1990.

John E. Roueche is professor and director, Community College Leadership Program, The University of Texas at Austin, where he holds the Sid W. Richardson Regents Chair. Suanne D. Roueche is director of the National Institute for Staff and Organizational Development (NISOD), The University of Texas at Austin.

Chapter 3

Leadership for Teaching and Learning

By Robert H. McCabe

Only a few decades ago, a college education was generally limited to an elite group of young, full-time students who were mostly white and mostly male. Few occupations required more than a high school education, and many did not require that. Today the majority of high school graduates continue their education past high school, and business indicates that even more should in order to prepare for information age employment. Most Americans will need continuing education to keep pace with shifting occupational opportunities and evolving job requirements. At the same time, high school graduates' academic skills continue to decline.

Our nation's demography is changing, with growing numbers of minorities, immigrants, and women in the work force. Higher education, with community colleges in the lead, must now undertake an awesome task—to prepare the broad spectrum of Americans for "new age" employment and for living effectively in a far more diverse and complicated society. The students are of all ages. A high percentage are part-time. All races are represented, and men and women are found in equal numbers. Too many of today's students are underprepared.

In this new environment, however, most educational practices remain as they were fifty years ago. The significant research on adult learning, the wonderful new and expanding capacities of information technology, and years of experience with the new students have had little impact. What we know about education has yet to be translated into what we do about education. Too many of us are satisfied with what we are already doing. Often our institutions are set up to be comfortable for faculty and administration rather than to achieve maximum benefits for students. The obstacles to improvement are substantial, which explains why there has been such limited progress. Those who would lead programs to improve teaching and learning must understand the difficulty before them, have unrelenting commitment, plan for the long term, be flexible, and have considerable patience.

The timing for major advancement in teaching and learning is both good and bad. It is good because there is broad agreement that teaching and learning should command the highest priority. It is good because we know so much more about how adults learn. It is bad because of the decline in public confidence and commitment. It is bad because of inadequate finances. We ask faculty and staff to do more, to try new and exciting methods, and to increase their commitment while resources shrink. Salaries are too low, and legislatures continue to demonstrate their lack of belief in community colleges by underfunding them. But improving student learning is immensely important to America, and the challenge must be accepted regardless of the obstacles. The extent to which we accept and act on this challenge is a true test of leadership.

THE PRESIDENT

In community colleges, major new programs and important advancements in teaching and learning will not take place without visible support and leadership from the president. Such complex changes are doomed unless the president gives these initiatives the highest priority and commits to direct long-term personal involvement. Although each institution operates differently based on the institutional setting and the makeup of its leadership, in the final analysis the president must decide what issues and programs are to be given the highest priority.

Each individual sees things from the basis of life experience and role. It is unreasonable to expect a mathematics professor to view events that deal with the educational program of the college from the perspective of the college's overall mission, and to be concerned with how the educational program fits with the needs of the surrounding community and the nation. That is the perspective the president must bring to the issue. It is within this broad perspective that the decisions concerning institutional policy must be made. It is also unreasonable to expect the president to fully understand the difficulties experienced by the mathematics professor in dealing with an array of students with different values, attitudes, and skills, and the impact of college policies on that individual's work. It is the president's role to set the overall direction for a project to improve teaching and learning in light of the needs of society and the impact on the institution. He or she must organize initiatives that include mathematics professors, with their special understanding and knowledge, for example, in the process so that there is an integration of values and perspectives.

The president must have and communicate a vision. He or she must work to emphasize the mission of the institution and to focus on values that are broadly shared as a foundation for advancement. Despite the authority that comes with the role, the president cannot force a new system into place. In order to be effective, those who will implement the system must believe in it. This can happen only if they are involved in the development of new systems and feel ownership for what they have helped create. Research continues to show that the involvement of many individuals with various perspectives and backgrounds in decision making and policy development results in superior policy decisions. In any major change, the expertise and views of all who hold a stake are essential. There must be a system for broad participation to foster a sense of communal ownership. A system of change cannot be cosmetic; it must give the participants real opportunities to shape the project and to be involved in all activities designed to achieve its goals.

THE FACULTY

Most human beings are uncomfortable with change, yet we live in a world in which change is the only predictable constant. No group is more resistant to change than college faculty. As a group they are liberal advocates of change in their fields, but there is strong commitment to maintaining the status quo with regard to academic affairs and college operations. College faculty are independent and often suspicious of administrative directives and organization. They are uncomfortable with constraints and with operating in systems.

Teachers know who among them does the minimum and who puts out extra effort for students. Yet faculty tend to hold stubbornly to the assertion that the quality of teaching cannot be measured. Teaching and learning are the domain of the faculty and without question the area most difficult to change. However, important improvement cannot occur without commitment and leadership from faculty. There are many individuals within the faculty who have excellent ideas and are excited by the growth of their students. The first task of leadership in bringing about needed changes in teaching and learning is undoubtedly to encourage the energy and ideas of faculty and to provide opportunity for faculty leadership in the venture.

Unfortunately, faculty still tend to value knowledge of discipline and academic achievement more than teaching skills. Even though it seems apparent that working with other human beings is the most complex and difficult activity teachers undertake, and that it takes tremendous skill, teachers still tend to act as if anyone who is knowledgeable in a discipline can be effective. There is a significant body of research about learning that should be essential to those engaged in teaching, but it is generally ignored. I have always thought that a teacher who is very knowledgeable in the subject, but who is not well-grounded in learning theory, is comparable to a heart surgeon who knows a great deal about the heart but has never held a scalpel in his hand. Yet it is normal to employ teachers who are knowledgeable in a discipline but not in learning.

With the population that enrolls in community colleges, successful teaching—the facilitation of learning—takes enormous skill and knowledge. Yet faculty tend to consider courses dealing with education and learning as simplistic, unimportant, and burdened with "educationese." Perhaps the best example is a case of a major university that produced a book about college teaching for its own faculty to read and use. The book's title indicated that it was a resource for graduate assistants in the belief that only under that guise would the faculty review the book and possibly use it.

The resistance is not only to information about education. Many consider anything that suggests improvement in how faculty do their work as an intrusion, a threat to academic freedom. Considerable time and effort must be placed on helping faculty understand that there are ways to improve in their work and that such improvement is related to student success. But more than anything else, the actions of the administration need to support the rhetoric. It is important that reward systems be aligned to coordinate with stated goals.

In 1986 Miami-Dade Community College initiated a major long-range project to reform teaching and learning. The overall goals of the Teaching/Learning Project were clearly stated: to improve the quality of teaching and learning at Miami-Dade Community College, to make teaching a professionally rewarding career, and to make teaching and learning the focal point of college activities and decision-making processes. The college changed its promotion system to one based on excellence in teaching and learning. The criteria are based on a statement of faculty excellence, developed over a two-year period, which emphasizes service to students. In addition the college is close to achieving its goal of raising private funds for 100 teaching chairs. These chairs will be awarded every three years and provide a supplement of $7,500 to each chair holder. An evaluation system was developed, and faculty were given a greater role in deciding about promotion in academic rank and the granting of tenure. In these ways the reward system supported the stated goals; institutional actions reflected institutional rhetoric. The most difficult area remains that of gathering and evaluating information to document success in teaching and learning.

INVOLVING THE WHOLE COLLEGE

At the first meeting of the Steering Committee to plan the Teaching/Learning Project, there was a long discussion of the need to help faculty learn more about how students learn; how to provide support; how staff development resources should be organized to help faculty improve in the classrooms; how to evaluate what faculty do for students; and how faculty could be encouraged to improve their teaching. During this meeting the president of the North Campus stood up and said, "On my campus, faculty are buying their own chalk at Kmart and carrying it in their pockets, because the chalk that the college provides is too hard and doesn't write well. How do we convince faculty that the institution puts its first priority on teaching and learning if we can't even provide decent chalk?"

The chalk story had considerable impact. It provided the impetus to broaden the scope of the Teaching/Learning Project to include everything that we do at the institution and to work on changing administrative behavior to ensure that administrators place teaching and learning issues first.

The administration must provide the best possible environment for teaching and learning, giving clear priority in budgets and in actions to those elements needed to support an excellent environment. Administrators must support faculty as individuals as they strive to achieve the demanding results that are expected. A key challenge will be realigning the reward systems to emphasize teaching and learning.

At Miami-Dade, an adjustment in the system for developing budgets places first priority on teaching and learning. Each organizational unit at the college works with the users of its services to evaluate those services; to work towards improvement; and to resolve issues like the hard chalk problem. For example, maintenance and custodial services review the condition of all teaching spaces daily and correct problems identified by teachers as quickly as possible. New faculty offices are designed to create an inviting environment that, it is hoped, will keep faculty on the campus and make them more available to students. Information systems are being developed to help faculty communicate better with colleagues and students.

Front-line academic administrators need special attention. Individuals often are appointed to important management responsibilities as department chairs and associate deans on the basis of performance as teachers, without consideration of management experience or training. If there is to be renewed emphasis on teaching and learning, which requires the development of an excellent environment and support system for faculty, the front-line administrators must be responsive to, thoroughly understand, and be committed to the teaching and learning improvement program. They must all be advocates. It is unfair to both faculty and those with instructional management responsibilities to place someone who is not well-trained in such positions. While few institutions of higher education do it, there should be a thorough program of preparation for those assuming department chair and other academic administrator responsibilities.

Another area that must be addressed by the administration is the participation of nonteaching personnel in the college. One of the unfortunate side effects of placing emphasis on faculty is the creation of an environment in which the remainder of the staff feel they are not important. Everyone who works at the college has a role in helping students. In a program developed to raise the status of teachers, it is especially important to work with all of the other staff to help them understand the value of the program. Nonteaching staff must be helped to understand and see the importance of the mission; the importance of service to students and to communities served by the college; and the importance of their role in helping carry out that mission.

Each unit of the college must understand how its role contributes to serving students. For example, the custodial staff needs to know that clean and comfortable classrooms are highly valued by faculty and students and play a key role in improving the conditions for learning. When the college is recognized for its leadership in teaching and learning, the custodial staff must share in the recognition for the contributions they make.

To sustain the commitment and morale of nonteaching employees, it is important that their reward systems be reconstructed to emphasize contributions to the college mission and to services to students. In this way, all employees can feel they are part of the college and part of the improvement of services.

STAFF DEVELOPMENT

Community colleges' hiring practices continue to emphasize discipline preparation. In most cases employees have earned an advanced degree in a discipline and taught for a number of years in their fields. Faculty have seldom been well prepared with regard to teaching and learning. We properly state that "you can't teach what you don't know," but we have not been equally concerned that "you can't teach if you don't know how."

In community colleges it takes great competence to be a successful teacher. The goal of teaching is not simply presenting information, but facilitating learning and often helping very needy individuals to grow. With rare exception, universities are not specifically preparing individuals for careers as community college faculty. Thus, colleges must take responsibility for developing excellent teachers.

Improvements in teaching and learning require application of the results of the last fifty years of significant research in learning, together with the knowledge that has been gained by successful faculty. While there is still much to be known about the special learning needs of the poor—particularly when malnutrition, conflict, and deprived environments provide additional obstacles to learning—there are many outstanding faculty who have developed the important skills and approaches necessary to be successful with these students. The volume of students with special needs continues to grow, and we must take advantage of the special abilities of those who have been working with these students for many years. New faculty must stand on the shoulders of those with experience and build on that experience.

The administration must provide new faculty with a view of the importance of the community college mission to encourage the enthusiasm and energy necessary for their success. The orientation program must offer a foundation carefully built on research about adult learners and the experience of successful faculty. Professional development activities must focus on more effective and affective means to help faculty internalize teaching and learning philosophy and demonstrate it in their behavior. For success with community college students, there must be committed, inspired, and knowledgeable faculty.

Almost half the successful and dedicated faculty in community colleges are reaching retirement age. When this factor is combined with continuing growth in enrollment, it is clear that a very substantial percentage of the faculty of the future will be hired in the next five years. This replacement faculty will be so large as to dominate the institution in the early twenty-first century. It is paramount that community colleges develop the very best programs that can be devised for orienting these new faculty. The programs should provide special sessions prior to beginning work that include attention to mission; ongoing support at least during the first year; and a substantial in-service educational program in teaching and learning.

A staff development program requires a significant commitment of resources by the college and should be comprehensive. There should be an organized program of workshops and seminars for all faculty, with special attention to the use of technology. Support should be provided to assist faculty members in design and implementation of their ideas for improving learning. Attention should be given to helping faculty continue their formal education.

At Miami-Dade, the program to bring new faculty on board and acculturate them has been carefully developed. New faculty begin one week before the opening of classes. They attend presentations by all major college administrators concerning college history and mission; orientation to the college and its services; and meetings with department chairs and deans to prepare for the opening term. Each new faculty member is assigned a mentor who will work with that faculty member for a two-year period. Workshops are planned for new faculty on each campus every month during the first year of service. In addition, the teaching load for the first semester is designed to ensure that no more than two preparations are required.

The college has developed two graduate courses to its prescription taught on the campuses by the University of Miami. These are required before a faculty member is eligible to apply for continuing contract (tenure), which in Florida can occur as early as the end of the third year. The courses deal with teaching and learning in the community college based on the concepts of classroom research and assessment developed by K. Patricia Cross, and are designed with strong input from veteran faculty. The granting of a continuing contract, once almost automatic, has become a major event based on a portfolio demonstrating the quality of work completed by each faculty member applicant. The recommendation is made by a committee of colleagues. At this point the quality of work being done by new faculty in this program supports our confidence that Miami-Dade will become even better at teaching and learning in the future.

THE DEVELOPMENT OF THE TEACHING/LEARNING PROJECT

In January 1993 Miami-Dade Community College won the first Theodore M. Hesburgh Award for Faculty Development to Enhance Undergraduate Teaching. The award was especially significant since the competition included all institutions of higher education. The award was made to Miami-Dade for its leadership in reforming teaching and learning through the Teaching/Learning Project. The scope of activities in the project are reviewed in Chapter 13 of this book. In the following section I have summarized briefly the major components of the program to indicate the complex array of activities that require leadership from the president.

50

For some time I had been concerned that growing numbers of students with poor academic skills and increasing diversity were presenting an increasingly difficult task to faculty. Since so many Miami-Dade faculty were hired in the 1960s, I was also concerned with the impending retirement of large numbers of very dedicated and skilled members. Adding to my concern was the failure of colleges to use what is known about adult learning and the difficult task of increasing productivity through technology.

At the 1986 convention of the American Association for Higher Education, I heard a presentation by K. Patricia Cross concerning classroom research. This innovative idea seemed to be a linchpin for a comprehensive approach to improving teaching and learning. It seemed to me that to be successful, community colleges had to become the experts in teaching and learning, and with the population now entering Miami-Dade, we had to be the very best.

I prepared a brief concept paper outlining the issues and proposed a major initiative for the college to address them. This paper was presented at an off-campus lunch meeting to 120 individuals from all areas of the college, with faculty the largest single group. The faculty were encouraged to take a leadership role in the proposed initiative, and a strong role was envisaged for veteran faculty. Responses to the proposal were solicited and were uniformly positive.

In fall 1986 a project director was appointed, along with a twenty-six-member steering committee composed primarily of faculty. Four subcommittees, with broad participation, were created to focus on institutional values, the teaching/learning environment, faculty excellence, and new faculty. By the end of the first year, thirty-eight Miami-Dade personnel were directly involved in the project.

In 1987–88 the focus was on raising awareness and expanding involvement. A Teaching/Learning Project *Bulletin* was published regularly; informational videos were produced; and meetings were set up with project subcommittees, myself, and individuals in small groups throughout the college. Three additional task forces were formed on classroom feedback, learning to learn, and faculty advancement. By this time nearly sixty personnel were directly involved. K. Patricia Cross spent three months in residence in fall 1987 to work with the committee on several of the projects. The subcommittees for Classroom Feedback and Learning to Learn concentrated on developing two graduate courses that would become requirements for all new faculty. Major work proceeded on the "Statement of Faculty Excellence," which would become the basis for the work of the Advancement Committee. The first draft of this statement was considered at a two-day retreat of seventy Miami-Dade personnel. In addition, I went to all five campuses in the Miami-Dade system and met with the 900 full-time faculty in groups of twenty-five to fifty to learn their views. By this time the Values Subcommittee had completed a "Statement of Values," which was adopted by the District Board of Trustees. The Endowed Teaching Chair Program was kicked off and funds raised for the first twenty-four chairs.

In the third year, 1988–89, committee work continued, and the number of people serving on committees increased to more than 100. New subcommittees were formed with regard to part-time faculty, the role of administrators, support for faculty and nonfaculty, and nonclassroom faculty. In August 1988 we implemented the first pre-semester one-week seminar for new faculty, and the two graduate courses, "Research in the Classroom" and "Effective Teaching and Learning," were piloted in the winter term. The essential "Statement of Faculty Excellence" was adopted by the District Board of Trustees. Most important was the adoption of the policy on faculty advancement. Once again a two-day retreat of more than 100 Miami-Dade personnel was held, and nine external consultants participated. At this retreat, the draft of the advancement document was reviewed in detail. As a result, a final draft of performance review, promotion, continuing contract (tenure), endowed chairs, and salary considerations was produced. In April 1989 the proposal was put to a referendum, and 69 percent of the faculty voted for the new plan. The evaluation system and a concomitant reward system was in place.

In 1989–90 efforts focused on institutionalizing various elements of the program. The new faculty preservice orientation was instituted permanently; the two graduate courses were regularly scheduled and made a requirement for new faculty; the "Statement of Faculty Excellence" was modified to include nonclassroom faculty; and a student feedback questionnaire, coordinated with the faculty excellence statement, was tested for the first time.

The fifth year, 1990–91, was a year in which a great deal of detail regarding implementation had to be addressed, and procedures of the faculty advancement program were formally adopted by the College Executive Committee and the faculty senates. A Monitoring and Review Committee was established, and there was agreement that changes could occur only with a recommendation from that committee and concurrence from the College Executive Committee and the faculty senates.

Teaching/Learning Support Center directors were appointed for each of the campuses, and all staff development and support activities were organized for delivery through these centers. In addition, the student feedback questionnaire was piloted, and by the end of the year the Institutional Research Department completed an analysis that found it to be valid and reliable.

In the sixth year, 1991–92, the faculty advancement process was fully implemented, and the first promotions were granted under the new system. Project staff and the appropriate committees identified and studied the various issues and problems associated with that process, which was a key element in the overall success of the project.

In 1992–93 the Monitoring and Review Committee made its report, and a process is underway to make necessary adjustments in the procedures for the promotion system. Additionally, the work dealing with advancement for office career and other support personnel is proceeding. There will be a parallel effort to recognize excellence for all staff at the college and to relate all activities to the improvement of teaching and learning.

The keys to the success of the Miami-Dade program are its comprehensiveness, breadth of involvement, and the patience and time we have taken to put it in place. In this sense, I believe it provides a useful model. Furthermore, I believe that all constituencies in the college would confirm the value of the president's role in providing committed and continuing leadership for this enormous systemwide effort.

NEW CHALLENGES AHEAD

The evolving information age and an evolving world society will continue to dominate our future. Everyone will need both more advanced education and lifelong education. More adults will return to college; more immigrants will require education; the underclass will continue to grow; and K–12 reform will be painfully slow. These conditions will result in a substantial increase in the number of underprepared students with special needs while business and industry demand higher skills.

Community colleges must respond to these circumstances by making important advances in teaching and learning. All of our priorities must be carefully reviewed, and harnessing the capabilities of information technology, both on campus and through distance learning, will be the key. There will be new alliances, more coordination among systems to develop seamless programs, and a public demand for more to be done with less.

The future of community colleges is promising. It will be dynamic, difficult, and challenging, and of great importance to the future of America.

Robert H. McCabe is president of Miami-Dade Community College, Florida.

Chapter 4

Policy to Support Teaching and Learning

By Kay M. McClenney

A policy is something usually devised and enacted at a level several degrees removed from a student. The major determinant of quality in teaching and learning is student-teacher interaction. Beyond that interaction, anything undertaken by "outsiders"—administrators, governing boards, state agencies, or legislators—is best understood as an attempt to create the circumstances under which good teaching and effective learning will be valued and practiced. More is known than is practiced, the pundits say, about good teaching and effective learning. More is known than is practiced about the kinds of institutional environments where teaching and learning will flourish. But it is fair to say that less is known than is needed about the policies that will best encourage the development of those supportive institutional environments and thus, for the most part indirectly, promote good practice in teaching and learning.

A constructive exercise for community college leaders to collaboratively undertake is a thoughtful review—a "policy audit"—to ascertain the extent to which college and/or state policy supports or inhibits teaching and learning. (For further discussion, see Jones and Ewell, 1992.) This chapter offers background for that policy review process by outlining a set of propositions about the nature of effective policy; briefly describing the current public context for higher education policy development; and reviewing selected categories of policy that would be important at the institutional or state level in a comprehensive effort to ensure support for teaching and learning.

PROPOSITIONS ABOUT EFFECTIVE POLICY

The failures of educational reform, as well as the successes, offer important lessons about what may constitute effective policy. The following propositions are offered for consideration and debate.

1. Effective Policy Takes into Account the Broader Public Context in Which Higher Education Operates. Very simply, no meaningful policy to support teaching and learning can be insensitive to salient contextual factors. The increasing diversity of the population, the changing demands of the workplace, and the growing public frustration over issues of cost and quality are all important realities. To ignore them is to risk irrelevance and decline.

2. Effective Policy Issues Form—or at Least Are Tested Against—a Vision of the Kind of Educational Institution and Educational System that Will Best Serve Student and Public Interests. Without that vision, that guiding sense of destination, there can be few benchmarks of progress and only ad hoc criteria for distinguishing good policy from bad.

3. Effective Policy Is Part of a Systemic Approach to the Achievement of Desired Ends. If a lake is pronounced dead and the single chosen remedy is to add phosphorous (a necessary ingredient), the result will be an overgrowth of weeds. Traditional policy making is incremental and fragmented. For example, funding formulas and other financing mechanisms often communicate priorities that are directly contrary to the espoused importance of

56

quality in teaching and learning. Funding mechanisms, admission standards, curriculum policy, and accountability initiatives are rarely examined in relation to one another. The results are confused priorities, mixed messages, and conflicting incentives. If anything has been learned from the piecemeal reform efforts of the past, it is that coherence in policy is necessary to fundamental and lasting improvement.

4. Effective Policy Is Aimed Less at Dictating Practice than at Promoting, Supporting, and Rewarding Good Practice. One of the predominant characteristics of traditional policy has been its bias toward centralization, standardization, and regulation. While there are important balances to be struck, a decade of experience in corporate restructuring and public school reform suggests that flexibility and empowerment, combined with high standards and accountability for results, are the more productive strategies.

THE CURRENT CONTEXT FOR HIGHER EDUCATION POLICY

For American higher education, the coming decade is likely to be a time of fundamental change. In the mid-1980s several national reports called for major improvements in undergraduate education (Study Group on the Conditions of Excellence in American Higher Education, 1984; Association of American Colleges, 1985), but the issues were debated primarily within the higher education community. By the late 1980s, the nation's governors, motivated by public concerns about college costs and questions about whether students were really learning what they should, began calling for fundamental reform (Education Commission of the States, 1986; National Governors' Association, 1986). Not until the sharp economic downturn of the early 1990s did higher education leaders begin to acknowledge publicly that basic changes might be needed. Now, an increasing number of nationally recognized leaders are challenging their colleagues to recognize the dilemmas of the next decade (Atwell, 1992; Bok, 1992).

In broad terms, American higher education faces three intersecting and conflicting realities: escalating expectations and demands, severe economic constraints, and increasingly negative public opinion (McGuinness, 1992).

Escalating Expectations and Demands

The United States has the world's highest college participation rates, and projections indicate continuing increases in enrollments (U.S. Department of Education, 1991). The impact will vary among states, with some experiencing declines while others, like Arizona, California, Florida, Texas, and Washington, experience extraordinary growth. Parallel to these pressures on access, numerous national reports have emphasized the message that American youth and adults must achieve far higher knowledge and skill levels if they are to be effective in future employment and citizenship (National Education Goals Panel, 1991 and 1992; Commission on the Skills of the American Workforce, 1990; U.S. Department of Labor, 1991). The nation still faces important challenges to increase the educational participation and achievement of growing minority populations.

Severe Economic Constraints

The 1980s were an affluent period for American colleges and universities, a time of real growth in resources per student (Mingle, 1992). But higher education is now experiencing an abrupt and far-reaching downturn in revenues that is projected to last well into the next century. State appropriations for higher education showed a two-year decline at the beginning of the new decade—the first such decline in 34 years of data collection. Predictions are that higher education's share of state budgets will continue to shrink, primarily because of other social priorities and mandates related to health care, criminal justice, environmental protection, and public school reform (Jaschik, 1991; Mingle, 1992; State Higher Education Executive Officers, 1992). There is also significant pressure on federal and local budgets.

A consequence of these resource constraints has been a move toward massive increases in tuition and fees. With these increases coming on top of significant tuition increases in the 1980s, there is a growing public backlash and consequently a growing prospect for legislatively mandated tuition caps. Colleges are caught in the crunch.

Increasingly Negative Public Opinion

Despite the demand for services, American higher education suffers from a negative wave of public opinion that goes far beyond any of recent experience. The public's anger and frustration appear to be focused primarily on the major research universities, but in this climate no sector is immune. Disenchantment is fed by escalating tuition costs, lack of attention to undergraduate education, and highly publicized stories of scandal, fiscal abuse, extravagance, and the exploitation of college athletes. The problems are exacerbated by the general alienation of the public from politics and public institutions.

THE CRUCIAL CONNECTION: LINKING POLICY TO GOOD PRACTICE

Extensive literature describes the principles and characteristics of good practice in undergraduate education, and in fact there appears to be very little disagreement about what constitutes good practice (Chickering and Gamson, 1987; Chickering, Gamson, and Barsi, 1989; Richardson, 1992; Roueche and Baker, 1987; Jones and Ewell, 1992). As part of a project sponsored by the Education Commission of the States (ECS) and supported by the Pew Charitable Trusts, Jones and Ewell (1992) have synthesized the research to produce this list (see Figure 1).

As Jones and Ewell point out, even a cursory review of this list will suggest how dependent good practice is on individual faculty motivation and skill. One can only be impressed by how difficult it is to influence these factors directly through state policy. Even at the institutional level, as clearly evident in the Roueche-Baker

---

FIGURE 1
Characteristics of Good Educational Practice

1. High Expectations
2. Coherence in Learning
3. Synthesizing Experiences
4. Integration of Education and Experience
5. Active Learning
6. Ongoing Practice of Learned Skills
7. Assessment and Prompt Feedback
8. Collaborative Learning
9. Considerable Time on Task
10. Respect for Diverse Talents and Ways of Knowing
11. Frequent Student-Faculty Contact
12. Emphasis on the Early Years of Study

Source: Jones and Ewell, 1992

Community College Excellence Model (Roueche and Baker, 1987), policy is but one factor in an interactive system where institutional climate, leadership, and faculty behaviors are determinative.

What this clearly suggests is that the role of policy—especially policy formulated beyond the institution—is far less to prescribe or direct behavior than to create conditions under which these desired practices will be encouraged, supported, and rewarded. "Good practice can be promoted by changing constraints and incentives in the external environment," assert Jones and Ewell, "and the particular cultures in which these practices will flourish can be actively cultivated. But few such practices can be instilled directly through mandate" (1992, p. 22).

Having witnessed for a decade the limited success and outright failures of policy mandates, policy makers may well consider a different approach: to emphasize the development of a coherent policy framework that encourages institutional cultures and structures—and in turn supports excellence in teaching and learning.

Again, there is extensive research that describes institutional environments where teaching and learning tend to be most effective. Which institutional characteristics seem to matter? The following factors are clearly important:

- A clear and shared sense of mission and purpose
- Top leadership that is actively and visibly committed to the teaching and learning mission
- A definition of faculty role that includes significant teacher-student interaction beyond the classroom
- Strong policies guiding the hiring, orientation, evaluation, advancement, and professional development of faculty
- Curriculum policies that reinforce good practice, including coherence in general education, synthesizing experiences, integration of learning and experience, etc.
- Clear statements of desired learning outcomes, both for the program area or major field and for general education
- Continuous assessment of institutional effectiveness by examining student and institutional performance relative to stated expectations and goals
- Limiting administrative/bureaucratic controls applied to the teaching function
- Consistent allocation of resources in amounts and configurations that demonstrate the priority given to teaching and learning
- Deliberate development of an institutional culture and tradition that values teaching and learning

Many important aspects of institutional leadership and culture are addressed in other chapters of this volume. Here the focus is policy, and the guiding question is, "What forms of policy are most likely to nurture good practice?"

The following overview is far from exhaustive; rather, it addresses selected policy areas in which institutions and states both tend to wield influence, though usually not in any coordinated way. These policy areas are necessarily part of a coherent and systemic framework to support teaching and learning.

POLICY OVERVIEW

Mission Definition

The obvious starting place in crafting policy to support teaching and learning is in the expression of college mission that makes those activities the institution's compelling first priority. Real change and improvement almost always issue from a clear and shared sense of where a college is going, of what it is fundamentally in business to do. At the state level, mission definition is often part of a strategic planning process for the state's higher education system. While such planning activities often leave considerable leeway for colleges to articulate the details of their mission, state policy can provide helpful guidance in designating special emphasis (e.g., teaching excellence) for certain institutions or requiring that the institutions clearly specify areas in which they will aspire to premier status.

Expectations and Standards

Following almost a decade of emphasis on general education reform and assessment of student learning outcomes, there is little debate within the higher education community about the value of articulating high expectations and clear standards for student learning. What is still argued (though more often in universities than community colleges) is the level at which expectations and standards should be set. Tradition long had the individual faculty member as the sole arbiter of such matters. During the 1980s many community colleges (and to a lesser extent baccalaureate institutions) made significant strides in developing statements of desired student learning outcomes at the program level, for general education, and for certificates and associate degrees. Graduation requirements are now far more often stated in terms of what students must know and be able to do rather than in terms of what courses they must take; and the emergence of "degree warranties" attests to the seriousness with which some colleges affirm their expectations of both students and teachers.

At present, state governments and higher education agencies express and monitor standards primarily through their mechanisms for setting admission standards and their requirements for institutional licensing or accreditation. These state policies tend to be most supportive of teaching and learning when they require that institutions be very clear about (1) the clientele they intend to serve (including its level of academic preparation), and (2) the institution's "exit standards"—what students should know and be able to do when they complete their educational experience.

Escalating concern at the state and national levels about the quality of undergraduate education is sparking a renewed debate about the desirability and feasibility of establishing a common set of performance standards for all college graduates, or all sophomores, or some other specified group. With a couple of notable exceptions, similar debates in the mid- and late 1980s resulted in policy decisions allowing individual institutions to handle their own standard setting in accord with their diverse missions and clientele. Given the current climate of public opinion and finance, there is an increasing possibility of renewed interest in standard setting at the state level, and a variety of federal initiatives are fueling discussion about national standards as well (Edgerton, 1991).

Curriculum Policy

At the campus level, policies pertaining to course and program approval will reflect the institution's commitment to rigor and coherence in education. Requiring that proposals for new curriculum options and evaluations of established courses address the criteria for good practice will reinforce those practices across the curriculum. Research indicates that student success in the community college can be strongly affected by policies that offer more structure and fewer choices to students, require early assessment and appropriate course placement, and provide for "early alert" and special help in the event the student encounters academic difficulty.

63

State-level involvement in curriculum matters is generally limited to two policy areas: program approval and review, and transfer and articulation. With reference to program approval and review, the key issue once again is how policies developed outside the institution can best reinforce good teaching and effective learning within the institution. Such a policy may be most helpful if it asks the institution to address whether the proposed program is consistent with institutional mission; how it contributes in a coherent way to the general education of students; whether it specifies learning expectations and offers creative and useful means for assessing their achievement; whether it incorporates a synthesizing or "capstone" experience; and so on.

Some people will argue that policy on transfer and articulation is more a matter of consumer protection than of supporting teaching and learning. Nonetheless, the process of developing transfer and articulation policy agreements at the campus level generally involves intense faculty-to-faculty conversations about desired learning outcomes for students, means for ascertaining achievement, and segments of the curriculum where learning is addressed. Those conversations almost inevitably will lead to greater attention to important principles of good practice. The policies themselves become institutional signposts pointing to the importance of academic achievement and progress.

Beyond the campus level, Jones and Ewell (1992) assert that transfer policies among institutions afford state authorities a rare opportunity for academic leadership:

> As students increasingly attend more than one institution to achieve a baccalaureate degree, the undergraduate curriculum becomes a joint product of the state's higher education system rather than the exclusive domain of a single college or university. More and more, this implies that the state act as an advocate for coherence and good practice to ensure that those attending multiple institutions are well served (p. 48).

Several authors have offered views about what constitutes helpful state policy on transfer and articulation (Knoell, 1990; Bender, 1990; American Council on Education, 1991). Jones and

Ewell summarize their own observations with the assertion that such policies will be most supportive of good practice when they:

- Establish transfer credit primarily on the basis of competencies rather than course titles and descriptions
- Base transfer on blocks or groups of courses rather than individual courses
- Establish fully transferable associate degrees, backed by appropriate assessments, eliminating the requirement for course-by-course approval
- Recognize the phenomenon of "reverse transfer" from four-year to community colleges
- Provide for monitoring of transfer patterns and effectiveness through statewide tracking systems

Assessment and Accountability

An important body of literature, much of it contributed since 1985, now addresses the role of campus assessment policy and practice in the improvement of teaching and learning. Simplistically stated, the benefits accrued from a great deal of work on assessment stem primarily from the collective attention brought to three simple but important questions: What do we want students to know and be able to do? How can we tell how well they are learning those things? Given our assessment results, how can we improve teaching and learning? Institutional assessment policy also can provide impetus for the collective inquiry about how the student's educational experience adds up, over time and across the curriculum. For many colleges, this inquiry has become the vehicle for defining the meaning of the associate degree.

Since the mid-1980s a number of states have instituted accountability policies; in fact, much of the campus-level assessment activity has been undertaken in response to those initiatives. Several years of experience and observation now suggest that state accountability policies have their most positive effects when they take into account the diversity of institutional missions and clientele, encourage and reinforce the institution's own assessment practices, provide resources to support assessment and improvement efforts based on assessment results, require assessment of general education as well as of discrete majors or program areas, and encourage attention not just to learning outcomes but to the processes that lead to them.

Faculty Policies

Among the most potent factors in supporting teaching and learning are institution's policies regarding its faculty: the role definition, the employment process, required activities for orientation and acculturation, performance evaluation, professional development, and criteria for tenure and promotion. A host of questions related to these policies will reveal an enormous amount about the college's commitment to student learning. Does the faculty role extend beyond the classroom to include involvement in recruiting, advising, and special help for students? Is a demonstration of teaching ability central to the faculty selection process? Are new faculty members expected to participate in serious and extensive orientation, including components dealing with the community college mission, pedagogy, and student diversity? Do faculty evaluation policies set high expectations, encompass a broad range of faculty responsibilities, and involve faculty, students, and administrators in regular, collaborative review of performance? Do promotion and tenure policies place predominant emphasis on demonstrated excellence in teaching?

Only rarely is there a direct attempt to influence faculty-related policies from outside the institution. Nonetheless, there are external forces that have enormous effects. The preeminent example is the extent to which federal and state funding for research skews the priorities of both institutions and faculty members away from teaching and toward research and publication. Even though most community colleges are relatively clear about the teaching mission, their faculties are often still susceptible to pressures from academic disciplines and to distortions in the broader higher education community's definitions of professional competence and prestige.

Governance

By themselves, institutional governance policies may have less impact on teaching and learning than does the spirit that motivates their creation and implementation. It is clearly important to establish explicit definitions for the role of faculty, administrators, and other groups in institutional planning and decision making. Such policies sometimes issue from the conviction that faculty involvement is critical to the quality of decisions and to keeping the college focused on academic achievement. In other settings, especially where there is a history of highly adversarial collective bargaining, governance policies may serve mainly to preserve an "armed camp" mentality, protecting the faculty from change in the status quo, from the administration, and even from students. As Richardson (1992) notes, the governance structures likely to be most supportive of teaching and learning are those that balance faculty and administrative influence and are based on shared values.

Beyond the campus level, there is the hazard that multiple layers of governance may result in conflicting bureaucratic controls and confused priorities, as each governing entity (district, system, state agency, legislature) attempts to influence institutions in accord with its own vision. Only serious and persistent efforts to align priorities and decentralize operational decision making can resolve the gridlock.

Finance

Clearly, one of the most powerful policy levers available at both the institutional and state levels is the manner in which dollars are allocated. For institutions, the proportion of resources allocated to support teaching and learning, the visible uses of discretionary funds, and the match between espoused values and actual expenditures are all compelling indicators of real priorities. Given the current public context for community college work (i.e., concerns about the interconnected issues of access, cost, and quality), the particular configuration of funding support for teaching and learning poses a real dilemma. For example, while access and efficiency may be served by increasing class size, teaching loads, and use of adjunct faculty, those policies may also threaten quality. As any community college leader knows, finding the appropriate balance is an important challenge.

State-level funding mechanisms for higher education incorporate both explicit and implicit incentives and disincentives. Among the policy features that may most directly affect teaching and learning in the community college are these: whether financial aid provisions allow students to attend primarily to learning rather than to unrelated employment; whether funding for undergraduate (and lower-division) instruction takes a back seat to funding for graduate education; whether funding supports developmental education, according to institutional mission, without encouraging a lowering of academic standards; whether there is support for institutional assessment activities; whether there is support for credits earned through internships and other work experience; whether there are incentives (e.g., a bias toward research) that would encourage institutions to diverge from their teaching mission; and whether there are special funding mechanisms (e.g., challenge grants) to encourage excellence in undergraduate education (Jones and Ewell, 1992).

TOWARD THE FUTURE: A NEW GENERATION OF POLICY

This rather cursory overview leads to an important conclusion: that is, that this discussion—especially as it pertains to state policy—is far too much a litany of the status quo. The challenges that face American higher education are so great, and the need to find, within limited resources, far more effective ways to educate an increasingly diverse student population is so critical, that mere preservation of existing policies will not suffice. If institutions of higher education are to be seen as deeply connected with serious issues of national interest—indeed, if they are to be seen as part of the solution rather than part of the problem—then concerted and collaborative effort must be applied to the work of creating a whole new generation of policy to support teaching and learning.

No sector is better equipped to provide leadership for that effort than community colleges.

REFERENCES

American Council on Education. *Setting the National Agenda: Academic Achievement and Transfer.* Washington, D.C.: American Council on Education, 1991.

Association of American Colleges. *Integrity in the College Curriculum: A Report to the Academic Community.* Washington, D.C.: Association of American Colleges, 1985.

Atwell, Robert. "Financial Prospects for Higher Education." *Policy Perspectives*, 1992, *4* (3), Section A, pp. 5B–12B.

Bender, Louis W. (Ed.). *Spotlight on the Transfer Function: A National Study of State Policies and Practices.* Washington, D.C.: American Association of Community Colleges, 1990.

Bok, D. "Reclaiming the Public Trust." *Change*, 1992, *24* (4), pp. 12–19.

Chickering, A. and Z.F. Gamson. "Seven Principles for Good Practice in Undergraduate Education." *AAHE Bulletin*, 1987, *39* (7), pp. 3–7.

Chickering, A., Z.F. Gamson, and Louis M. Barsi. *Inventories of Good Practice in Undergraduate Education.* Racine, Wis.: The Johnson Foundation, 1989.

Commission on the Skills of the American Workforce. *America's Choice: High Skills or Low Wages!* Rochester, N.Y.: National Center on Education and the Economy, 1990.

Edgerton, Russ. "National Standards Are Coming!...National Standards Are Coming!" *AAHE Bulletin*, 1991, *44* (4), pp. 8–12.

Education Commission of the States. *Transforming the State Role in Undergraduate Education: Time for a Different View.* Denver: Education Commission of the States, 1986.

Jaschik, S. "State Funds for Higher Education Drop in Year: First Decline Since Survey Began 33 Years Ago." *Chronicle of Higher Education*, November 6, 1991, p. 1.

Jones, Dennis P. and Peter T. Ewell. "The Effect of State Policy on Undergraduate Education." Paper prepared for the Education Commission of the States. Boulder, Colo.: National Center for Higher Education Management Systems, 1992.

Knoell, Dorothy. *Transfer, Articulation, and Collaboration: Twenty-Five Years Later.* Washington, D.C.: American Association of Community Colleges, 1990.

69

McGuinness, Aims C., Jr. "Lessons from European Integration for U.S. Higher Education." Paper presented at the Eleventh General Conference, Programme on Institutional Management in Higher Education, Organisation for Economic Development and Cooperation, Paris, September 1992.

Mingle, James R. "Funding Higher Education in the 1990s: The Choices We Face." Remarks to the Quality Reinvestment Conference of the University of Wisconsin, Madison, April 3, 1992.

National Education Goals Panel. *The National Education Goals Report: Building a Nation of Learners.* Washington, D.C.: National Education Goals Panel, 1991.

_____. *Report to the Goals Panel from the Task Force on Assessment of the National Goal Relating to Postsecondary Education.* Washington, D.C.: National Education Goals Panel, 1992.

National Governors' Association. *Time for Results.* Washington, D.C.: National Governors' Association, 1986.

Richardson, Richard C., Jr. *Creating Effective Learning Environments: Report of a Study Funded by the Ford Foundation.* Tempe: College of Education, Arizona State University, 1992.

Roueche, John E. and George A. Baker, III. *Access and Excellence: The Open-Door College.* Washington, D.C.: Community College Press, 1987.

State Higher Education Executive Officers. *State Higher Education Appropriations 1991–1992.* Denver: State Higher Education Executive Officers, 1992.

Study Group on the Conditions of Excellence in American Higher Education. *Involvement in Learning: Realizing the Potential of American Higher Education.* Washington, D.C.: U.S. Department of Education/National Institute of Education, 1984.

U.S. Department of Education. *Projections of Education Statistics to 2002.* Washington, D.C.: Superintendent of Documents, 1991.

U.S. Department of Labor Secretary's Commission on Achieving Necessary Skills. *What Work Requires of Schools: A SCANS Report for America 2000.* Washington, D.C.: Superintendent of Documents, 1991.

Kay M. McClenney is vice president of the Education Commission of the States.

PART TWO:

The Practices and

Programs

Chapter 5

The Assessment Movement

Implications for Teaching and Learning

By Peter T. Ewell

Now some ten years old, the national assessment movement in higher education contains a particular imperative for the community college. Far more than any other sector, the proof of effectiveness for the two-year college lies in the judgments of those whom the institution is bound to serve—students, employers, other colleges and universities, and members of the local community. If shortcomings occur here, there are no ivy-covered walls behind which to shelter. The escalating challenges provided by a new environment of financial stringency and growing diversity are far more immediately apparent in the two-year college world than in higher education generally. Because of these factors, it is likely that the nation's community colleges will need to become more effective and to demonstrate their effectiveness far more than will other types of institutions.

Assessment and, more importantly, a systematic process of improvement in teaching and learning based on its results, have become critical to mission fulfillment and survival. And community colleges generally are in the forefront of those institutions paying serious attention to assessment. Yet the community college also provides a particularly challenging environment for assessment. Enormous diversity in student abilities and backgrounds, relatively slim databases about student characteristics and activities, and, above all, the variety of ways in which students experience instruction often preclude the use of techniques "proven" in other settings. The result is, as it should be, a distinctive community college approach to assessment that must be developed on its own terms.

The intent of this chapter is to describe this evolving approach, but also to provide some direction for its future. Two-year colleges are more often seeing the wisdom of combining assessment with more comprehensive quality initiatives—often under the rubric of Total Quality Management (TQM)—intended to transform teaching and learning and to improve administrative processes. This chapter consists of four main sections reflecting this growing emphasis. The first presents briefly the evolution of the national assessment movement, with emphasis on the special problems faced by two-year colleges. Among the most salient is the fact that the typical community college is a multifunction, multiconstituency institution whose assessable goals are both numerous and quite often differently interpreted by its constituencies. An initial challenge is to specify these goals in a manner that can better guide assessment and the improvements that we expect assessment to inform. The chapter's second section addresses this issue. Beyond goals, however, the community college environment provides substantial technical challenges for the practice of assessment. These challenges, and some unique opportunities as well, suggest approaches to assessment that experience with two-year colleges shows to be fruitful—approaches that are presented in the chapter's third section. But as demonstrated on far too many campuses, assessment is useless without application. Accordingly, the chapter's final section provides three core injunctions intended to improve instructional practice and to cement the linkage between information and action.

74

A key assumption cutting across all four sections is that the community college is preeminently a "practice" environment. If assessment techniques do not apply directly to improvement or are not easily accommodated within the institution's distinctive and flexible approaches to teaching and learning, they will not be legitimate or effective.

THE ASSESSMENT MOVEMENT AND THE COMMUNITY COLLEGE: COMMON ROOTS, DISTINCTIVE SETTINGS

The forces behind the emergence of the current national assessment movement have much in common with the forces attending the birth of most two-year colleges two to three decades earlier. Both movements embodied a conscious reform agenda and a desire to return the needs of the student to the center of attention. Both incorporated this agenda in a broader notion of service to community and society, emphasizing the proposition that higher education could no longer function as an isolated enterprise.

The stimulus for the current movement came from two simultaneous developments in the mid-1980s. The first involved issues internal to higher education—in particular, the compelling need to promote greater coherence in instructional design and delivery, to provide more frequent opportunities for feedback and active learning to students, and to accommodate an increasingly diverse and underprepared student body. For community colleges, these concerns were apparent in two ways: a demand to fuse traditional and applied learning in practical ways acceptable to the demands of an older, more product-conscious student; and a need to develop effective mechanisms to quickly identify basic skill deficiencies. Assessment, when initially proposed by such national reports as *Involvement in Learning* (National Institute of Education, 1984) and *Integrity in the College Curriculum* (Association of American Colleges, 1985), embraced these themes as part of a broader academic agenda: coupled with an emphasis on high expectations and an actively involving curriculum, faculty might

75

through assessment consciously and systematically redirect undergraduate teaching and learning in desired directions.

Because the message of these two reports was couched in the rhetoric of the traditional four-year residential college, much of the community college world initially felt excluded from the conversation—despite the fact that most of them had practiced assessment for far longer than their four-year counterparts. But the movement's initial emphasis on diversity of approaches, faculty-ownership, and the overall effectiveness of the institution remained highly consistent with community college sentiments.

The other stimulus for assessment came from outside, fueled in the mid- to late-'80s by growing public and political concerns about higher education's declining quality, and often directed at community colleges. To some degree, these concerns were a natural carry-over from K–12 education, where quality problems were more severe and the perceived need for external solutions more pressing. But external pressure for higher education assessment in this period was also a product of more fundamental and permanent shifts in the notion of accountability, away from an exclusive concern with access and efficiency and toward "return on investment" as demonstrated in such areas as state-level economic development and work force competitiveness. The result of both these forces in the period 1986–92 was a significant increase in state-mandated assessment of student performance and a realignment of the focus of regional accreditation from inputs and processes toward educational results (Ewell and Boyer, 1988). By 1992 more than three-quarters of states had in place a requirement that all public institutions engage in a systematic process of assessment and report on the results, while all six regional accrediting bodies enacted similar provisions.

For a number of reasons, these mandates often affected community colleges disproportionately. First, their visibly public nature did not allow avoidance of such requirements, and their political clout to resist or reshape them was generally weaker than that of more established institutions. In a few states, such as California, accountability for community colleges was established through special legislation independent from the balance of higher education. Second, because of their access mission, the problems of community colleges were more publicly visible, and thus two-year institutions were often under greater public pressure to comply with any such directives.

The result by 1990 was substantial institutional action on assessment within the community college sector, but much of it was reactive to external pressure and concentrated on basic skills, rather than directed toward broader instructional improvement (El-Khawas 1988–92). From these reactive beginnings, however, many two-year campuses had by 1992 evolved a distinctive and innovative approach to assessment, more aligned with the movement's initial philosophy of ongoing internal, student-centered improvement of practice. At the same time, many had also recognized that adopting the goal-centered core philosophy of assessment helped to legitimize the distinctive mission of the community college by de-emphasizing an exclusionary view of quality. If, as most now argued, mission attainment—rather than the pre-enrollment characteristics of admitted students—could be seen as the ultimate mark of a quality institution, community colleges might begin to remove from the public's minds the perception of quality traditionally imposed by the academic pecking order.

In implementing assessment, however, community colleges quickly felt the need to alter traditional approaches, developed in far different settings, to fit their own distinctive environment. On the positive side, two-year institutions began with the advantage of a strong organizational focus on the core function of teaching and learning: people in community colleges know what they are trying to accomplish far more concretely than their counterparts in other parts of higher education. At the same time, the community college environment is distinctively permeated by a spirit of innovation and flexibility: relatively unencumbered by customary methods, people in community colleges are not afraid to try new things if they appear to have the potential of paying important dividends. Assessment practice benefitted greatly from these attributes.

But assessing student learning in the typical two-year college setting also involved some unusual challenges. Some are rooted in the mission of the community college and the students it is bound to serve. The typical community college is generally in several "businesses" at once—including traditional transfer education, occupational/technical training, developmental education, and avocational/service instruction—and most of these "businesses" operate in relative independence. In this respect, the typical community college is more like a holding company than a single-purpose industry. Similarly, typical two-year college students can range from the traditional 18- to 21-year-old population through a gamut of individuals, each with a different set of needs and ambitions. These characteristics suggest that many of the goals of assessment should be separately conceived for different constituency and mission areas—a challenge explored in the next section.

At the same time, the typical community college provides a particularly intractable setting for the deployment of traditional assessment methods. For example, most two-year colleges have relatively slim databases about their students, particularly in the area of prior educational attainments and experiences. More importantly, the typical community college student will not sit still for assessment. Most are unwilling to engage in testing that does not benefit them directly, and, as commuting students, most are not routinely available for data collection. In fact, relatively few take the curriculum as designed (or in many cases even complete it), effectively precluding in many programs the use of "capstones" or other curriculum-embedded assessment devices that depend upon students taking courses in a particular order. As noted in the section on Evolving Appropriate Assessment Methods, these features have led to a distinctive pattern of practice that continues to evolve.

CLARIFYING GOALS

It is an old and honored axiom in assessment that clear goals are necessary to guide evidence gathering and improvement. Indeed, as considerable experience in assessment suggests, developing clear goals for instruction may be beneficial in itself (Banta and Moffett, 1987). Only rarely are higher education institutions

78

accorded the opportunity to specify the outcomes they intend to pursue collectively. When such an opportunity arises, it often provides an occasion to discuss long-neglected cross-curricular issues that can have an immediate impact on course content and instructional delivery.

But where should such collective instructional goals come from? When considering the typical domains of community college performance, it is traditional to begin with the litany of program areas contained in most two-year college mission statements. These at least include college transfer, occupational/technical, and developmental instruction. But while broadly descriptive of what community colleges do, these statements rarely specify performance terms; still less (with the possible exception of developmental education) do they directly imply a specific set of student knowledge and skill levels against which to assess performance. Nevertheless, these three core instructional functions provide an excellent place to begin a discussion of collective learning goals. What, for example, do each of these three functions imply in performance terms? As summarized in Figure 1, a first answer in each case addresses what students actually know and can do when they leave the institution (Evidence of Student Capacity). A second and equally important answer addresses how well former students actually perform in the context for which they were prepared (Evidence of Student Behavior). Useful goal statements for guiding both assessment and instructional improvement should involve both and should get quite specific within each.

"Effective learning" in transfer education, for instance, implies that students possess fundamental knowledge in a range of disciplines and requisite skills of college functioning to successfully pursue baccalaureate study. "Knowledge" in this context generally refers to knowledge of the basic content of core disciplines in the humanities, sciences, and social sciences, together with some familiarity with the modes of inquiry typical of different disciplinary areas (for example, scientific/experimental method). "Skills" in this context generally refers to such higher-order integrative thinking skills as critical thinking, creative thinking, or problem

79

FIGURE 1
Community College Functions as Statement of Intended Performance

Function	Outcome/Goal	Evidence of Student Capacity	Evidence of Student Behavior
Transfer	Students possess fundamental knowledge in a range of disciplines and requisite skills of collegiate functioning to successfully pursue baccalaureate study at a four-year college or university	Assessed knowledge of: –core discipline content –disciplinary modes of inquiry Assessed skill levels in: –collegiate skills (e.g., critical thinking/problem solving) –academic/study skills Academic attitudes/values	Successful transfer to or performance in four-year institution
Occupational	Students possess requisite technical knowledge and competence to perform effectively in identified fields of employment –for job entry –for job upgrade	Assessed competencies in completing specific job tasks in actual job settings Work-related attitudes/values	Success in obtaining/maintaining employment in field of training Job performance in field of training
Developmental	Students possess requisite knowledge and basic skills to successfully undertake college-level work	Assessed skill levels in: –reading –writing –computation	Success in subsequent college-level work

solving; often these include higher levels of communication (both oral and written) and quantitative abilities as well. Alternatively, such skills have been described as general intellectual skills, including such abilities as "gathering information, analyzing information, and presenting information" (College Outcomes Evaluation Program, 1987). Finally, appropriate student capacities in this area may embrace such skills as how to use a computer or the resources of a library, and such academic attitudes as value neutrality, intellectual persistence, and tolerance for diversity. Student capacities in all these areas are reflected behaviorally in subsequent performance at a senior institution. Relevant performance characteristics here include successful transfer of credits, persistence at a senior institution, baccalaureate degree completion, grades earned, and course completion rates.

"Effective learning" in occupational/technical education, in turn, implies that students possess the requisite technical knowledge and competence to perform effectively in identified fields of employment. Properly specifying intended instructional results in this domain first requires recognition that two quite different student groups may be involved, each with a somewhat different criterion for success. For students seeking job entry, effective learning is manifested in obtaining and maintaining initial employment in their fields of training. For those seeking job or skills upgrades, continuing technical skill development, or recertification, the appropriate test of effective learning is promotion and enhanced job performance. In either case, earning the associated community college credential (degree or certificate) is only an indirect indication of success because program completion may not be necessary to attain these primary goals. As in the case of transfer instruction, moreover, further distinctions are needed among those student capacities targeted by instruction. One set of these, of course, has to do with the particular knowledge and skill base required for the occupation or profession in question—a set of outcomes that usually is already well-specified in most two-year occupational/technical programs. Equally important but generally less well-specified is a set of more basic work-related knowledge-building skills required to learn new procedures, instructions, and technologies, and to communicate effectively with fellow workers. As in the case of transfer education, appropriate vocational outcomes may finally include such critical affective domains as motivation, tolerance, responsibility, team membership, and proper work habits.

"Effective learning" in developmental education implies that students possess the requisite knowledge and skills to successfully undertake college-level work. Such basic skills include reading, writing, and computational abilities that are already defined operationally at most two-year colleges through initial diagnostic testing and placement, and often through post-testing. The true behavioral "test" of the effective acquisition of these basic skills is not an examination score but subsequent performance in related college-level coursework by students previously assessed as deficient in comparison with students who did not receive or did not require basic skills instruction. Relevant performance requirements here include persistence in college, degree completion, overall course-completion rates, and particularly performance in the first college-level course encountered that demands proficiency in a previously deficient skill. Another common component of developmental instruction in community colleges addresses the acquisition of additional societal competencies—for example, GED (high school equivalency) training or English as a Second Language. In both cases, behavioral evidence of learning effectiveness is provided by persistence in and eventual completion of these programs; if students achieving these competencies continue with regular college-level transfer or occupational study, additional evidence of effectiveness is provided by their performance in these curricula and their ultimate success in completing them.

Different institutions will, of course, differ markedly in their relative emphases on these generic instructional functions. More importantly, because community colleges are principally service institutions, each of these basic functions (and the goals that compose them) may need to be explicitly investigated from the perspectives of clients and constituents. In most cases, this means partially recasting goals from a range of identified "customer" viewpoints. Indeed, at many colleges the subsequent adoption of total quality practices that demand a systematic identification of customers and customer requirements has a significant impact on the conduct of assessment (e.g., DeCosmo, Parker, and Heverly, 1991).

For individual community college students, for example, success in learning ultimately implies fulfillment of their own goals for attendance—goals that may or may not include program completion per se, or indeed, any of the specific competencies that the faculty intends to teach. Determining the effectiveness of learning from the student's perspective thus demands some knowledge about initial student goals and the degree to which these goals have changed or been fulfilled in the course of attendance. Taking the student's perspective may also entail collecting information on the future likelihood, based on past performance, that student goals will in fact be fulfilled—for example, information on the probability that a student with given characteristics will obtain a job as a result of completing a particular program, or will even complete the program. A parallel group of clients in this regard consists of area employers. Effectiveness from their perspective may embrace qualities not always covered in faculty-established program goals—for instance, the need for teamwork and oral communications skills among potential employees.

EVOLVING APPROPRIATE ASSESSMENT METHODS

Taken collectively, the many domains of the community college and the multiple perspectives and behavior patterns of its constituents help determine what is most useful and what is most practical for assessment. Based on analysis and emerging practical experience, the following four priorities for assessment have emerged as most appropriate for community colleges as devices to improve teaching and learning.

1. Develop Longitudinal Information on Student Experience and Performance. Because patterns of attendance and course taking are so varied in community college settings, it is often difficult to determine precisely which of many possible curricula a given body of students has taken. But without such knowledge about the instructional stimulus, there will be little hope for improvement, no matter what results an outcome asessment may show. Experience has demonstrated that a major assessment priority for community colleges is to construct an integrated longitudinal student database capable of investigating such patterns (Palmer, 1992; 1990; and Bers, 1989). Based on a cohort methodology, such a database typically allows monitoring of overall persistence, course completion rates, and the fulfillment of various curricular requirements. Adequately constructed, it can also contain information on student goal fulfillment, the adequacy of developmental education as reflected in subsequent performance in college-level work, and placement and performance in senior institutions or in the workplace (Ewell, Parker, and Jones, 1988).

2. *Carefully Target Special Assessments of Student Performance.* Assessing actual learning outcomes is a formidable undertaking, and community colleges provide a particularly challenging environment for such work. As a result, two-year colleges will generally and appropriately deploy fewer formal assessment techniques than their four-year counterparts, with these carefully focused on particular student populations or outcomes. Only rarely will large-scale general-purpose testing be either possible or beneficial, but several targeted assessment activities are especially fruitful for guiding improvement in a two-year college setting. Post-testing of basic skills after the completion of developmental coursework is among the most beneficial and easily implemented. Most two-year colleges already engage in substantial testing in reading, writing, and computation for course placement, so the selection of a valid and accepted instrument is generally not an issue. Exit testing using the same instrument not only provides a final certification of the fact that remediation has occurred, but if subscore and item scores are available, the process can also serve to identify remaining areas of weakness in learning.

A second fruitful locus for carefully targeted direct assessment is in the occupational/technical areas, many of which already include formal internships or practice projects as part of their curricula. Practice experiences that involve a demonstration of

84

learned skills in actual practice settings provide admirable opportunities for more formal assessment, if multiple judges and defined rating scales are used (Erwin, 1991). Assessors can in this case be drawn not only from faculty, but also from members of the local practice community, many of whom may already be involved in the program through membership in a program advisory committee. Because the objective here is to detect overall patterns of strength and weakness across student populations, the rating scales employed should be designed to assess multiple dimensions of performance, not just the individual student's overall adequacy or fitness to practice.

3. *Capitalize on Collecting Additional Information at Existing Points of Contact with Students.* Because of the volatile nature of community college enrollment, there usually are few occasions to systematically collect information from students. This makes it more important to take advantage of existing opportunities to collect additional information about instructional effectiveness—even when these opportunities were not originally designed for this purpose. Two of the most prominent points of contact are basic skills testing and instructional course evaluation. Because the first is often a mandatory activity (at least for degree seekers), it reaches a large volume of students. Not only can scores on such examinations be used as part of an overall assessment program, but the opportunity can also be taken to administer additional instruments; among the most fruitful here are surveys that examine student goals for attendance and/or anticipated difficulties in enrollment. Similarly, instructional course evaluations are often completed by thousands of students but are almost exclusively concerned with course characteristics and instructor behaviors. But such instruments can easily be modified to include additional items on student behavior associated with the course—for example, numbers of hours spent studying, discussions of class materials with classmates or peers, and reported use of the library—or to include additional items on self-reported learning gain in specified areas.

Among the most important points of contact, of course, is the classroom. Beyond initial admissions processing, the individual classroom provides what is often the only feasible setting for assessing the typical community college student. As a result, indirect assessment approaches that rely on the use of already-produced student work, such as portfolios and work samples, have become particularly attractive in a two-year college setting. In transfer courses, for instance, compilation of student writing portfolios can be useful both in assessing individual student progress and in determining the strengths and weaknesses of student writing more in general (Elbow and Belanoff, 1986). Similarly, such techniques as systematically collecting the examinations and exercises of the "median student" in each class within a particular discipline group can allow useful patterns of average performance to be explored without the typical disruptions of mass testing. Where multiple-choice tests are used, simply compiling and disseminating results for discussion among faculty can be extremely useful in discussing and better targeting instruction.

4. Develop Better Mechanisms for Getting Information to Those Who Need It. All too often, assessment data collection leads to reports that no one reads. This is particularly true of the decentralized academic setting provided by the community college, in which few natural opportunities occur for collective faculty dialogue. As important as collecting assessment information is developing means for disseminating and discussing it with those who need it—those in direct contact with students. In place of reports packaged around particular data collection efforts (for example, a follow-up survey of students who complete occupational programs), reports are often far more fruitfully packaged in terms of perceived problems—for example, the challenges of placing individuals who have been long out of the work force or older women who are returning to work. Problem-oriented reports of this kind must be actively disseminated and discussed—most effectively in such special problem-solving work group settings as are now becoming popular in community colleges through the application of TQM. Finally, individual faculty members and advising personnel need more and better information about the goals, strengths, and weaknesses of the students with whom they have direct contact. Individual "course reports," which aggregate previously collected assessment information about the students in a particular classroom for immediate faculty use (as at Mt. Hood Community College, Oregon), and computer-generated integrated advising profiles (as at Miami-Dade Community College, Florida) provide excellent examples of use-oriented reporting.

All four of these priority approaches have the virtues of practicality and concern for use. Each of them can be pursued independently and incrementally as opportunities arise. This last is a particularly important lesson as many community colleges initially attempted assessment as a grand design, dependent on one-shot, all-or-nothing, and often very complex data-gathering approaches. Experience suggests that getting something practical in place early and gradually refining it to meet new needs is a far superior approach.

PUTTING ASSESSMENT TO WORK IN IMPROVING TEACHING AND CURRICULAR DESIGN

Setting appropriate learning goals and collecting appropriate evidence of their achievement is, of course, only the first prerequisite for improving curriculum and teaching practice. Systematic application of these results is required on a continuous basis at all levels—from curricular monitoring and design to the development and adjustment of teaching strategies in individual classrooms. This requires that assessment increasingly be undertaken by faculty and academic administrators not as something extra but as a kind of second nature, essentially indistinguishable from everyday practice. Assessment activities have evolved to have much in common with the current quality revolution in business and industry, and many TQM concepts are appropriate as integral parts of instruction in two-year college settings. Three specific injunctions seem particularly germane in this respect and can be used to inform assessment design and to improve instructional practice. Each is applicable to many levels of academic organization within the college—from the institution as a whole, through specific instructional programs, to the individual classroom.

1. Get Specific About Intended Results. Faculty at community colleges are often extremely adept at developing specific learning goals for individual classes. But with the exception of a few well-specified occupational and technical areas, they are generally much less able to agree immediately on common goals for instruction at the program or institutional level. Assessment forces such attention as a critical condition of gathering evidence, and, as many observers have noted, the goal-development process forced by assessment may have important independent effects on curriculum and instructional delivery. But all too often, faculty see the process of goal development as linear. They believe that fully developed, agreed-upon goals are a necessary prerequisite to beginning assessment of any kind, unaware that in practice the two often go hand in hand. Indeed, the most fruitful linkages between assessment and teaching practice often occur at the outset of the process, when faculty must wrestle with the question of how the achievement of a given student competency or attribute might be practically recognized, taught for, and assessed.

This is not to say that all such goals must be in the narrow sense "measurable"—another common faculty perception that makes a mistake of a different kind. But assessment's demand that goal achievement at least be subject to recognizable description will often lead to important and refreshingly concrete faculty discussions about the strengths and weaknesses of existing student work, in an attempt to agree on the abilities they would like to assess—discussions that inevitably have an impact on how they behave in their own classrooms. One of the most commonly reported positive effects of assessment is that faculty directly involved in the design process become far more adept at constructing their own examinations and local grading procedures (Boyer, 1989).

Once intended results are fully described, it is a reasonable further question to ask what is to be taught where. While educational processes are certainly not production lines, in which components are assembled in a rigidly defined order, they do occur at least in principle according to a particular design. Yet only rarely do faculty examine systematically the degree to which their curricular designs match their expectations. Are faculty indeed teaching the overarching common skills which in a different forum they all agreed are important, or are these assumed to be taught in other peoples' classes or made the students' responsibility? Again, curriculum descriptions provide a good place to start in addressing this question, but such descriptions are rarely approached as a basis for a wider set of discussions about improvement.

Given these issues, experience suggests some particular techniques inspired by the Total Quality Movement, which can have a positive effect on both assessment and instruction:

- **Benchmarking.** External benchmarking of expected performance is common in many professional programs through the establishment of standards for individual certification and specialized program accreditation. Required standards are increasingly being recast (and assessed) in performance terms as complex abilities rooted in actual practice settings. Detailed knowledge about these settings, how they operate, and how they embody the skills to be taught is fundamental to the process. So is some familiarity with what others in the same instructional business—already recognized as effective by the practice community—are expecting and doing. Such concepts are not commonly applied to more traditional academic areas such as writing or the development of quantitative skills, where practice settings are more difficult to specify, but they can be. Revising an expectation for written communication in an occupational program, for instance, from an abstractly defined level of functioning to the far more concrete question of how a given individual is able to prepare a business memo or a problem report on a particular piece of equipment, provides a useful example of what might be accomplished here.
- **Flow-charting and curricular mapping.** Though loosely intended as learning plans, most curricula are rarely analyzed as such. An often successful approach is to map the curriculum to note the points and levels in required course sequences where identified skills are to be reinforced. This process quickly reveals gaps and can immediately suggest

points of collective attack to close them. Flow-charts of this kind can be even more useful when the unit of analysis employed to build them is not what is taught but what is tested. Constructing a theoretical portfolio of expected student performance for a particular curriculum—consisting of the sum total of all tests, papers, exercises, etc. that are required to complete it—can reveal a good deal about the degree of reality in those expectations. This view of the curriculum, after all, is the one the student most often sees and is often what really shapes behavior. In turn this leads to a final empirical form of flow-charting to determine whether students are taking the curriculum as designed. As noted earlier, the behavioral curriculum often only approximates the designed curriculum as students make their own choices about what classes to take and in what order. A longitudinal database that allows computerized tracking of course-taking patterns and other aspects of enrollment behavior can be a major asset in this process. Explicitly mapping all three curricula—designed, expectational, and behavioral—can provide faculty with a particularly effective starting point for improvement.

2. Make Sure that Connections Are Happening. Faculty are also generally more adept at designing good curricula than ensuring that instructional processes assumed by the design are working properly. A telling example often lies in the assumed connections among courses set up in a prerequisite sequence. Instructional research often reveals that skills learned in one class may not be effectively transferred into an alien context, either because they have been forgotten or because instruction has not emphasized and rehearsed such transitions. Because community college faculty are typically dispersed across discrete classrooms with little incentive to cooperate, addressing this condition can prove to be challenging. One increasingly used approach is to develop specific exercises that assess the transition of key skills between classrooms and that assess such skills in new contexts. This technique is already practiced with writing and can be successfully extended to other skills. Using such techniques may also involve the identification of behavioral "course clusters"—classes generally taken together or in sequence by large numbers of students, regardless of original curricular design. Once these are identified, faculty in such clusters can work together to design instructional contexts and exercises that will help rather than hinder the transition of common skills.

Among the specific techniques potentially applicable to this set of issues are the following:

- **Identifying "internal customers."** It is often a surprise to discover that faculty resistance to the term "customer" can evaporate when it is applied not to students or potential employers, but to themselves in relation to one another. Structures of prerequisite courses, if they work at all, are in essence based upon an internal network of supplier-customer relations. Faculty are quick to grasp the power of this idea in community colleges if it helps them address what they see as a principal problem in teaching: the need to continually re-teach what should have been learned earlier. Such exercises are best kept small and should involve only a few key courses and skills in a defined prerequisite sequence. Some of the best candidates here are communications ability and basic math in connection with later courses that require these skills. Less obviously, it has proven important to keep faculty attention focused on the relatively few core competencies that need to go forward, rather than focusing on the far larger portion of disciplinary content that any given course will generally contain. "Supplier" faculty who teach basic math should be fully aware of the specific kinds of calculations that their students will face in business courses, for example, and should employ such applications wherever appropriate; but this by no means dictates that a cookbook approach be used for their course as a whole.
- **Identifying patterns of deficiency.** Once the notion of establishing internal supplier-customer relationships takes root, a next step is often to systematically determine what

skill transitions are not taking place. A simple and appropriate assessment technique is to classify the errors students typically make when attempting to apply particular skills or concepts, ranking them according to frequency and using the resulting information to help target earlier instruction to address deficiencies (see, for example, Cross and Angelo, 1988). A common vehicle for doing this is a simple first-day-of-class exercise that can simultaneously serve to provide direct feedback to the student about readiness and areas of deficiency, provide information to the instructor about the overall readiness of the class and what needs to be covered again, and provide information to support discussions with "suppliers" about what needs to be emphasized for the future.

3. Reorient Faculty Grading to Provide Information About the Instructional Process as well as Individual Performance. In individual classrooms faculty constantly assess student performance. But because their judgments are typically focused on students taken one at a time, they are rarely able to retrieve the complex mental decision process associated with determining and assigning a particular grade. If these complex, multidimensional decision processes and criteria can be captured—as faculty in a nursing program often do in their observation of clinical practice—the result is a record that can also help guide further collective improvements in instruction.

At the same time the role of grades as critical elements of internal and external communication is currently undervalued. Internally, faculty rarely look at grades in prerequisite courses as data for a number of reasons. Laudably, they want to make an independent judgment of performance and fear that they may be unduly influenced by the results of prior assessment. But more often they discover that an examination of prior course performance records fails to really tell them anything. Externally, with the often revealing exception of key occupational courses, most employers rely on their own independent assessments of student capacity in making hiring decisions. In both cases, the occupational course exception is telling, because grades in such courses are much more likely to be graded against specific competencies. The development of dimensional grading techniques defined in terms of specific competencies is far less common in transfer courses and need not fully displace traditional grading. But it can certainly pay considerable dividends for improvement. Here, experience suggests, it is important to start with a few carefully selected courses that contain such competencies and allow faculty to experiment with different grading approaches.

Given these conditions, the following approaches appear applicable:

- **Looking at grade patterns more systematically.** Any outcomes data collected over time should be examined statistically to distinguish those cases that are exceptional from those that are part of a larger pattern of common variation. Because many current grading processes are norm-based, built on the variation of a given classroom of students around its own mean of performance, they unconsciously reinforce the assignment of such variation to "special causes" assumed to be outside the process of instruction. Most of these are attributed to students' presumed differences in ability, motivation, or time on task. Examination of the resulting grading pattern may tell us something about individual students, but it is virtually useless for informing the instructional process. Competency-based grading systems—particularly when they allow the independent identification of discrete dimensions of performance—are more promising in this respect. So long as criteria remain stable and rating assignments reliable, such results can be meaningfully analyzed over time to begin separating "special" from common causes of variation. Once the latter are truly isolated, they can provide a good point of departure for systematic improvement.
- **Cross-grading and team grading.** For grading patterns to be collectively useful as data for instructional improvement, they must also be reliable. Attaining this condition requires

more than abstract agreement about standards; it requires practice. Team grading in key courses is reappearing at some institutions and never disappeared from a few others. In writing and occasionally other fields, multiple readers are also widely used for high-stakes assessment exercises. When posed as a systematic assessment device, however, most community colleges reject team-grading approaches as too expensive to seriously consider. But useful approximations of team grading are far cheaper and easier to implement. One is cross-grading across course sections, in which only one reader per section is used, but each examines the work of students in another class. A variant in a multisection course is to design a common exercise, each portion of which is rated for all students by a different instructor. A final alternative is to leave current grading practice unaltered, but to cross-rate occasional samples of performance and discuss the results. Like other attempts to develop common assessments of performance, these techniques have the virtue not only of ultimately providing more reliable grading standards, but also of promoting the kinds of team-building discussion required for collective improvement. Indeed, if past experience in assessment is any guide, discussions of this kind are probably the most important outcome of all.

In sum, assessment in community colleges has grown and is being transformed into something of much greater significance for teaching and learning. Beginning on many campuses as an act of compliance in response to outside directives, assessment has become a critical tool to inform a process of continuous improvement. And to meet tough times and the challenge of diversity, this process will be sorely needed in the years to come.

REFERENCES

Association of American Colleges. *Integrity in the College Curriculum.* Washington, D.C.: Association of American Colleges, 1985.

Banta, Trudy W., and Marian S. Moffett. "Performance Funding in Tennessee: Stimulus for Program Improvement." In Diane F. Halpern (Ed.), *Student Outcomes Assessment: What Institutions Stand to Gain.* New Directions for Higher Education, no. 59. San Francisco: Jossey-Bass, 1987.

Bers, Trudy H. (Ed.). *Using Student Tracking Systems Effectively.* New Directions for Community Colleges, no. 66. San Francisco: Jossey-Bass, 1989.

Boyer, Carol M. *Improving Student Learning: The Outcomes Program at Kean College of New Jersey.* Union: Kean College of New Jersey, 1989.

"College Outcomes Evaluation Program, State of New Jersey, Final Report to the New Jersey Board of Higher Education from the Advisory Committee to the College Outcomes Evaluation Program." Trenton: New Jersey Department of Higher Education, 1987.

Cross, K. Patricia, and Thomas A. Angelo. *Classroom Assessment Techniques: A Handbook for Faculty.* Ann Arbor: National Center for Research to Improve Postsecondary Teaching and Learning, 1988.

DeCosmo, Richard D., Jerome Parker, and Mary Ann Heverly. "Total Quality Management Goes to Community College." In Lawrence J. Sherr and Deborah J. Teeter (Eds.), *Total Quality Management in Higher Education.* New Directions for Institutional Research, no. 71. San Francisco: Jossey-Bass, 1991, pp. 13–26.

Elbow, Peter, and P. Belanoff. "Portfolios as a Substitute for Proficiency Examinations," *College Composition and Communication,* October, 1986.

El-Khawas, Elaine. *Campus Trends Survey(s).* Washington, D.C.: American Council on Education, 1988–1992.

Erwin, T. Dary. *Assessing Student Learning and Development: A Guide to the Principles, Goals, and Methods of Determining College Outcomes.* San Francisco: Jossey-Bass, 1991.

Ewell, Peter T., and Carol M. Boyer. "Acting Out State-Mandated Assessment," *Change,* 1988, *20,* pp. 40–47.

Ewell, Peter T., Ronald Parker, and Dennis P. Jones. *Establishing a Longitudinal Student Tracking System: An Implementation Handbook.* Boulder, Colo.: National Center for Higher Education Management Systems, 1988.

National Institute of Education. *Involvement in Learning: Realizing the Potential of American Higher Education.* Report of the Study Group on the Conditions of Excellence in American Higher Education, Washington, D.C.: U.S. Government Printing Office, 1984.

Palmer, Jim. *Accountability Through Student Tracking: A Review of the Literature.* Washington, D.C.: American Association of Community Colleges, 1990.

_____. "Implementing Student Tracking Systems: Concepts and Issues," *Community, Technical, and Junior College Journal*, 1992, 62 (4), pp. 15–19.

Peter T. Ewell *is senior associate, National Center for Higher Education Management Systems.*

Chapter 6

Improving Opportunities for Underprepared Students

By Richard C. Richardson, Jr. and Diana B. Elliott

For as long as records have been maintained, students attending community colleges have been characterized as less well-prepared and less traditional than their senior-college counterparts. Apart from having lower grades in high school courses and scoring lower on tests of academic aptitude, they are older, less certain of their educational objectives, more likely to work while attending school, less likely to earn a degree, and more likely to be minorities or women.

The level of diversity is increasing (Cohen and Brawer, 1991). Trends during the past two decades include increasing numbers of lower-ability students, lower academic skills among entering freshmen, and low prior school achievement.

More than half of all students entering community colleges lack the basic skills required to do creditable academic work (McCabe, 1988). In urban institutions these numbers often range from 75 percent to more than 95 percent of the student body.

97

While the concentration of minority students in urban institutions, which lack the resources and diversity of the surrounding suburban areas, contributes to the visibility of minority preparation problems (Orwell et al., 1984), most students in most community colleges need learning environments that are user-friendly and nurturing.

Community colleges have responded to increased student diversity by expanding the curriculum and by enhancing the number and variety of developmental offerings. They also rely more heavily on part-time faculty who may impart information as effectively as their full-time counterparts, but who clearly are less available for advising, out-of-class assistance, and committee assignments. In the growing community college commitment to part-time intermittent students and faculty, some observers have seen a plot to preserve existing social arrangements by diverting students from earning degrees that might increase their social mobility (Brint and Karabel, 1989).

A recent analysis of National Longitudinal Study (NLS) data for the class of 1972 (Adelman, 1992) takes critics to task, describing the accusations of class-based social tracking as "bizarre" and the analyses on which arguments are based as "hocus pocus" (p. 26). In contrast to the four-year college population, Adelman describes community college students as reflective of the general population in "just about everything" and likely to go to school on their own terms (p. 31). Differences in curricular backgrounds distinguish students who go to college and earn degrees from those who do not. Adelman adds, "The few highly talented students in the NLS-72 simply did not attend community colleges regardless of socioeconomic background" (p. 16).

The way a problem is defined determines the range of solutions likely to be explored. Identifying community college students as underprepared places the blame for academic failure on them rather than on the college. In this chapter, the results of survey research and case studies[1] funded by the Ford Foundation

---

1. Institutions participating in the case study phase of the four-year project were Bronx Community College (NY), El Paso Community College (TX), Essex County College (NJ), Erie Community College (NY), Northern Essex Community College (MA),

will provide a richer and more contextual description of diversity among community college students; will describe the needs of diverse students in their own words; and will report responses to these needs by a nationally representative sample of community college faculty. We conclude by summarizing implications for community college leaders. We suggest community colleges can improve the quality of their education by emphasizing practices that help faculty respond more effectively to student diversity.

CHARACTERIZING STUDENTS IN MORE PRODUCTIVE WAYS

Community colleges serve students with a wide range of preparation and opportunity orientations (Skinner and Richardson, 1988). The term "diverse" is more descriptive of these students than "underprepared." Diversity suggests key differences among all students that may affect their chances for academic success. Several examples illustrate diversity and its influence on the way a student experiences a learning environment (Richardson, Matthews, and Finney, 1992, p. 1):

- African American, Latino, or American Indian students enrolled in predominantly Anglo colleges (or Anglo students enrolled in predominantly African American, Latino, or American Indian colleges).
- First-generation college students of any race or ethnicity.
- Students whose previous academic preparation is a poor match for campus expectations. (Such students can properly be referred to as underprepared.)
- Women enrolled in historically male programs or institutions.
- Older students attempting to earn degrees while concurrently managing employment and family responsibilities.
- Students with developmental or physical disabilities.

Penn Valley Community College (MO), Richland College (TX), Sacramento City College (CA), Sinclair Community College (OH), Triton College (IL), Valencia Community College (FL), Wayne Community College (NC).

These categories are not mutually exclusive. Students are underprepared when they do not meet the entering expectations of the institution in which they enroll. Students are at risk when they differ from a campus' traditional clientele.

The preparation/diversity issue is arguably the most important challenge community colleges confront. It cannot be neutralized by redefining outcomes downward so that underprepared students can achieve them. Nor can the issue be avoided in open-access institutions by excluding students assessed as extremely high-risk. Increasing the number of students who attend without also increasing the number who attain outcomes to which the public attaches priority aggravates the problem. Changing the learning environment by improving the quality of student-faculty interaction offers the most hope for long-term improvement in acceptable outcomes.

DIVERSITY MANDATES CHANGE

Faculty are key to any strategy for improving educational opportunities for the increasingly diverse students enrolling at community colleges. Students who are uncertain about their abilities, their aspirations, and the value of attending college need help from faculty outside as well as inside the classroom. In this section, we report the range of faculty behaviors that community college students described in our recent study as important to their persistence and subsequent success (Elliott, 1992).

The community college context is highly interactive. Students, faculty, and administrators together create the academic and social milieu for teaching and learning. Actions of faculty members are critical, strongly influencing the conclusions students reach about their ability to meet their own goals by attending college. As diversity among students increases, so does the degree to which they rely on faculty guidance and interventions. Many of the behaviors students described as helpful depart from traditional conceptions of appropriate faculty roles.

Most students in this study had not experienced the involvement of community college faculty members during recruitment or orientation, although a few were aware that teachers met them at the registration tables. As a result, student comments typically emphasized faculty behaviors after entering the classroom.

> I was real apprehensive about going back to school.... The first semester I had a teacher who was very helpful, just encouraging. He felt if the student was willing to work, he was also willing to work with you. (American Indian woman)

Students reported that effective teachers created highly structured learning experiences, assignments that were easy to understand, and efforts that were consistently evaluated. Memorable faculty members used a variety of teaching methods. Exposed to such teachers, students learned to successfully complete assignments, pass tests, establish in-class and out-of-class relationships with students and teachers, and accrue credits.

Faculty members assisted students in applying academic concepts in terms most familiar to the students.

> He taught us how to take the time and to really let concepts sink in rather than just trying to superficially look at a concept, memorizing it.... You could bring out problems in everyday life and he would turn them around, show you how to think about them. (Hispanic man)

> We would read chapters and then try to apply them to things going on with us. Nobody shamed us.... It was very personal. (American Indian woman)

Very few students reported any involvement in campus clubs, student government, or even attendance at campus sports events. Their time on campus was spent primarily in attending classes, although they valued the social context while there. Students were grateful to faculty members who assisted them in making connections with other students.

> It makes it so much easier when the teacher breaks the ice for the students.... It could take you four to five weeks until you get to know someone. And by that time, class could be almost over. (African American woman)

Faculty needed to help students locate on-campus resources, describe ways students might improve grades, and explain how present goals might be broadened or even changed in the light of emerging student insights and competencies. Students relied heavily on faculty to help them understand context, options, abilities, and progress.

[The faculty member] let me know there was more to life than just getting married and having children. She let me know there are a lot of opportunities for young Black women. (African American woman)

When I was first at the community college I had a misconception of school altogether...that changed. I needed to put more emphasis on college to do the things I wanted to do in life...[to] get my degree...[and] this is the first step. (African American man)

Students reported needing assistance in understanding the relationships between community college course content and standards and those they would encounter at the university.

[The faculty member] really introduced you to what the engineering college would be like...(Hispanic man)

Although having faculty role models from similar ethnic/racial backgrounds was helpful, students also emphasized the importance of teachers who were open and accessible, regardless of race or ethnicity.

[The faculty] would offer extra credit or let you turn in things later or ask you what your problem is and what they can do to help. (African American man)

We discussed our personal attitudes or aspirations. It was helpful to me to compare what the [faculty member] had gone through to some of the similar problems I had in getting through school. (American Indian woman)

Students assumed faculty had subject matter competence, although they reported varying levels of apparent faculty commitment to the profession of teaching. First-generation college-goers expressed a great deal of curiosity about the nature of faculty members' professional lives and could report in some detail the comments faculty made about their activities outside the classroom, their recreational choices, and their extra-professional involvements such as freelance writing or consulting in the community. And students expressed concern that faculty were not always informed on current articulation agreements between institutions.

Because many students lacked family and personal or worklife friends to describe college life and advise them through the difficulties, they relied heavily on faculty members to forecast events and expectations in the community college. Transfer students needed to understand what they would encounter later at the baccalaureate institution. One struggling student described her dilemma:

> Nobody ever told us how we're going to get the credits, get the B.A. and stuff like that. [Faculty] were there [in the university]. They graduated. I looked at the catalog one time.... I thought, well, maybe they graduated so long ago they forgot how it works. They went to school so long ago and it was such a bad memory they don't want to discuss it again.... She told me what I was capable of doing to bring up my GPA. There was no need to tell me I was doing badly.... She gave me something I could do...[and] that kind of support is important. (Anglo woman)

At some point in their academic progress, transfer students began the process of disengagement from the community college. For some the leaving was difficult. Students felt anxiety about the size of the university student body and campus. They valued the time and effort exerted by community college faculty members to encourage or in some cases to push them to take the next step, describe the expectations, advise them on the admission process, and occasionally actually lead a physical tour of the university campus.

> When it got to be time to register, he began the process of helping me. He even took me over there for a tour. (African American woman)

[The faculty member] gave me options. Like he asked me what I really wanted to go into. Then he gave me a variety of things that I could look at, and he knew some people and told me what they were like. (American Indian woman)

Although many transfer students received assistance from a faculty member who described the differences in expectations, other students were dismayed later to encounter more demanding standards and less flexibility from their teachers at the university.

At the community college level you are just learning to go to college. And then when you're ready to do the really tough work, and you really need to concentrate on your homework, you've got that two years of adjustment under your belt. I misread my first [university] teacher, the first class I took over at [the university]. So I don't know, maybe I wasn't prepared for people who have been dealing with students who have learned to "play college" [in the community college]. (Anglo woman)

Students experienced the college context differently depending on their characteristics of diversity. Some first-generation college students moved relatively smoothly through the community college, following the catalog and advice from carefully selected advisers, selecting courses, and meeting the expectations of the faculty and institution without encountering serious difficulty. Most of these students found individual faculty members who served as their primary and sometimes only consistent link with the institution. Largely through faculty-guided experiences, students began to understand the expectations of higher education, to decide whether they could succeed, to determine what constitutes professional life, and to assess their own potential for setting and reaching higher academic and professional goals.

Through the community college experience, students learned self-worth. They internalized positive messages from their teachers about their abilities and potential, enjoyed handshakes with respected professionals, obtained advice from busy people who appeared to care about them, responded to individuals who believed in them, and, in the words of one Hispanic woman, "opened up like a flower." It is easy to see in these student comments the critical roles faculty members play as teachers, links, models, and academic standard definers and maintainers. By their actions, faculty interpret the higher education context, the local college, the university, and the intellectual and humanistic role of higher education in adult life.

Community college faculty actions are essential in helping students construct for themselves an accurate sense of their competence as they take the next steps in their academic careers or (re)assume roles in the various communities to which they relate.

THE FACULTY RESPONSE TO STUDENT DIVERSITY

A model explaining how colleges respond to diversity without relinquishing a commitment to high-quality learning outcomes (Richardson and Skinner, 1991) was used as a conceptual tool for creating eight categories of the student-success-related faculty behaviors identified in the interviews with students, faculty members, and administrators reported above (Richardson, 1992). Behaviors were also drawn from the Miami-Dade Teaching/Learning Project (Miami-Dade Community College, 1988) and from an extensive review of the literature.

The forty-four behaviors making up the eight categories were combined in a survey that was administered to full-time faculty in a nationally representative sample of 52 community colleges during the spring and fall semesters of 1989. The overall response of 68 percent provided 3,124 surveys that were analyzed to determine the extent to which faculty reported practicing the following behaviors.[2]

---

2. Further information about the study, including procedures used in its development and reliability coefficients for subscales, can be found in: Murphy, B.J. *The Role of Community College Faculty in Improving the Learning Environment*. Tempe: Arizona State University, unpublished doctoral dissertation, December 1992. The Community Colleges of Hawaii participated in a full pilot test of the survey in 1988.

1. *Outreach and Student Recruiting.* Faculty members engage in collaborative efforts to improve student preparation and motivation at the junior high school and senior high school levels. They serve as mentors, provide enrichment experiences for students, and work with senior high school faculty to ensure that competencies required in related courses help students make smooth transitions.

Most community college faculty members reported little, if any, involvement in these behaviors.

2. *Mentoring and Advising.* Faculty members advise in majors related to the courses they teach. They serve as mentors to high-risk students and participate in special advising programs where they receive training and extra pay. They help students fill out class schedules and make sure courses count toward educational objectives. They help students cope with the administrative requirements for registration and course withdrawal, and they provide advice and assistance to students transferring to four-year institutions.

Faculty are not heavily involved in serving as mentors or providing academic advising, although practices vary widely among institutions. There was no consensus among faculty in the study that these behaviors should be an expected part of their role.

3. *Academic Support/Learning Assistance.* Faculty members help students learn by being available for individual assistance outside of class. In addition to keeping required office hours, they set up and staff open laboratories and train tutors. They participate in early-alert programs and refer students experiencing problems to appropriate sources of academic support.

Faculty reported high involvement in providing learning assistance, and there is little difference of opinion about the importance of this faculty role.

4. *Campus Climate.* Faculty encourage students to remain in school by participating in efforts to make the campus more hospitable to cultural diversity. They support efforts to make faculty and staff composition more diverse. They develop programs for special populations, including the high achieving. They contribute to the sense of community by participating in campus activities,

sharing personal and scholarly experiences, and by sponsoring student organizations.

There is relatively low faculty involvement in these behaviors along with substantial disagreement about the degree to which faculty should be involved.

5. *Student Assessment*. Faculty ensure that students have the academic skills necessary for success in their coursework by setting standards and documenting outcomes. They help design assessment procedures and evaluate student performance. In their classes, they check learning and provide students with frequent assessments of progress.

Faculty reported very high levels of involvement in student assessment and very little disagreement about the importance of these behaviors to faculty role.

6. *Good Teaching Practices*. Faculty help students learn by preparing consistently, communicating effectively, and using regular student feedback to improve instruction. They treat all students with respect and are fair in assessment practices. They structure content and use technology effectively. They exhibit a sense of humor and show enthusiasm for their subject matter. They are competent in their discipline and meet objectives of their syllabi.

These are defining behaviors for community college professionals. There is high faculty involvement and little variation across all institutions.

7. *Adaptive Instruction*. Faculty members adapt their teaching to a more diverse student clientele by providing alternative ways of learning and making content applicable to the ages, experiences, and cultures of their students. They try to make learning environments comfortable and use a variety of methods to access student achievement. They teach study skills and student success courses, and tailor methods to student characteristics.

Faculty are substantially less likely to engage in adaptive teaching behaviors than more traditional forms of learning assistance, student assessment, and teaching practices. Faculty members in community colleges with higher proportions of minority and nontraditional students are the most likely to emphasize adaptive teaching strategies.

8. *Emphasize Achievement*. Faculty members emphasize academic achievement by balancing caring behaviors with high standards. They expect all students to achieve. They incorporate reading and writing requirements and teach study skills in all classes to encourage critical thinking and problem solving.

Faculty engage in high levels of these behaviors, and there is relatively little disagreement about their importance.

The pattern of involvement in the eight categories of faculty behaviors varied significantly as a function of disciplinary identification. Faculty members in allied health, vocational fields, business, and media and the arts reported significantly higher levels of involvement in most categories. Faculty members in the physical sciences, mathematics, and engineering-related areas were at or near the bottom in most categories.

EXPLAINING DIFFERENCES IN FACULTY RESPONSE PATTERNS

The survey data raised intriguing questions about institutional effectiveness in encouraging faculty behaviors identified as important to student success. Some institutions were significantly more successful than others. To find out why, case studies were undertaken at twelve of the institutions surveyed. From the analysis of the case study and survey data, three explanations emerge as worthy of detailed consideration by community college administrative and faculty leaders (Richardson, 1992).

The first has to do with the extensive use of part-time faculty. Full-time faculty members at most case-study institutions identified as a preeminent concern the impact of part-time faculty on quality. Perhaps the archetypal expression of administrative sentiment came from a senior administrator in a state hit hard by resource reductions, who nonetheless remained steadfastly committed to enrollment expansion: "More and more of our teaching will be done by part-timers; part-timers are as good in the classroom as full-timers; however, they don't do the advising or committee work. As long as we have a core of full-time faculty, at least a third of whom will do the work, we are not worried about the percentage of instruction done by part-timers."

Some of the disengagement of faculty members from involvement in outreach and student recruiting, mentoring and advising, and campus climate interventions clearly arises from a sense of being overwhelmed by the number of students who needed assistance in relation to the number of faculty available to provide it. In a growing number of community colleges, faculty receive extra pay for any assignment beyond meeting their scheduled classes and posting some minimum number of office hours for which they may or may not be present. Even committee assignments qualified for extra compensation under the collective bargaining agreements in some case-study colleges. This narrowing definition of faculty role complicates institutional efforts to serve a more diverse student population, as do the shallow or nonexistent linkages between full-time and part-time faculty reported in many of the case-study institutions.

A second explanation has to do with disciplinary differences in approaches to the learning process. Bloom (1956) identified three domains of learning: the cognitive, the affective, and the psychomotor. Our 1983 study of literacy in open-access institutions found all three of these domains present and influential in community colleges. The study also indicated that these domains accounted for important differences in the ways faculty members structured the learning process and interpreted their roles. The disciplinary differences described above are in some ways a reprise of the 1983 report.

The cognitive domain has to do with the recall or recognition of knowledge and the development of intellectual skills. It describes the hierarchical view of learning to which math and science faculty subscribe. It is arguably the aspect of the community college curriculum that receives the least attention and emphasis during this period of expansion and diversification of student bodies. To some degree, faculty members in these fields have given up striving to reconcile their disciplinary commitments with the aspirations of those they teach. The results are apparent; few students transfer to or graduate in these fields in most community colleges.

The affective domain deals with changes in interest, attitudes, and values as well as the development of appreciations and adequate adjustment. The commitment of many community colleges to nurture high-risk students helps account for the preeminence of this model in the case-study institutions. The affective domain describes the view of learning held by social scientists and humanists.

The developmental approach to student deficiencies also fits in this domain, either in its earlier "right to fail" version or in its more recent advisory approach. With this approach, colleges correct reading or writing deficiencies that may be crippling student success in other courses. Only mathematics has achieved reasonable success in requiring mastery learning for student progression. While social scientists and humanists are not as disaffected as mathematicians and scientists, they still describe compromises and concerns in their approach to classroom responsibilities. The issue is complicated by faculty dependence on extra classes for extra pay, an arrangement that compromises willingness to take a tough stance on entrance or exit requirements for social science or humanities offerings.

The manipulative or motor skills domain was described by Bloom as "so little done...in secondary schools or colleges" (1956, p. 7) as not to warrant the development of a classification. In the contemporary community college, vocational and career education places considerable emphasis on this domain. Those who teach in related fields are most likely to display the range of success-related behaviors conducive to student success, and their fields produce disproportionately high numbers of all graduates. Why is this so?

The answer seems relatively straightforward. Vocational and career education is the community college curricular response to increased student diversity. These are the programs characterized by Brint and Karabel (1989) as diverting because they are designed to provide students with immediate access to skills leading to employment. Beyond responding to a more diverse clientele, career programs in high-demand areas like allied health are also selective, freeing faculty from coping with the same range of student diversity that their liberal-studies colleagues encounter daily.

So some differences in faculty response patterns appear attributable to differences in disciplinary affiliations and to disciplinary variations in the proportion of classes taught by part-time faculty. But there is a third, and equally important, set of explanations, which might be broadly subsumed under the general concept of "institutional culture."

Culture is defined by the assumptions and beliefs shared by members of an organization (Kuh and Whitt, 1988). The learning environment consists of the interventions and strategies an institution employs to help students achieve outcomes. The learning environment can be thought of as the observable product of an institution's invisible culture.

At case-study colleges where faculty reported higher levels of student-success-related behaviors, administrators created and defended cultures where faculty input was sought out, valued, and used. The faculty role was broadly defined. Behaviors valued in faculty were modeled by administrators. Priorities were clearly identified and focused on teaching and learning. Administrators were open and fair in the internal distribution of available resources. A jointly defined accountability structure balanced administrative and faculty influence. Administrators supported rituals and told stories that illustrated and reinforced the attitudes and beliefs that defined culture.

In community colleges where faculty reported lower levels of student-success-related behaviors, complex administrative and governance structures substituted for shared values and mutual accommodation. There was no consensus about priorities. Faculty members were oriented toward meeting the minimum standards spelled out in restrictive contracts or board policies. Administrators relied on extra compensation to encourage faculty to become involved beyond minimum requirements. In many of these institutions faculty seemed to be dominant, or at least well-protected.

In institutions with higher levels of success-related behaviors, administrators made decisions and provided leadership, however low-key. In institutions with lower levels of success-related behaviors, administrators persuaded, influenced, supported, or in some instances confronted. But they did not seem to develop any sort of shared vision of what the institution hoped to achieve. The institutions with higher levels of effective behaviors had cultures that brought people together. While in some instances these cultures tolerated a lack of involvement, they did not encourage it. Among the institutions with lower levels, the presence of competing cultures and formal safeguards allowed faculty members to opt out of active participation.

PROMOTING EFFECTIVE FACULTY BEHAVIORS

Each of the three explanations for the significant differences in the levels of faculty behaviors found among the institutions in the Ford study offers opportunities for faculty and administrative leaders to improve the environments they provide for diversity and quality.

Despite constrained resources, many community colleges have made valiant efforts to reduce their reliance on part-time faculty. Full-time faculty have been given release time to mentor and monitor their part-time colleagues. While some progress was evident among a number of the case-study institutions, problems remain. The pressure points are discipline-specific rather than institution-wide. At one community college committed to having 60 percent of its credit offerings taught by full-time faculty, there were no part-timers in some disciplines while 90 percent of the instruction was offered by part-timers in some business-related areas.

Our study demonstrated the importance of a wide range of faculty behaviors inside and outside the classroom. The most effective case-study institutions defined faculty role broadly and expected more from their faculty than less-effective institutions. Getting faculty to accept responsibilities not mandated in current contracts or board policies depends on convincing them that new tasks will be manageable because they will not have to cover for a large cadre of "invisible" part-timers.

Community colleges might also consider the degree to which their definition of appropriate responses to underpreparation has turned off faculty members in the physical sciences, mathematics, and the engineering fields. Math and science faculty reported less involvement in effective behaviors. They also reported significantly less involvement in professional development or governance. The community college literature is full of interventions based on differences in student learning styles. Largely missing is any similar treatment of the interventions that might be appropriate as a function of differences in the way disciplines view knowledge and the nature of learning. At institutions where interventions designed to respond to student diversity are faculty-specific, math and science faculty invent different solutions than their colleagues in the humanities and social sciences. Community colleges might do well to encourage math and science faculty to invent their own solutions rather than trying to persuade them to accept currently predominant models.

Community colleges can also work to alter organizational cultures that define the range of student diversity their learning environments serve effectively. Altering organizational culture is difficult and time-consuming, but it may offer the best hope for augmenting approaches to deficiency with alternatives that emphasize achievement. And it is the only approach that has much potential for revitalizing faculty in mathematics and the hard sciences.

A more diverse student population depends on faculty members in ways that are only now beginning to be understood. The ways in which faculty members define their role as well as their willingness to move beyond minimum behaviors specified in collective bargaining agreements or board policies depends upon institutional policies and administrative practices in such critical areas as setting goals, making decisions, and structuring opportunities for professional renewal. Institutions that have succeeded in providing environments where faculty are encouraged to be more responsive to student diversity can offer important insights to colleges where failure is still seen primarily as the fault of the underprepared student. The process of institutional transformation begins with administrative and faculty leadership.

REFERENCES

Adelman, C. *The Way We Are: The Community College as American Thermometer*. Washington, D.C.: U.S. Government Printing Office, 1992.

Bloom, B.S. *Taxonomy of Educational Objectives Handbook I: Cognitive Domain*. New York: David McKay, 1956.

Brint, S. and J. Karabel. *The Diverted Dream*. New York: Oxford University Press, 1989.

Cohen, A.M. and F.B. Brawer. *The American Community College, Second Edition*. San Francisco: Jossey-Bass, 1991

Elliott, D.B. *Community College Faculty Behaviors Impacting Transfer Student Success: A Qualitative Study*. Unpublished doctoral dissertation, Arizona State University, Tempe, 1992.

Kuh, G.D. and E.J. Whitt. *The Invisible Tapestry: Culture in American Colleges and Universities*. Washington, D.C.: Association for the Study of Higher Education, ASHE/ERIC Higher Education Report, No. 1, 1988.

McCabe, R.H. "The Educational Program of the American Community College: A Transition." In J.S. Eaton (Ed.), *Colleges of Choice*. New York: ACE/Macmillan, 1988.

Miami-Dade Community College. *Faculty Excellence: Teaching/Learning*. Miami: District Board of Trustees, October 1988.

Orwell, G. et al. *The Chicago Study of Access and Choice in Higher Education*. Chicago: University of Chicago Committee on Public Policy Studies, September 1984.

Richardson, R.C. and E.F. Skinner. *Achieving Access and Quality: Case Studies in Equity*. New York: ACE/Macmillan, 1991.

Richardson, R.C. *Creating Effective Learning Environments: Report of a Study Funded by the Ford Foundation*. Tempe, Ariz.: Education Policy Studies Laboratory, October 27, 1992.

Richardson, R.C., D.A. Matthews, and J.E. Finney. *Improving State and Campus Environments for Quality and Diversity: A Self-Assessment*. Denver: Education Commission of the States, June 1992.

Skinner, E.F. and R.C. Richardson. "Making It in a Majority University: The Minority Graduate's Perspective." *Change*, 1988, *20* (3), 1988.

Richard C. Richardson, Jr. is professor, Arizona State University. Diana B. Elliott is president, EFG and Associates, Inc.

114

Chapter 7

Transformative Faculty Development

Realizing the Promise Through Classroom Research

By Thomas A. Angelo

T hey sometimes feel lonely and unappreciated. They often wonder if their efforts really make any difference. Nonetheless, every year, on campuses across the United States, thousands of skilled, dedicated, idealistic community college teachers choose to invest their hours and energies in faculty development programs. They get involved year after year, despite doubts and misgivings, because they believe in the bright promise inherent in faculty development. They believe, in other words, that the quality and effectiveness of teaching and learning can—and should—be improved. And they believe that working with colleagues on faculty development efforts offers the best chance of realizing that bright promise.

Those who take part in faculty development are not alone in their convictions. In the face of mounting economic, demographic, and social challenges, there is a growing sense in the United States that the effectiveness and quality of higher education must be im-

115

proved. Because community colleges enroll nearly half of all undergraduates nationwide and because they play a preponderant role in educating traditionally underserved groups in the society—as well as in training and retraining the work force—the educational effectiveness of two-year colleges is clearly linked to the nation's economic and social well-being (El-Khawas, Carter, and Ottinger, 1988). For these reasons, improving the quality of teaching and learning is the primary mandate for community colleges in the 1990s. To fulfill that mandate, they must find ways to realize the promise of faculty development.

Over the past two decades, faculty development has become widely accepted throughout the community college sector. Overall, however, there is little evidence that it has effectively improved teaching and learning. To increase the effectiveness of faculty development in its third decade, this chapter proposes a new agenda for the 1990s. This "transformative" agenda would shift the focus of current efforts toward realizing the promise of faculty development: higher quality in higher learning.

Faculty developers—working closely with community college teachers and academic administrators—can meet the challenges and capitalize on the opportunities of the 1990s by developing clearly focused transformative program goals, creating programs based on research and practice guidelines, and employing effective and appropriate methods to achieve their goals. This chapter focuses on classroom research, one promising approach to transforming faculty development and improving higher learning in community colleges.

This chapter is organized around prime numbers, mostly threes and sevens. After notes on three assumptions and three definitions, it offers a brief review of seven political, economic, and educational trends that pose challenges and opportunities for faculty development in community colleges. It then describes seven barriers that limit the effectiveness of most current faculty development programs. Next, it outlines seven shifts in focus that could help lower or remove those barriers, and suggests seven ways that faculty developers can use classroom research to accomplish those shifts. Given that classroom research works best when embedded within broader faculty development programs, the chapter concludes with eleven general research-based guidelines for planning and implementing successful campuswide efforts.

THREE KEY ASSUMPTIONS

Like a stool that rests on three legs, this chapter rests on three main assumptions. If these assumptions are sturdy and well made, then like the legs of that stool, they should support the arguments balanced upon them. The first assumption is that true higher learning is transformative and not merely additive. In an additive model of higher education, more is always better, and quantity of learning is the measure. In a transformative model, it is the quality of learning that matters most. While the accumulation of knowledge and skills is necessary, it is not sufficient to constitute higher learning. Higher learning takes place only when students actively transform the continuously added knowledge and skills into personally meaningful and useful learning, and in so doing, transform the ways they learn, understand, think, and act.

The second assumption is that the central purpose—and promise—of faculty development efforts in community colleges should be to help teachers improve the quality of higher learning in their classrooms. The third assumption is that faculty development programs must shift their focus to become transformative learning experiences in order to accomplish their purpose and realize their promise.

THREE KEY DEFINITIONS

Faculty Development

The terms "staff development" and "faculty development" are employed in so many different ways that they require some definition. In terms of intended participants at least, the distinction is clear: Faculty development involves only the teaching staff. But exactly which activities are included under the umbrella of faculty development is less obvious. On many campuses, faculty development

117

refers to a variety of efforts focusing on the professional, personal, curricular, organizational, and instructional development of college teachers (Mathis, 1982). All these areas merit attention, and each has its advocates. Nonetheless, given that teaching and learning are at the heart of the community college mission, I would suggest that instructional development—aimed directly at improving teaching effectiveness—should be the primary focus of faculty development efforts in the 1990s. Throughout this chapter, then, "faculty development" refers to explicit institutional efforts to improve the effectiveness of college teaching and learning.

Classroom Research and Classroom Assessment

Since 1986, K. Patricia Cross has developed and disseminated the concept of classroom research, which she defines as the systematic, careful, and patient investigation of student learning by faculty in their own classrooms. "In simplest terms, ...classroom research involves stating in assessable terms what students should be learning in the class, designing feedback measures to assess the extent to which they are learning those things, and then experimenting with ways to improve learning" (Cross, 1990, p. 18).

Cross and I have written and spoken extensively on classroom assessment, one method of gathering data on student learning within the broader approach of classroom research. The relationship between classroom assessment and classroom research is analogous to the relationship between lecturing (one method) and teaching (a broader approach). Classroom assessments are the most highly developed and widely used method of classroom research. They are quick and simple data-gathering exercises through which teachers obtain feedback on what and how well their students have learned during a single class session. Classroom Assessment Techniques (CATs) are the simple tools faculty use to gather this limited, focused feedback (Angelo and Cross, 1993). Since 1987 thousands of college teachers nationwide have received training in this method and have adapted it to assess and improve their students' learning. The great majority of faculty engaging in classroom research and classroom assessment are community college teachers.

Classroom research is sometimes referred to as "classroom-based research" in community colleges, and many campuses use the terms "classroom research" and "classroom assessment" interchangeably, even though Cross and I do not. To simplify matters in this chapter, the umbrella term, classroom research, refers both to the broader approach and to classroom assessment.

FACULTY DEVELOPMENT IN THE 1990S: CHALLENGES AND OPPORTUNITIES

Over the past several years, seven interrelated trends have created challenges and opportunities that make the 1990s a promising time for faculty development in the community colleges. These trends are:

- Continuing public and political pressures to improve the quality of higher education
- An increasing level of competition for funding
- A rise in educational consumerism
- Changing faculty demographics
- Growing diversity in the student body
- An expanding base of useful, relevant research about college teaching and learning
- A rising level of faculty development expertise

Public and Political Pressure to Improve Higher Education

Beginning in the mid-1980s, higher education reform reports such as *A Nation at Risk* (National Commission on Excellence in Education, 1983) and *Integrity in the College Curriculum* (Association of American Colleges, 1985) signaled a fundamental shift in focus from concerns with *quantity*, defined mainly as access to higher education, to an emphasis on the *quality* of college outcomes. The earlier political and public policy goal of "equal access for all" has gradually moved toward one of "access to a quality education for each." To some degree, this shift can be understood by viewing higher education as a maturing market. As happened with many once-scarce goods, the quantity of higher education became sufficient to meet consumer demand, and product quality increasingly became the criterion of choice. At the same time, widespread political concerns about the nation's economic and scientific competitiveness have helped sustain a public policy debate about the quality of higher education.

Competition for Funding

Economic trends also influence the growing emphasis on educational quality. During the past decade, new public priorities emerged to compete with higher education for available funds. In the 1990s governments and private foundations alike face ever-growing pressures to clean up the environment, provide health care for an aging population, combat drug abuse and related health problems, and invest in public schools. Years of recession and high budget deficits further restrict possible spending on higher education.

These macroeconomic pressures, together with the focus on quality, have generated and fueled the assessment movement, which has swept U.S. higher education over the last decade. Documenting how much, how well, and how many students are learning is the primary focus of most state-mandated assessments. Consequently, to successfully compete for funds, public colleges and universities increasingly find it necessary to demonstrate the quality of their "products."

Educational "Consumerism"

Changing public attitudes and expectations also favor an emphasis on quality. The current cohort of college students is more likely to have college-educated parents and siblings than was any previous generation. As a result, these students and their families are increasingly demanding and well-informed "consumers" of

120

higher education. Adult learners, who are entering community colleges in ever-greater numbers, and the employers who sometimes sponsor them, tend to be demanding consumers as well. As a result community colleges have to "sell" the quality of their product as never before to legislators, foundation officers, parents, prospective students, business and industry, and the tax-paying public. The growing interest in Total Quality Management (TQM) and Continuous Quality Improvement (CQI) among community college administrators and faculty is, like assessment, a response to student consumerism, economic pressures, and concerns about education quality.

Changing Demographics of the Community College Faculty

Faculty demographics also play a role in stimulating demand for faculty development. The World War II generation of G.I. Bill faculty is already largely retired, with the Korean War wave right behind them. Within the next ten years roughly half the nation's present college faculty will reach retirement age. Until they retire, however, older faculty are expected to remain current in their fields and in their teaching methods. Most of the new faculty hired to replace them may be more up-to-date in their disciplines but will have no more preparation for teaching college than their predecessors—that is, little or none. Thus faculty development efforts should not only address the differing needs of these generations, but should also serve as a bridge connecting them. New and veteran faculty working together to improve teaching and learning can achieve synergy, as older faculty renew their freshness and enthusiasm while younger faculty benefit from their elders' hard-won experience and skill.

Another important shift in the makeup of the community college faculty is the result of their ever-increasing reliance on part-time instructors. By 1989, for example, part-time faculty outnumbered full-time faculty in thirty-six of the fifty public community college systems in the nation. Currently 63 percent of all community college faculty are part-time (Mahoney and Sallis, 1991, pp.

121

55–56). This growing reliance on part-timers, at a time when pressures for quality assessment and assurance are rising, suggests that faculty development programs that focus most or all of their energies on full-time faculty are aiming wide of the mark.

An Increasingly Diverse Student Body

The community college student population is becoming ever more diverse in terms of race, ethnicity, age, gender, prior educational experience, and educational goals. Yet few community college faculty—whether old or young, full-time or part-time—are prepared by experience or training to instruct the range of students they encounter. Faculty development programs can help faculty meet this challenge. But to do so, they must go beyond prevalent consciousness-raising and attitude-adjustment activities to help faculty develop practical skills and strategies for helping every student learn effectively.

A Rapidly Expanding Knowledge Base

The sixth trend in support of quality is the explosion of potentially useful knowledge about teaching and learning. During the past three decades, researchers have discovered much about human learning in general and about college student learning in particular (McKeachie et al., 1986; Menges and Svinicki, 1991). Solid research by cognitive scientists, educational psychologists, ethnographers, and other qualitative researchers offers more direction to today's college teachers than ever before.

Although we may still know relatively little when compared to fields such as medicine or engineering, the college teaching profession already knows much more about effective practice than we apply. To remedy this lack of application, faculty developers can and should play a central role in translating and disseminating the relevant research to community college teachers. Faculty developers can also help teachers determine potential applications of this research to their particular disciplines, their students, their classroom settings, and their unique teaching styles.

A Wealth of In-House Expertise

Since the early 1970s thousands of community college faculty have played key roles in faculty development efforts on their campuses as program coordinators, advisory committee members, workshop leaders, and faithful participants. Hundreds have become faculty development leaders at state, regional, and national levels. This human capital represents a valuable resource base that faculty development efforts can build on and extend in the 1990s. Because many of these faculty development leaders are nearing retirement age, it is particularly important that their expertise be tapped and transmitted soon.

FACULTY DEVELOPMENT IN COMMUNITY COLLEGES: STRONG COMMITMENT, WEAK RESPONSE, AND LIMITED RESULTS

Strong Commitment

No segment of U.S. higher education is more dedicated to effective teaching and learning than the community colleges. This dedication is borne out by the fact that no segment invests as much time, money, and energy in faculty development to enhance instructional effectiveness. Florida, for example, has reportedly spent more than $50 million on staff and program development in its community colleges over the past 25 years (Smith, 1989, p. 178). Though none has equaled Florida's level of commitment, California, Texas, and other states have also invested millions in community college faculty development since the 1970s.

Nationwide, faculty development is big business in community colleges. A.B. Smith's 1980 survey of all U.S. community colleges found that 60 percent of the respondents reported having some type of staff development program, and 56 percent reported having a specific unit and/or person responsible for staff development activities (Smith, 1989, p. 192). Those percentages may well have risen since that survey.

Since the mid-1980s, as noted above, faculty development efforts have been spurred on by broad reform movements in higher education, larger societal trends, and changes within the community colleges. As a result, the need for and interest in faculty development have increased. Given the seven trends discussed above, institutional commitment to faculty development efforts is likely to remain steady or grow throughout the 1990s.

Individual community college faculty are also strongly committed to faculty development activities, if we allow a broad definition. For example, Miller and Ratcliff found that Iowa community college faculty reported participating, on average, in 160 hours of faculty development activities in the course of a year. They also found that most participation in faculty development activities (73 percent) occurred outside of normal working hours; that 44 percent of these activities were self-financed; and that only 11 percent of the total faculty development time was spent on activities leading to promotion or salary increases (Miller and Ratcliff, 1986). While these data are from only one state, it seems likely to be indicative of many.

Weak Response and Limited Results

Although the level of interest in and commitment to faculty development is strong in community colleges, in terms of impact the story is less impressive. As Maxwell and Kazlauskas put it:

These [faculty development] programs are widespread in community colleges and generally approved, yet they muster only moderate or even little participation, often are relatively ineffective, and have particularly little impact on those who most need to improve their teaching (1992, p. 352).

Survey research and anecdotal evidence confirm that most campuswide instructional improvement programs suffer from these three problems. First, a relatively small percentage of the faculty takes advantage of development programs. Second, those faculty who participate most in teaching improvement efforts are often those who need them least. And third, most faculty development efforts result in little if any measurable or long-term improvement in teaching and learning.

Yet community college faculty overwhelmingly view teaching as their primary role. If we assume that most community college instructors are motivated to teach well, why do so few participate in instructional improvement programs? This general reluctance is not simply a product of complacency or intransigence, although these attitudes may contribute in some cases. Nor can we attribute it to the conflict between teaching and research, or lack of rewards for teaching, as may be the case in four-year colleges and universities. Lack of time is the most common reason given, but that response simply begs the question of priorities. Since most community college teachers appear to invest a significant amount of time in faculty development activities on their own, why do so few choose to become involved in organized faculty development efforts on campus? And why does faculty development so often fail to achieve measurable success with those faculty who do participate?

THE LIMITS OF "ADDITIVE" FACULTY DEVELOPMENT

Some answers can be found in the implicit model of learning behind most faculty development efforts. It is a quantitative, additive model. That is, the underlying assumption is that by participating in a number of faculty development activities, regardless of content or coherence, teachers will somehow improve. What matters most is the quantity of participation, not the quality.

These additive faculty development programs in community colleges often encourage or require teachers to earn a given number of faculty/staff development "credits" during the year. Faculty typically accrue these credits by selecting from a smorgasbord of workshops, lectures, seminars, field trips, and individual projects on topics ranging from syllabus design to stress reduction to dressing for success. In such programs, which are often stipulated in faculty contracts, little attempt is made to make connections or achieve coherence. This scattershot, additive approach to learning is unfortunately a familiar one, since it characterizes the curriculum and course requirements students face in most colleges.

SEVEN BARRIERS TO GREATER AND MORE EFFECTIVE PARTICIPATION IN FACULTY DEVELOPMENT

Why do organized faculty development programs in so many community colleges fail to realize their promise to improve teaching and learning? One major reason is that they fail to involve many faculty. And one plausible explanation for limited faculty involvement is that most teaching improvement programs contain barriers to participation unwittingly built into their frameworks. Some of these spring directly from the additive model of learning. Others are primarily psychological or logistical. Individually and in concert these barriers serve as disincentives, discouraging teachers from investing time and effort by lowering the expected benefits of participation and/or raising the expected costs. To actively involve a greater percentage of faculty in improving teaching and learning, development advocates must recognize and remove, or at least lower, the seven common barriers discussed below.

1. Most Faculty Development Efforts Focus Primarily on Improving Teaching and Only Secondarily, If at All, on Improving Learning. They focus on changing faculty knowledge, skills, attitudes, and behaviors. While improving teaching is a potentially powerful means to improve student learning, it is hardly the only means. In many cases helping students develop their study skills and strategies is a more direct, productive route to improved learning. Thus programs that focus only on improving teaching may not be the most effective at improving the quality of student learning.

By focusing on teaching and teachers, rather than on learning and learners, faculty development programs also may inadvertently threaten faculty status and professional autonomy. Some faculty see participation in such programs as a tacit admission of inadequacy or failure as teachers, or at least of a lack of self-confidence in one's performance. Since status and face saving are critically important in academic life, faculty are prone to avoid any situation that threatens their professional image.

Another characteristic value in academic culture is professional autonomy, a central component of academic freedom. Most college teachers are accustomed to developing and teaching courses entirely on their own without depending on or even turning to others for help or advice. Participation in instructional improvement programs that involve videotaping, observation by faculty developers or peers, team projects, or even discussions with other faculty can threaten a college teacher's sense of professional autonomy and control over the classroom. Given this individualistic orientation, even well-meaning suggestions for improvement may be resented as intrusions. Faculty will tend to avoid programs that threaten their sense of professional autonomy.

2. Many Programs Try to "Develop" Faculty, Rather than Helping Them Become Truly Self-Developing. Instead of trying to foster self-awareness in teachers and the skills needed to diagnose and improve their teaching and students' learning, they simply try to teach faculty information and techniques. By not helping faculty transform their higher-order skills and abilities, these programs are, in the language of the famous parable, giving participants fish rather than teaching them to fish. This additive approach limits faculty development to relatively trivial short-term outcomes at best.

3. Many Programs Do Not Recognize the Importance of Discipline-Specific "Ways of Knowing," Teaching, and Learning in Colleges. Faculty develop these within disciplinary frameworks (Eisner, 1985). As a consequence, the intellectual world view of a biologist is likely to be quite different from that of a specialist in English literature, a psychologist, or even that of a chemist. Surveys of community college teachers in 1988 and 1990 showed that faculty's instructional goals differed more significantly by academic discipline than by gender, age, race, or type of institution (Cross and Fideler, 1988; Angelo and Cross, 1993). These differing goals reflect the fact that the skills and knowledge students must master to succeed differ greatly from field to field. As a result, teaching and learning have their own particular characteristics in each academic field. What works well in general may not work at all in a specific setting.

Given these differences among disciplines, it's not surprising that many faculty are skeptical of the idea that anyone outside their particular disciplines can understand its specific teaching and learning issues. Even those faculty who avidly participate in faculty development often have trouble understanding the relevance of teaching innovations or suggestions presented by teachers from other disciplines. This difficulty occurs partly because general teaching ideas must first be translated into discipline-specific terms and concepts before they can be understood or acted on. Such translations are most powerful and convincing when made by faculty for themselves by identifying analogous issues within their own realms of experience.

4. Many Teachers Fail to Recognize the Need for and Potential Usefulness of Faculty Development Activities in Their Own Teaching. While this barrier is related to and sometimes exacerbated by a lack of translation across different disciplines, it has more to do with faculty's lack of awareness of how well they are doing. Most community college teachers probably think they are doing a better job teaching than they actually are. In their survey of nearly 300 community college teachers, Blackburn et al. (1980) found that 92 percent believed their own teaching was above average. Faculty in other types of colleges express similar views, which I call the "Lake Wobegon Effect." (According to radio celebrity and author Garrison Keillor, Lake Wobegon is a town where all the women are strong, all the men are good-looking, and all the children are above average.) Most faculty probably overestimate their teaching effectiveness, not because they are immodest or statistically illiterate, but because they lack specific, accurate information on how well, or how poorly, their students are learning. They also lack a basis for comparison, since most faculty rarely or never observe their colleagues' teaching.

Most college teachers receive little or no formal training in assessing student learning. At the same time, they often have limited experience in identifying and diagnosing teaching and learning problems, and even less experience in discussing them productively with other teachers. When faculty meet to discuss educational matters, a rather rare occurrence, it is usually to consider the content or structure of the curriculum or to set requirements—not to talk about classroom teaching and learning. Therefore it should come as no surprise that many college teachers cannot or do not perceive the problems their students have learning course material.

Research on student evaluations indicates that the faculty most likely to change in response to feedback are those whose student ratings are lower than their self-ratings (Levinson-Rose and Menges, 1981). Similar gaps between expected feedback and what is received seem to motivate faculty who use classroom research to change their teaching. Until faculty can see those problems and gaps for themselves, which is not at all the same as having them pointed out by others, there is little use in trying to interest teachers in potential solutions.

5. Many Programs Fail to Capitalize Effectively on Faculty Motivation. Simply lowering barriers and removing disincentives are not enough to ensure broader participation—it is also necessary to increase incentives. Community college teachers are probably closer to the intrinsic end of the motivation scale than are members of most other professions. By their very choice of vocation, college faculty have indicated that they are not likely to be highly motivated by extrinsic rewards (McKeachie, 1979). In their study of professional development programs, Miller and Ratcliff found that Iowa community college faculty typically "chose activities that were not rewarded on the salary schedules over those that were" (1986, p. 342). When community college teachers do get involved in organized faculty development, they tend to be motivated by professional pride, intellectual challenge, and the fulfillment that comes from helping students learn and develop.

This does not mean that money and recognition cannot motivate faculty. They obviously can and do. But in terms of their power to change teaching behaviors and improve learning, extrinsic rewards probably have little effect. While identifying and rewarding outstanding teachers with public praise and cash awards are not necessarily bad ideas, they are unlikely to motivate the winners or their colleagues to teach better once the plaques and checks are handed out. Under most circumstances, it is equally unlikely that simply releasing faculty from teaching will improve their classroom performances.

Even when faculty are self-aware and motivated to improve their teaching, the generic nature of many faculty development efforts, such as presentations and workshops, often fails to assess individual teachers' highly personal and specific needs. Faculty concerns tend to be problem-centered, while faculty development programs are often topic-centered. Even when discussions or training sessions are explicitly problem-centered, it is usually the faculty developer or presenter who has defined the agenda, not the teachers. Many faculty are not motivated to invest time and energy in programs not directly related to their immediate, very specific teaching goals and needs.

6. Many Programs Are Perceived to Lack Intellectual Substance. In trying to interest teachers in participating, they search for new and different topics, themes, or speakers to highlight each year. This can give faculty the sometimes accurate impression that faculty development is faddish and superficial. Many will shun efforts perceived as lacking content or as trendy knock-offs of educational fashions. A great deal of good research on teaching and learning exists, and some faculty development activities are solidly grounded in that research. Too often, however, the faculty who are asked to participate are not made aware of the scholarship behind the innovations being proposed. Only intellectually substantive, credible programs are likely to convince the majority of faculty members to reconsider and change deep-rooted attitudes and teaching behaviors.

7. Many Programs Are Not Planned and Organized for Success. They lack the planning, leadership, support, and long-term follow-through necessary to improve teaching and learning. The dispositions, attitudes, and habits that guide so much of teaching behavior develop over many years, perhaps even before the future teacher's college experiences. Any program that seeks to change teaching behavior must plan for the long term. On many community college campuses, the director of staff/faculty development is a part-time position, often held by a different person each year or two. While inexpensive and seemingly democratic, this approach to leadership makes it almost impossible to achieve coherence and continuity.

Although most college faculty react against having structure imposed on their teaching from outside, they tend not to take unstructured activities very seriously. They prefer well-planned, well-organized, well-led enterprises. Most faculty development programs also undercut their potential effectiveness by failing to invest sufficiently in follow-up and ongoing support for long-term efforts, choosing instead to offer a large number of less demanding one-shot or short-term options. For example, Miller and Ratcliff report that Iowa community college faculty members took part in an average of twenty-four different faculty development activities in the course of a year, averaging less than seven hours on any one (1986, p. 330). Research on effective faculty development suggests that a few well-organized, long-term efforts are a better investment if change is the goal (Levinson-Rose and Menges, 1981; Miller and Ratcliff, 1986).

TRANSFORMATIVE FACULTY DEVELOPMENT: A PROMISING NEW AGENDA FOR THE 1990S

To this point, I have asserted that most faculty development programs are based on an additive, or primarily quantitative, view of learning. To overcome the barriers to effectiveness mentioned above, community colleges need to adopt a transformative model of learning—one in which the quality of learning matters most—and a transformative faculty development agenda.

At first glance, this proposed faculty development agenda may seem no more than a new label pasted on an old bottle of wine. There are, however, three ways in which focusing on improving the quality of higher learning would represent a significant shift from most current faculty development practice. First, a transformative agenda would focus directly on helping faculty help their students improve learning, and only indirectly on improving teaching. Second, it would promote faculty and student self-awareness, self-assessment, and self-improvement. And third, it would help faculty understand and evaluate the potential applications of traditional research on teaching and learning to their own courses and students.

Faculty developers can use classroom research to help shift the focus of their programs to realize the promise of transformative faculty development. While it is not possible to provide discipline-specific examples here, dozens of detailed examples of the transformative use of classroom research in a range of disciplines can be found in Angelo and Cross (1993), Angelo (1991), Cuevas (1991), and Fideler (1991).

OVERCOMING BARRIERS: SHIFTING THE FOCUS OF FACULTY DEVELOPMENT TO REALIZE ITS PROMISE

Once the barriers to involvement in faculty development are recognized, the challenge is to overcome or lower them. The seven shifts in focus suggested below parallel and respond to the seven barriers mentioned above. They should help faculty developers increase both the quantity and quality of faculty participation. With more and better participation, efforts to improve teaching and learning are more likely to succeed.

Classroom research is already being used on many community college campuses to find a new focus for faculty development programs and lower barriers to participation. Examples follow of how faculty developers can use classroom research to help accomplish each shift.

1. Shift the Focus from Improving Teaching to Improving Learning. Shift from considering faculty's teaching interests first to considering students' learning needs first. Shift from trying to make teachers better performers to helping faculty help students perform better.

By focusing programs directly on improving student learning, faculty developers can avoid or lower many of the barriers

132

discussed above. First, making improved learning the goal of instructional development focuses everyone's attention on the desired outcome and encourages use of a wider range of approaches to achieve that goal. Second, focusing on learning is more inclusive than focusing on teaching. The former can involve administrators, faculty, and students in a common enterprise, while the latter usually involves only faculty. In a related way, focusing on learning improvement encourages students to accept more responsibility for the outcomes of their classroom experiences. Third, focusing on learners and learning is less likely to threaten faculty status and autonomy and more likely to lower emotional barriers to participation.

Classroom research is a learner-centered activity, intended to help faculty—and students—evaluate learning and find ways to improve it. Unlike teacher evaluation, classroom research focuses faculty attention primarily on students' learning and only secondarily on students' perceptions of teaching performance. Several commonly used classroom assessment techniques (CATs) prompt students to assess their own problem-solving approaches, use of study time, and prior knowledge. Faculty and students then use the feedback to improve learning. Because classroom research is a voluntary activity, controlled and directed by individual teachers in their own classrooms, it poses little or no threat to status or academic freedom.

2. Shift the Focus from Providing Answers to Helping Define Questions. Shift from providing general teaching solutions to helping faculty discover, define, and respond to the specific questions and problems in their classrooms.

Programs can promote self-awareness by encouraging and assisting faculty to become skilled observers of their own teaching and assessors of its effects on student learning. To develop these skills, programs should offer practical ongoing training, support, and consultation for teachers who are interested in learning to more effectively assess and improve student learning.

Classroom research promotes self-questioning and self-awareness by providing faculty with simple techniques of observation and assessment. By engaging in assessment in their classrooms, faculty discover and clarify the most important questions and problems.

On the most basic level, classroom research can help teachers help students improve their learning. And by actively participating in such projects, students and teachers can improve their self-awareness as learners. By assessing their teaching effectiveness, individual faculty members can continually improve their practical knowledge and teaching skills as they deepen their understanding of their disciplines. And by collaborating on classroom research projects and sharing lessons learned, college teachers can greatly improve what the academic disciplines, and the profession as a whole, know over the longer term about effective practice.

3. Shift the Focus from the General to the Specific. Shift from treating faculty as consumers to encouraging them to be creators of knowledge on teaching and learning. Shift from offering faculty general teaching tips and information to engaging them in teasing out the implications and applications of research to their specific disciplines, courses, and students.

Programs should respect discipline-specific ways of knowing by recognizing faculty members as potential experts on teaching and learning in their fields. They should encourage faculty to adapt and apply their discipline-specific research skills to study and improve learning in their own classrooms. They should capitalize on shared world views by organizing project working groups along disciplinary and departmental lines.

Since classroom research is carried out by individual faculty in specific courses, the focus is necessarily discipline- and context-specific. The faculty developer's problem then becomes one of helping teachers from different disciplines find common threads among their very specific projects. Over time, involvement in group training sessions, ongoing project meetings, and structured seminars can help faculty see those commonalities and develop a cross-disciplinary language for talking about teaching and learning.

4. Shift the Focus from Individuals to Communities. Shift from assisting isolated individual faculty members to assisting faculty as members of departmental, program, and institutional teaching-learning communities. Shift from only considering the needs of certain groups within the faculty—such as full-time, tenured teachers—to engaging the entire community in helping one another.

Programs can create personal investment by helping individual faculty define and pursue questions and problems they want to address while helping faculty connect their individual concerns to the larger departmental or institutional agenda. Providing a clear procedure allows the participating faculty to define and plan individual and collaborative learning improvement efforts. Respect for faculty autonomy shows in allowing and encouraging faculty ownership of learning improvement programs. Programs should let faculty participants in each program determine the appropriate level of administrative involvement and support and involve part-time and full-time, as well as novice and veteran, faculty.

Classroom research focuses on the class as a learning community, rather than on individual students. Classroom assessment techniques usually provide teachers with brief anonymous responses to prompts such as, "What was the most important thing you learned this session?" or "Give one practical application of the principles you studied in your last homework assignment." Faculty collect and quickly analyze feedback in order to gain a better sense of how the class as a whole is doing. Armed with that information, teachers then respond to the class, rather than to specific individuals. Focusing on the group lowers students anxiety levels and defensiveness, helps build a classroom community, and takes the faculty member far less time than would responding to individuals. Since most teachers who use classroom assessment continue to grade and comment on assignments and tests, students continue to receive individual feedback.

Classroom research can also help create a learning community among faculty. As mentioned above, when faculty engage in group training workshops and follow-up discussions, a common language of concepts and terms can be built over time, which allows them to discover shared problems and concerns—as well as to assist one another. Once created, these classroom research groups can form the foundation for ongoing faculty development efforts.

135

5. Shift the Focus from Extrinsic to Intrinsic Motivations. Shift from appealing primarily to faculty's short-term, extrinsic motivations to appealing to a wide range of more intrinsic, longer-term motivations to participate.

This can be done by focusing on teaching and learning issues that capture the intellectual interest of faculty. Programs should offer clear-cut, step-by-step procedures to help faculty set and achieve their goals and objectives. They should help faculty collaborate productively with departmental colleagues and with those from other disciplines. Teachers often find the personal and social rewards of such collaboration highly motivating.

Participants should be recognized and praised publicly for their interest, involvement, and efforts. Programs should encourage and celebrate risk taking and experimentation, not just success. These types of extrinsic motivation cost little or nothing and yield many benefits. Use high-status awards and monetary rewards to recognize extraordinary performance or improvement, not just participation. When funds are available for classroom research, consider providing support for clerical help and research assistants, rather than directly subsidizing faculty participation. Consider using extrinsic rewards primarily as a way to tip the scales—to convince those who need only a slight nudge to get involved.

Classroom research capitalizes on three powerful sources of faculty motivation: intellectual curiosity, interest in helping students learn more effectively, and the desire to share teaching experiences with other faculty. Teachers who have practiced these approaches for more than a year indicate that enhanced collegiality, positive student response, and intellectual stimulation are the three most important benefits of participating in classroom research projects. Obviously, these benefits represent, at least potentially, renewable and sustainable sources of motivation for improvement.

6. Shift the Focus from Adopting New Ideas to Adapting Promising Ones. Shift from asking what works to asking what works for whom, when, where, how, and why.

Faculty development programming should help participants make explicit connections to the relevant research on teaching and learning in their specific disciplines. Fortunately, there are useful general principles for effective college teaching and learning based on research (Gamson and Chickering, 1987; McKeachie, et al., 1986; Murray, 1985; Pintrich, 1988; Sherman, 1985; Svinicki, 1991; and Weinstein and Underwood, 1985). Faculty developers need to help teachers build on that base by discovering discipline-specific and context-specific principles for effective teaching and learning. Put another way, we already know a great deal about what works in general. Now we need to discover what works specifically. Faculty members are in the best position to answer these questions.

There are at least two ways in which classroom research can help teachers and faculty developers discover for themselves what works. First, these approaches provide simple, systematic ways to assess the effectiveness of teaching and learning innovations. A cardinal axiom of classroom research is "adapt, don't adopt," and the CATs are constructed to be highly flexible and easily adapted. Faculty can reshape these tools to find out whether new teaching techniques or materials really are more effective. But more importantly, as faculty become experienced in these approaches, they develop the habit of carefully adapting new ideas and assessing them, thus becoming more systematic and successful at improving their own teaching and student learning. Over time, many classroom researchers become interested in traditional research and in exploring the relevance of general research findings to their unique classrooms.

7. Shift the Focus from Short-Term Quantity to Long-Term Quality. Shift from envisioning, measuring, and evaluating program success only in terms of faculty participation and satisfaction rates to aiming for and assessing long-term improvements in teaching and learning performance.

Building a faculty development program to achieve lasting improvements in student learning is a much more daunting task than putting together a calendar of workshops and speakers for a semester or two. A long-term focus requires adequate planning time, ongoing human and material support, stable leadership, and a well-organized but flexible process within which faculty can define and accomplish individual agendas linked to the overall plan. To encourage ongoing faculty involvement, create a structure that allows participants to start small, build incrementally, and set limits on the amount of time and energy invested in such programs.

Classroom research is about quality, first and foremost. Most faculty who persevere in these approaches find they focus more on making sure their students learn the most important course content, and less on covering as much content as possible. The most successful classroom research programs on community college campuses are well planned, well led long-term efforts that provide practical ongoing training, support, and consultation for teachers who are interested in learning to assess and improve student learning more effectively. See Stetson (1991) for a description of an exemplary program at the College of Marin, California, and Cuevas (1991) for an evaluation of Miami-Dade's intensive classroom research course for faculty.

DESIGN GUIDELINES FOR IMPLEMENTING TRANSFORMATIVE FACULTY DEVELOPMENT

While classroom research and classroom assessment are approaches that faculty developers can use to promote more successful, coherent, and transformative programs, they are only part of the equation. The literature provides us with some general implementation guidelines from research and practice. The following proven and practical guidelines are a synthesis of suggestions found in Levinson-Rose and Menges (1981), Genthon (1989), Quinlan (1991), and Maxwell and Kazlauskas (1992).

In general, community college faculty development efforts are likely to be more successful if they:

- Support and reinforce the institution's mission, goals, academic programs, and institutional culture of teaching and learning
- Plan and program for the long-term with a few major projects, building in support for follow-up activities, assessment, and revision

- Benefit from strong, stable, and continuing administrative support
- Are led by well-respected, competent individuals with strong academic credentials and good interpersonal skills, who serve as program leaders for significant periods of time
- Involve a variety of faculty members, including several high-status senior faculty who are opinion leaders, in the planning and implementation of faculty development, not just as participants
- Develop programming that connects the very specific needs and interests of individual faculty to those of their colleagues, to the needs of students, and to those of the institution as a whole
- Connect programming explicitly to the best current research and practice in college teaching and learning
- Communicate with, engage, and involve the widest possible sample of the faculty—full-time and part-time, new and veteran
- Offer a range of incentives—intrinsic and extrinsic—to motivate faculty to invest their time and energies in improvement efforts over the long term
- Help faculty develop skills and knowledge they can adapt and apply to their specific disciplines, courses, and students
- Engage in ongoing assessment of faculty development's effectiveness at the level of the institution, program, and individual participant

Faculty development in community colleges has weathered twenty turbulent years of growth and retrenchment and is likely to survive into the foreseeable future. But as the faculty development movement enters its third decade, its goal should not be merely to survive, but to thrive. In order to realize its promise during the 1990s, faculty development must play a pivotal role in the transformation and improvement of teaching and learning in community colleges. If faculty developers adopt a transformative agenda for the 1990s, classroom research can serve as a powerful lever for raising the quality of higher learning.

REFERENCES

Angelo, T.A. (Ed.). *Classroom Research: Early Lessons from Success.* New Directions for Teaching and Learning, no. 46. San Francisco: Jossey-Bass, 1991.

Angelo, T.A. and K.P. Cross. *Classroom Assessment Techniques: A Handbook for College Teachers, 2nd Edition.* San Francisco: Jossey-Bass, 1993.

Association of American Colleges. *Integrity in the College Curriculum: A Report to the Academic Community.* Washington, D.C.: Association of American Colleges, 1985.

Blackburn, R.T., A. Bober, C. O'Connell, and G. Pellino. *Project for Faculty Development Program Evaluation: Final Report.* Ann Arbor: Center for the Study of Higher Education, University of Michigan, 1980.

Cross, K.P. "Teaching to Improve Learning." *Journal on Excellence in College Teaching,* 1990, *1,* pp. 9–22.

Cross, K.P. and E.F. Fideler. "Assessment in the Classroom." *Community/Junior College Quarterly of Research and Practice,* 1988, *12* (4), pp. 275–285.

Cuevas, G.J. "Feedback from Classroom Research Projects." *Community/Junior College Quarterly of Research and Practice,* 1991, *15* (4), pp. 381–390.

Eisner, E. "Aesthetic Modes of Knowing." In E. Eisner (Ed.), *Learning and Teaching the Ways of Knowing: Eighty-Fourth Yearbook of the National Society for the Study of Education, Part II.* Chicago: University of Chicago Press, 1985.

El-Khawas, E., D.J. Carter, and C.A. Ottinger. *Community College Fact Book.* New York: American Association of Community Colleges/American Council on Education/Macmillan, 1988.

Fideler, E.F. (Ed.) *Educational Forum.* Wellesley Hills, Mass.: Windsor Press, 1991.

Gamson, Z. and A.W. Chickering. "Seven Principles for Good Practice in Undergraduate Education." *AAHE Bulletin,* 1987, *39,* pp. 5–10.

Genthon, M. "Helping Teaching and Learning Centers Improve Teaching." *Accent on Improving College Teaching and Learning.* Ann Arbor: National Center for Research to Improve Postsecondary Teaching and Learning, 1989.

Levinson-Rose, J. and R.J. Menges. "Improving College Teaching: A Critical Review of the Research." *Review of Educational Research,* 1981, *51,* pp. 403–434.

Mahoney, J. and L. Sallis (Eds.). *Community, Technical, and Junior Colleges Statistical Yearbook, 1991 Edition*. Washington, D.C.: American Association of Community Colleges, 1991.

Mathis, C.B. "Faculty Development." In H.E. Mitzel (Ed.), *Encyclopedia of Educational Research*, Vol. 2. New York: Free Press, 1982.

Maxwell, W.E. and E.J. Kazlauskas. "Which Faculty Development Methods Really Work in Community Colleges? A Review of Research." *Community/ Junior College Quarterly of Research and Practice*, 1992, *16*, pp. 351–360.

McKeachie, W.J. "Perspectives from Psychology: Financial Incentives Are Ineffective for Faculty." In D.R. Lewis and W.E. Becker, Jr. (Eds.), *Academic Rewards in Higher Education*. Cambridge, Mass.: Ballinger, 1979.

McKeachie, W.J., P.R. Pintrich, Y-G Lin, and D.F. Smith. *Teaching and Learning in the College Classroom: A Review of the Research Literature*. Ann Arbor: National Center for Research to Improve Postsecondary Teaching and Learning, 1986.

Menges, R.J. and M.D. Svinicki (Eds.). *College Teaching: From Theory to Practice*. New Directions for Teaching and Learning, no. 45. San Francisco: Jossey-Bass, Spring 1991.

Miller, D.J. and J.L. Ratcliff. "Analysis of Professional Development Activities of Iowa Community College Faculty." *Community/Junior College Quarterly of Research and Practice*, 1986, *10* (4), pp. 317–343.

Murray, H.G. "Classroom Teaching Behaviors Related to College Teaching Effectiveness." In J.G. Donald and A.M. Sullivan (Eds.), *Using Research to Improve Teaching*. New Directions for Teaching and Learning, no. 23. San Francisco: Jossey-Bass, 1985.

National Commission on Excellence in Education. *A Nation at Risk*. Washington, D.C.: U.S. Department of Education, 1983.

Pintrich, P.R. "Student Learning and College Teaching." In R.E. Young and K.E. Eble (Eds.), *College Teaching and Learning: Preparing for New Commitments*. New Directions for Teaching and Learning, no. 33. San Francisco: Jossey-Bass, 1988, pp. 71–86.

Quinlan, K.M. "About Teaching and Learning Centers." *AAHE Bulletin*, 1991, *44* (2), pp. 11–16.

Sherman, T.M. "Learning Improvement Programs: A Review of Controllable Influences." *Journal of Higher Education*, 1985, *56* (1), pp. 85–100.

Smith, A.B. "Innovations in Staff Development." In T. O'Banion (Ed.), *Innovation in the Community College*. New York: ACE/Macmillan, 1989.

141

Stetson, N.E. "Implementing and Maintaining a Classroom Research Program for Faculty." In T.A. Angelo (Ed.), *Classroom Research: Early Lessons from Success*. New Directions for Teaching and Learning, no. 46. San Francisco: Jossey-Bass, 1991, pp. 117–128.

Svinicki, M.D. "Practical Implications of Cognitive Theories." In R.J. Menges and M.D. Svinicki (Eds.), *College Teaching: From Theory to Practice*. New Directions for Teaching and Learning, no. 45. San Francisco: Jossey-Bass, 1991, pp. 27–37

Weinstein, C.E. and V.L. Underwood. "Learning Strategies: The How of Learning." In J.W. Segal, S.F. Chipman, and R. Glaser (Eds.), *Thinking and Learning Skills: Relating Instruction to Research*, Vol. 1. Hillsdale, N.J.: Erlbaum, 1985.

Thomas A. Angelo *is director, Academic Development Center, Boston College.*

Chapter 8

Involving Faculty in TQM Through Classroom Assessment

By K. Patricia Cross

For those who experienced the missionary zeal and momentum of the community college movement of the 1960s, the decade of the 1990s is a real downer. In the 1960s access to higher education was the national priority; resources were plentiful, and there was a direct correlation between access and resources. Improving access required more resources—more money, more colleges, more faculty, more programs. In such projections, the future is a simple extension of the past. Colleges expand and extend; they do more of what they have been doing. But at some point—and it may have been reached in education—the direct relationship between challenges and opportunities breaks down. "Paradigm shift" is the academic term for changed perspectives, and "restructuring" or "re-engineering" is the corporate term.

A decade ago, some hard-pressed American industries began the process of "restructuring" their organizations when it became apparent that business as usual was no longer an option. Tinkering at the margins—downsizing and economizing—would barely make a dent in restoring health and vitality to their organizations. Michael Hammer argues in the *Harvard Business Review* (1990, p. 104) that industry must "radically redesign...business processes in order to achieve dramatic improvements in their performance." He observes that "heavy investments in information technology have delivered disappointing results—largely because companies tend to use technology to mechanize old ways of doing business. They leave the existing processes intact and use computers simply to speed them up." The challenge for American industry, says Hammer, is to "stop paving the cow-paths." Education has some cow-paths of its own, and some pioneering colleges are calling for radical redesign, not only to meet what appears to be a continuing budget crisis, but to meet the dramatically different requirements of the 21st century.

The need for a paradigm shift in higher education is vividly illustrated by the currrent crisis in California. Viewing the California Master Plan through the lens of the 1960s shows declining access and/or quality as an inevitable result of declining resources. If the money is not forthcoming to support and extend the familiar paradigms for education, the argument goes, then the public must expect restricted access or a decline in the quality of education—or according to the plan, both. Public four-year institutions in California are refusing to accept more students because, they say, they are already at the limit of their resources. Since the California Master Plan calls for access to higher education for all who can benefit, community colleges are faced with absorbing student demands for access, albeit without additional resources.

If the old paradigms still hold, it appears that four-year institutions will opt for maintaining quality by reducing access, whereas community colleges must opt for the other alternative—that of maintaining access, but at the cost of reducing quality.

IMPROVING QUALITY THROUGH INCREASING PRODUCTIVITY

As anyone involved in the education wars of the 1990s knows all too well, the "productivity" of educators, especially faculty members, is being questioned. For all higher education institutions, whether community colleges or research universities, one pertinent measure of productivity is the quality of student learning. And assessment of student learning outcomes is the handle that state legislators use to determine the "accountability" of higher education. Are college faculty members productive, in the sense that they turn out students who can use their developed intellectual knowledge and skills to contribute to society as workers and citizens?

The demands for attention to the quality of student learning—for the most part without increased budgets—started in the 1980s with the nationwide assessment movement. Today virtually every college, private or public, has some sort of assessment plan. The good news is that the sincerity with which higher education responded to the calls for accountability has resulted in less strident demands from state legislators for "assessment for accountability," and more support for "assessment for improvement." Legislators in most states are backing off from earlier mandates and prescriptions for standardized assessments, in favor of support and encouragement for self-study assessments that will help institutions improve the quality of their education.

The bad news is that many institutions are confirming through their assessments that the quality of student learning is poor and—if the old paradigm holds—community colleges must make a choice between using limited funds to increase access or to improve quality—an intolerable situation for community colleges with their promise of equal opportunity, where "equal" means not just access to education but to quality education that meets students' needs.

TOTAL QUALITY MANAGEMENT (TQM)

The challenge then of the 1990s, in education as in industry, is to improve quality through increasing productivity. The opportunity, many believe, lies in the application of Total Quality Management (TQM) to higher education. TQM or SLI (Something Like It) is already at work in more than half of the Fortune 1000 firms, and leaders in education, especially in research universities and community colleges, are exploring its potential for higher education (Marchese, 1991; Seymour, 1991; Mangan, 1992).

Admittedly, TQM has its advocates, agnostics, and detractors, but it appears that education has "hit the wall." State budgetary crises have forced reductions of 25 to 30 percent over a three-year period, resulting in unprecedented tuition hikes, layoffs of tenured faculty members, abolition of entire academic programs, and restriction of student admissions. Even these Draconian measures, however, are not enough. Deeper cuts are required and higher quality is demanded. Without a dramatic paradigm shift, higher education is headed toward challenges that it cannot possibly meet. It is time to look at the opportunities to rethink on education in fresh and innovative ways.

The goal of course is to do more with less. Hammer (1990) relates the dramatic success of the Ford Motor Company in reducing costs in its accounts payable department. Management estimated they could reduce personnel costs by 20 percent by applying new technology and increasing efficiency. That looked good until they found they could reduce personnel costs by an astounding 75 percent by revamping the procedures of accounts payable. Not surprisingly such success stories caught the attention of educators. Daniel Seymour (1991) surveyed twenty-two pioneering colleges and universities with experience in TQM and found mixed reactions to early efforts, but concluded that in general the results were promising.

There is considerable irony, however, in the approach of educational institutions to TQM. While the rhetoric calls boldly for paradigm shifts, restructuring, and dramatic change, the educational practitioners of TQM start very timidly. In the colleges in Seymour's survey (1991, p. 11), the five most common applications of TQM were in registration procedures, mail distribution, physical maintenance, construction and remodeling projects, and payroll. While today's TQM practitioners talk boldly about totally new organizational cultures and about "barrier busting" (bringing people together from all over the institution to work on training teams), it appears that the barriers busted so far are usually between employees of different departments in the same management division. Today, TQM's application in higher education is far from the dramatic reforms that seem called for in the language of TQM and in view of the challenges faced by higher education. TQM, says Marchese (1991, p. 4), "is a call to leadership for the reform of American enterprise. Its advocates want more than a change in management practice; they want an entirely new organization, one whose culture is quality-driven, customer-oriented, marked by teamwork, and avid about improvement."

While it is certainly to everyone's advantage for the culture of the mail distribution center to be "quality-driven, customer-oriented, marked by teamwork, and avid about improvement," even total success in the implementation of TQM in the management divisions of colleges and universities would not begin to meet the demands of the 1990s for improved quality in student learning and the increase in faculty productivity that such a goal implies. After all, it is the faculty who constitute the major portion of any college's budget, and it is they who control quality. If the classroom doesn't work, the college doesn't work, no matter how well the support services are managed.

"But," experienced colleagues in the administrative trenches will say, "everyone knows you can't 'manage' faculty." Right! And the whole point of TQM is to get people to manage themselves—to assume individual responsibility for working toward common ends.

When Miami-Dade Community College, Florida, started its Teaching/Learning Project five years ago, TQM was not even in the lexicon of higher education. But Miami-Dade's total-college push toward improving the quality of education for students is an excellent example of TQM's ideals. The goal of the project was defined in this way:

> The college would attempt systematically to change the way that it does business in order to raise the status of teaching; improve teaching and learning at the college; relate all of the reward systems to classroom performance; and change the decision making process such that the first priority is teaching, learning, and the classroom environment (McCabe and Jenrette, 1990, p. 183).

While the major focus of the project is on the classroom and improving the productivity of teachers and students, changing the culture of the total institution is clearly the goal. Miami-Dade President Robert McCabe tells a story about changing the decision-making process at the college that captures the essence of what TQM advocates in higher education are talking about. It seems that since the purchasing department was buying cheaper chalk that was too hard to write with, some teachers were buying good chalk and carrying it with them from classroom to classroom. As the Miami-Dade community continued their discussion of quality, other stories about defective light bulbs, dirty classrooms, and the like began to surface. The result was the Marriott Plan. Much as "a good hotel does not wait for an irate guest to report a lack of soap or a broken towel rack," so Miami-Dade would not wait for faculty, who were "like hotel guests, constantly passing through an assigned room," to report less than satisfactory classroom conditions; the college would send a housekeeper around with a list of standards for classrooms and laboratories (McCabe and Jenrette, 1990, p. 184).

Had TQM been applied to the purchasing department or the physical plant alone, the Marriott Plan would not have been the result. Only when the attention of everyone who works for the college is directed toward the common mission of improving education does restructuring take place. When someone in the registrar's office carries out her bureaucratic duties efficiently by focusing on the proper procedures and forms to be filed by students, she is doing one job. But when she focuses on contributing to the quality of education at the college, she may see her job quite differently—a paradigm shift. TQM requires a paradigm shift throughout the institution, but to date its application in higher education has ignored the single most critical element in educational change—the faculty.

TQM AND CLASSROOM ASSESSMENT

Fortunately, thousands of faculty members pursue the quality-oriented activity of classroom assessment (See Chapter 7 in this book; Cross, 1988; Cross and Angelo, 1988; Angelo and Cross, 1993). Its purpose is to maximize learning through frequent assessment of how well students meet the goals of instruction. Classroom assessment procedures involve periodic data collection from students throughout the term or semester and then use that information to modify teaching, constantly experimenting to see how teachers can more effectively maximize learning.

Quizzes and tests are a timeless way to assess learning, but much of the appeal of classroom assessment is that it offers a variety of simple techniques that teachers of any discipline can use to provide quick and immediate assessments of student responses to instruction. The second edition of *Classroom Assessment Techniques* (Angelo and Cross, 1993), describes fifty classroom assessment techniques (CATs) grouped in the following categories: techniques for assessing course-related knowledge and skills; techniques for assessing learner attitudes, values, and self-awareness; and techniques for assessing learner reactions to instruction.

Classroom assessment is designed to improve the productivity of teachers and students through continuously focusing the attention of both on the quality of students' learning. Merging management-oriented TQM with academically-oriented classroom assessment offers an unprecedented opportunity for addressing the quality challenge.

Marchese (1991) has identified twelve major themes of TQM. There is remarkable congruence between these and the principles of classroom assessment. Marchese's themes can be used as a framework to illustrate how faculty can be involved in TQM.

TQM Focuses on Quality. "Quality," says Marchese, is "a mind-set, the soul of the company itself, an all-pervasive drive of such intensity that it defines the corporate culture" (p. 4).

Education, like American industry, has been harshly criticized recently for lack of attention to quality. The oft-quoted report from the National Commission on Excellence in Education (1983, p. 5) warned that "the educational foundations of our society are presently being eroded by a rising tide of mediocrity that threatens our very future as a Nation and a people." Unfortunately, the public's concern about "the rising tide of mediocrity" in the schools arrived at about the same time as the rising tide of red ink in state budgets. Under the old paradigm, in which higher quality requires more resources, there is a temptation to concentrate reform in the business office or development office. But the quality of a college is determined in its classrooms. If teachers fail to set high standards for learning in their own classrooms, then TQM's pervasive drive for quality in institutional culture is impossible.

Classroom assessment addresses the quality issue by running a continuing quality check on learning to find out how it can be improved. One of the best-known CATs is the "minute paper," which asks students to write a sentence or two about the most important thing they learned in class that day. This extremely simple technique directs the attention of students to monitoring and articulating their own learning and provides immediate information to the teacher about what class accomplished that day.

The total impact of hundreds of students and teachers asking themselves what they learned or taught that day is potentially enormous. It can result in a cumulative mindset that determines the campus culture.

TQM Is Customer-Driven. "The cardinal rule," Marchese writes, "is to identify explicitly who your customers are, know their needs systematically, and commit to serving those needs" (p. 4).

Higher education has many customers, but first and foremost is the student. The purpose of classroom assessment is to systematically determine how well instruction is meeting student needs. This requires continuous assessment. Twelve CATs in Angelo and Cross (1993) are grouped under the heading "Assessing Learner Reactions to Instruction." "Chain notes" is a simple CAT enabling teachers to find out how students respond to the work of the class at any given moment. The teacher passes around a large envelope on which she has written one question about the class. When the envelope reaches a student, he or she spends less than a minute writing a response to the question, then drops the answer in the envelope and passes it on. The question most often used is some variation of, "Immediately before this envelope reached you, what were you paying attention to?" Student responses provide the teacher with a running commentary on the work of the class as it is perceived by students.

Other CATs may ask students to evaluate an assignment or an exam. I routinely ask my graduate students to rate the value of assigned readings as learning tools. The question they are to answer is not, "How good is the research or the chapter?" but "How useful is it to you as a learner?" Since students' responses vary, their evaluation of the material enriches discussion, and the ratings and discussion are used to revise next year's outside reading assignments. CATs such as "chain notes" and "assignment assessments" keep teachers continually informed about the value of the class to students. Through such information teachers can commit to serving the needs of their students.

TQM Emphasizes Continuous Improvement. "Customers, markets, technologies change every day," Marchese says. "What's good enough now is suicide tomorrow" (p. 4).

Every teacher has had the experience of teaching the same subject matter to very different groups of students. English 101 may go extremely well with an 8 a.m. class and fail with a 4 p.m. class—perhaps because the morning class is mostly younger full-time students, whereas the afternoon class is older working adults. Classroom assessment is conducted in the classroom, assessing the quality of teaching and learning in a specific classroom with a particular group of students. It takes account of the changing demographic characteristics of students—age, ethnicity, work patterns, and the like—but goes beyond such broad categories to reassess teaching effectiveness in each class. The question for classroom assessment is, "What are *these* students learning in *this* classroom as a result of *my* efforts *today*?"

Whereas institutional assessment provides information about the long-term quality of students' learning, classroom assessment places the emphasis on continuous improvement, modifying teaching and classroom procedures while learning is in process. Institutional assessments and final exams are summative evaluations, providing information on what students *have* learned. The most likely changes instituted as a result of a summative evaluation are changes for "next time," e.g. changes in curriculum and requirements. Classroom assessments are formative evaluations; they provide information about what students *are* learning. Improvements are likely to call for changes in instruction and classroom procedures. Both types of evaluation are valuable and both are concerned with improvement, but classroom assessment places the emphasis on continuous improvement—on fixing inadequacies in learning as they are discovered.

TQM Concentrates on Making Processes Work Better. "The aim," Marchese says, "is to identify those processes; enable the people who work in them to understand that work in relation to customer needs" (p. 5).

The major process of any college or university is learning. And it is the faculty who need to understand that process and take responsibility for improving it. Few college teachers have any formal training in cognition and human learning. Yet teachers have an exceptional opportunity every day to observe the process of learning. Classroom assessment capitalizes on illuminating that process for both teachers and students .

David Ausubel (1977), a pioneer in the study of meaningful learning, made that point more than fifteen years ago, but the importance of learning as a continuous process is receiving renewed attention today. He said, in essence: Find out what a student knows and teach accordingly. Learning is not so much additive, with new learning simply piling on top of existing knowledge, as it is an active dynamic process in which new information interacts with old, reformatting and changing the cognitive structure.

CATs are designed to make teachers more sensitive to the processes of learning. The "background knowledge probe," for example, provides information about the level and range of students' preparation for a class, enabling the teacher to know where to start and how to build on what students already know. This use of classroom assessment is concerned with the learning process, with building connections between new and existing knowledge.

But there also is a use of classroom assessment concerned with the *educational* process, with assuring that the institution's methods work for quality in education. In industry, TQM is usually concerned with process as a smooth and efficient work flow. Transitions are important, and therefore teamwork within and between departments is important, as is articulation between the various levels of education. The teamwork and articulation aspects of classroom assessment are addressed below.

TQM Extends the Mind-Set. "Quality concerns," Marchese says, "reach in all directions.… No longer will it do for automakers to say, 'We know our cars aren't very good, but our lowest bid suppliers send us so-so goods' " (p. 5).

Today's educators are encouraged to think of education as a unified system with a "seamless flow" of students from grade school through college. Teachers at all levels need to know the backgrounds, interests, and preparation of students entering their classes, just as they need to know what students take from their class into the next one.

A useful device for helping teachers extend their mind-set to the lives of students before and after class is the "interest/knowledge/skills checklist," which asks students to rate their level of interest in various topics and their self-assessment of knowledge or skill in those topics. This CAT was used by a psychology professor in designing a capstone course whose purpose was to help students integrate and evaluate what they had learned in the previous three-and-a-half years of psychology coursework. It might also be useful in assessing what students think they need or want to know as they prepare for work after college (Angelo and Cross, 1993).

Marchese's further elaboration that "TQM companies attempt to develop stable relations with a smaller set of suppliers who agree to be partners in the quality-improvement process" (p. 5) applies directly to the cooperation of community college faculty members with teachers at high schools and four-year colleges in the articulation of coursework. Increasingly, teachers from different segments of the educational system—high school to community college and community college to four-year college—are getting together to articulate where students have been and where they are going in the study of a particular discipline.

TQM Involves the Discipline of Information. "If you're serious about quality," Marchese says, "everybody has to know how they're doing" (p. 5).

The relationship between classroom assessment and TQM on this principle is so obvious that little explanation is needed. Classroom assessment *is* the continuous collection of information, a disciplined activity used regularly by teachers in the practice of their profession. It may be important, however, to point out that an additional requirement of classroom assessment is that the data collected must be shared with students. Feedback on students' learning tells teachers how effectively they have taught the lesson, but equally important, it provides students with information about how well they have learned. Through classroom assessment, both teachers and students are continually faced with the discipline of using information to improve their performance.

TQM Eliminates Rework. "An aim of all this attention to work processes is to ferret out the 'scrap, waste, and complexity' from a system" (Marchese, 1991, p. 5).

Critics of education have been especially sharp in their complaint about the waste in remediation. When students fail to learn what they should at any point in the educational system, waste piles up and work has to be done over. Teachers in community colleges are all too familiar with the material and human costs resulting from poor learning the first time around. Because classroom assessment involves continuous checking on the quality of learning, it enables teachers and students to identify weaknesses when they first appear.

Every teacher has had the experience of giving what appeared to be a masterful teaching performance, only to be surprised and disappointed at the misperceptions and lack of understanding shown by students' learning. Classroom assessment, with its emphasis on assessing specific teaching/learning experiences while they are still fresh in mind, shows both teachers and students what does and does not work. Some classroom assessors find that they have been doing wasteful and ineffective things for years .

Discovering weaknesses in student learning at midterm, or worse yet in the final exam, is wasteful in the extreme. It is too late for students—and too late for the next teacher who receives inadequately prepared students. While teachers may use the results of a final exam to prepare for next semester's classes, the next class may be different, and in any case, when teaching and the assessment of learning are widely separated in time, it may be difficult to pinpoint where and when teaching and learning parted company.

TQM Emphasizes Teamwork. "Teams," Marchese observes, "are not your familiar committees; they are self-directed work groups with their own required competencies and protocols" (p. 5).

While classroom assessment was originally proposed as an independent activity that teachers could use in their own classrooms without consulting others, experience shows that independence is not highly valued for teachers who become active in classroom assessment. Quite the contrary; classroom assessment appears to promote interaction and conversations about teaching. Once teachers begin to raise questions about their own teaching and to collect data about its impact on learning, there is a self-generated pressure to discuss findings with colleagues and to form voluntary study groups. One of the most common outcomes on campuses where classroom assessment is practiced is the voluntary formation of faculty groups who wish to share findings with colleagues and to develop innovative approaches (Angelo and Cross, 1993 and Chapter 7 in this book).

Study groups may of course be multidisciplinary or interdisciplinary, but some of the strongest teamwork in classroom assessment is found at the departmental level, at least in part because members of a department share a set of common values regarding teaching goals and priorities. Our research on the Teaching Goals Inventory (TGI) shows conclusively that teaching priorities are related more to teaching discipline than to any other factor (Angelo and Cross, 1993; Cross, 1992; Cross, 1993).

Departments are also natural sites for teamwork on quality because they are the "key organizational unit within virtually every American college and university" ("Testimony from the Belly of the Whale," 1992, p. 4A). Indeed, the scholars who participated in the Pew Higher Education Roundtable contend that "departments must be the 'agents of reform' for the quality of undergraduate education." They go on to say that, "We believe that departments, more than individual faculty, ought to be vested with the responsibility for the quality of undergraduate teaching" (p. 4A).

If that is the case, then departmental teamwork is required, and classroom assessment is one promising route to the development of faculty teamwork.

TQM Empowers People. "Who, in TQM," Marchese asks, "reviews work processes? ....not distant managers or external evaluators but the people closest to the processes, those who do the work itself" (1991, p. 5).

Although classroom assessment is part of the nationwide institutional assessment movement, it moves assessment into the classroom and under the control of the people who do the work of teaching and learning—students and faculty. Its major principle is that it is *self*-assessment. It shares the assumption with TQM that teachers want to teach as well as they can and students want to do the best job of learning that they can. Classroom assessment empowers teachers and students to "take charge" of the learning process.

TQM Invests in Training and Recognition. "TQM firms invest heavily in human resource development" (Marchese, 1991, p. 5).

Classroom assessment is a powerful form of faculty development. The major difference between traditional faculty development and classroom assessment is that in the former attention is directed toward the improvement of teacher performance, whereas in the latter attention is focused on student performance as the ultimate criterion. In traditional forms of faculty development, the teacher is the subject of observation by peers, experts, videos, and the like. Without question there are many things that experts and peers can point out that will improve teaching performance. Nevertheless, the ultimate criterion of good teaching is effective learning; it makes no difference how perfectly the teacher is teaching if students are not learning. Classroom assessment places the emphasis on teachers as observers rather than as the observed. By observing the impact of their teaching on students' responses, classroom assessors develop a repertoire of teaching techniques that work for them in their subject matter with their students. But classroom assessment is not a substitute for traditional approaches to faculty development. Rather, the combination of peer collaboration and self-evaluation is a powerful form of human resource development.

156

TQM Requires Vision. "Unlike the lofty piffle of 'mission' statements," Marchese writes, "TQM urges compelling down-to-earth language that gets all parties focused on the right things to do" (p. 6).

Most classroom assessment starts with teachers making explicit their teaching goals—their vision of what they want students to learn. The revised handbook on *Classroom Assessment Techniques* provides a self-scorable version of the TGI. The TGI consists of fifty-two concrete and specific goals. Through taking the TGI, teachers make their teaching goals explicit. The handbook then guides teachers to the CATs that are most useful in assessing their priority teaching goals. The point is that teachers must have some vision about their role in the educational process. Classroom assessment helps to implement the vision by evaluating how well concrete goals are accomplished.

While classroom assessment gives credence to the visions of individual teachers, educational quality at the institutional level is more than the sum of its parts. One of the most concrete ways to find out if a college is directing its teaching efforts toward accomplishing the goals of its mission statement is to obtain an institutional profile of the faculty's teaching goals. If, for example, the "lofty piffle of the mission statement" promises to develop in students an appreciation of other cultures, but only 14 percent of the faculty members consider such a goal essential to their own teaching (our actual finding from administering the TGI to nearly 1,800 community college teachers), then questions must be raised about how well the institution is implementing the collective vision of its mission statement.

TQM Requires Leadership. "TQM partisans want fewer managers, at least of the old type—powerful figures in sole command of vertical authority structures. Instead, they want leaders, and of a new type—vision givers, listeners, team-workers, committed to quality and customer needs, avid but patient for long-term ends, orchestrators and enablers of people-driven improvements" (Marchese, 1991, p. 6).

Classroom assessment is most successful on campuses where it is supported and encouraged by leaders of the type desired by

TQM. Miami-Dade's McCabe is the prototype of a TQM leader. His leadership provided the vision and support for the Teaching/Learning Project. Faculty were not only heavily involved in committees and task forces, they carried out the institutionwide vision of excellence in their own classrooms (See Chapters 3 and 13 in this book). It is significant that a requirement of the Miami-Dade program is the development of faculty human resources through the participation of all new faculty in a graduate-level classroom assessment course taught by the University of Miami.

The challenges to the community colleges of the twenty-first century are enormous, but they basically boil down to offering high-quality education to the widest diversity of learners anywhere in the world, at a cost that will be supported by society. This chapter is not an argument for "squeezing the fat" out of education by cutting budgets and hoping higher education can adjust to underfunding and lack of community support. It is an appeal for careful and systematic analysis of the current processes, procedures, and structures of education to determine how best to meet the challenging demands of the next century. Current unprecedented pressures for change require dramatic response. TQM is one possible response that appears bold enough—at least in concept—to meet the challenge. And classroom assessment is one way to involve faculty in the substantial restructuring required by TQM. The challenges to community colleges have never been greater—nor have the opportunities.

REFERENCES

Angelo, Thomas A. and K. Patricia Cross. *Classroom Assessment Techniques: A Handbook for College Teachers.* San Francisco: Jossey-Bass, 1993.

Ausubel, D.P. "The Facilitation of Meaningful Verbal Learning in the Classroom." *Educational Psychologist,* 1977, *12*, pp. 162–178.

Cross, K. Patricia. "In Search of Zippers." *AAHE Bulletin,* 1988, *10* (4), pp. 3–7.

_____. "Classroom Assessment for Academic Departments." Keynote speech, AAHE Assessment Forum, Miami Beach, June 22, 1992.

_____. "On College Teaching." *Journal of Engineering Education,* 1993, 82 (1), pp. 9–14.

Cross, K. Patricia and Thomas A. Angelo. *Classroom Assessment Techniques: A Handbook for Faculty*. Ann Arbor: National Center for Research on the Improvement of Postsecondary Teaching and Learning, 1988.

Hammer, Michael. "Reengineering Work: Don't Automate, Obliterate." *Harvard Business Review* 1990, July/August, pp. 104–112.

Mangan, K.S. "TQM: Colleges Embrace the Concept of 'Total Quality Management.'" *The Chronicle of Higher Education,* August 12, 1992, pp. A25–26.

Marchese, Ted. "TQM Reaches the Academy." *AAHE Bulletin,* 1991, *44* (3), pp. 3–9.

McCabe, Robert H. and Mardee S. Jenrette. "Leadership in Action: A Campuswide Effort to Strengthen Teaching." In P. Seldin and Associates, *How Administrators Can Improve Teaching*. San Francisco: Jossey-Bass, 1990.

National Commission on Excellence in Education. *A Nation at Risk*. Washington, D.C.: U.S. Department of Education, 1983.

"Testimony from the Belly of the Whale." *Pew Policy Perspectives*, 1992, *4* (3).

Seymour, Daniel. "TQM On Campus: What the Pioneers Are Finding." *AAHE Bulletin*. 1991, *44* (3), pp. 10–13.

K. Patricia Cross is Elizabeth and Edward Conner Professor of Higher Education, University of California at Berkeley.

Chapter 9

The Community College Teacher as Scholar

By George B. Vaughan

Speaking at a 1992 national conference on student transfer, Stephen Trachtenberg, president of George Washington University, proclaimed: "I find myself increasingly uneasy with the term 'scholar' and what the term implies." What made him uneasy about a term that has been used and accepted by the higher education community for centuries? Trachtenberg feels that forces other than scholars, notably business leaders and government mandates, are increasingly setting the standards for what is taught and what is expected of graduates. This encroachment on the historic territory of the professoriate has made the scholar's role unclear, even in large universities with major research components.

In an address to the faculty, George Johnson, president of George Mason University, lamented that two decades ago one knew what to do to get promoted: one had to be a scholar. And,

Johnson noted, in those days everyone agreed on what was meant by scholarship (in Vaughan and Palmer, 1991).

While the encroachment of outside forces into the academic world is not new, and while being a scholar remains the route to promotion at universities such as those led by Trachtenberg and Johnson, these examples illustrate how the role and the concept of the scholar, and therefore of scholarship, are changing throughout higher education. Leading the discussion of changing scholarship concepts should be community college faculty members. Since they have defined their roles as teachers and not researchers, they are uniquely positioned within the higher education community to discuss, define, and fulfill the role of teacher-scholar.

Other voices are calling for a clarification of the term "scholarship." Ernest L. Boyer, in his 1990 report for the Carnegie Foundation for the Advancement of Teaching, acknowledges the need for a redefinition of scholarship: "We believe the time has come to move beyond the tired old 'teaching versus research' debate and give the familiar and honorable term 'scholarship' a broader, more capacious meaning, one that brings legitimacy to the full scope of academic work" (p. 16). Boyer calls for the scholarship of discovery, the scholarship of integration, the scholarship of application, and the scholarship of teaching. While he does not define scholarship, he nevertheless broadens the boundaries within which the scholar works.

Boyer's report continues to attract attention. An article in the October 28, 1992, *Chronicle of Higher Education* notes that Boyer's broader definition of what counts as scholarly work would reward professors for teaching and for working on the curriculum, even though that work is not groundbreaking research. R. Eugene Rice, who assisted Boyer on the report and who is now dean of the faculty at Antioch College, says with approval that he is amazed at how many campuses are discussing a broadened definition of scholarship. Rice believes that a current priority of higher education should be to rethink what it means to be a scholar (Mooney, pp. 17–19).

One report related specifically to community colleges calls for their faculty members to be both teachers and scholars. The report of the Commission on the Future of Community Colleges, of which Boyer was a member, concludes that, "While not every community college faculty member is a publishing researcher, each should be a dedicated scholar—including those involved in technical and applied education. But for this to be a realistic goal, the meaning of scholarship must be broadened" (1988, p. 26). David Pierce, president of the American Association of Community Colleges, repeatedly refers to the commission's report as the community college's blueprint for the future.

With the above providing the setting, this chapter proposes to do the following: define scholarship and suggest that community college professionals adopt a definition of scholarship compatible with the community college mission; briefly discuss some of the writings on scholarship's role in the community college; suggest ways some of the barriers to scholarship might be lessened or eliminated; and offer practical suggestions for engaging in scholarship and publishing the results of one's scholarship.

DEFINING SCHOLARSHIP

Scholarship is a concept in search of a definition, for definitions do indeed define boundaries. In the spring 1988 issue of *Educational Record*, I defined scholarship in a way that is compatible with the mission of most higher education institutions and specifically compatible with the community college mission and its emphasis on teaching. Prior to its publication, this definition of scholarship was reviewed by a number of scholars and practitioners. Included among the reviewers were two community college presidents and three community college faculty members; also included were Ph.D.s in chemical engineering, botany, and chemistry. One of these reviewers was the director of a prestigious national scholarly organization. After much debate and revision, the following definition emerged:

Scholarship is the systematic pursuit of a topic; an objective, rational inquiry that involves critical analysis. It requires the precise observation, organization, and recording of information in the search for truth and order. Scholarship is the umbrella under which research falls, for research is but one form of scholarship.

163

Scholarship results in a product that is shared with others and is subject to the criticism of individuals qualified to judge the product. This product may take the form of a book review, an annotated bibliography, a lecture, a review of existing research on a topic, or a speech that is a synthesis of the thinking on a topic. Scholarship requires that one have a solid foundation in one's professional field and keep up with the developments in the field (Vaughan, 1988, p. 27).

The reaction among community college professionals to the definition has been unanimously positive. Nevertheless I did not feel that the definition quite captured the essence of scholarship as it applies to the work of community college faculty. I later broadened it to include art exhibits by teacher-artists; original essays and poems by faculty members; scholarly articles in journals and other publications that are not research-based or which may not be "refereed"; the development of original texts designed for using computers in teaching and learning; inventions related to one's teaching field; and classsroom research when related to one's own teaching. I would now add original plays and musical compositions by faculty members as constituting legitimate scholarly activities. While one cannot continue to expand definitions without sinking into the quicksand of semantics, it is nevertheless important that the definition of scholarship be in concert with the community college mission and the faculty's role in defining and fulfilling that mission. The definition must speak to what community college faculty members do, or should do, in their roles as scholars-teachers. An example will serve to illustrate how a topic might be approached by applying the above definition.

Members of the art world in particular and the population in general are shocked when a revered painting or other piece of art is revealed to be a forgery or the work of students of the great master, as has been the case with some of the paintings attributed to Rembrandt. When a forgery is revealed, the *good* teacher will certainly discuss it with students, often drawing upon the news media or popular weekly magazines as sources. On the other hand, the *great* teacher, who I believe must be a scholar, might seize the opportunity as a vehicle for further scholarly work. For example, if the painting has been accepted for years as one by the grand master, what does it tell us about our ability to judge art? If the market price of the work drops drastically, as it surely will, what does this say about our value system? Is the piece less attractive? What does Rembrandt's signature on a painting that was done by someone else say about the ethics of the day? The scholar-teacher could pursue the topic of art forgery in many ways. The point is that to tell the students that the painting is a forgery or assistants' work is simply bartering information. The *scholar* will engage in some scholarly work to support and enhance the discussion.

BUILDING A CASE FOR SCHOLARSHIP

Two recent monographs are devoted to a discussion of scholarship and its relationship to the community college. *Enhancing Teaching and Administration Through Scholarship*, published by Jossey-Bass in its New Directions for Community College Series (Vaughan and Palmer, 1991), contains chapters by three community college presidents, as well as chapters by community college faculty members and university professors. This volume examines the importance of scholarship to the community college professional and suggests how community college leaders can promote professionalism built around scholarship. The second volume, *Fostering a Climate for Faculty Scholarship at Community Colleges*, published by the American Association of Community Colleges, contains chapters by a community college president, an executive dean, a community college faculty member, and three university professors. The short volume discusses scholarship under three umbrellas: the leadership required to enhance scholarship on campus; the connection between scholarship and teaching; and the obligation of community college educators to be scholars (Palmer and Vaughan, 1992).

While these volumes do not constitute a revolution in the thinking regarding the role of scholarship among community college professionals, they do indicate that there is keen interest in the subject among some scholars and practitioners. Indeed, *Community College Week*, in its "Faculty Issues: Emerging Concerns of the Two-Year Professoriate" section, discusses the role of scholarship in the lives of community college professionals. Unfortunately, in discussing faculty interests, the writer turned to information from the National Education Association that defined the debate as teaching versus research, not the teacher as scholar (Brodie, 1992).

Why should community college faculty members concern themselves with scholarship? Why should they be scholars as well as teachers? After all, they teach fifteen to eighteen credit hours per week as part of their normal teaching load. Many teach additional courses for additional pay. Not only do they have multiple class preparations, but many teach in more than one discipline. One outstanding community college faculty member in one semester taught the introductory transfer chemistry course, a course on the metric system, two courses in transfer mathematics, a course in developmental mathematics, and a credit physical education course in beginning tennis. While this may not be typical, it is not unusual for community college faculty members to teach subjects whose content extends well beyond the pale of their graduate degrees. Moreover, community college faculty members, like other members of the higher education community, serve on an endless number of committees that seem to meet perpetually; they advise students (many states mandate that faculty members have a minimum of 10 office hours per week); and they do any number of things such as attend graduation (again, often mandated) and in general fulfill their roles as professionals. It is not surprising that the reason most often given by community college faculty members for not producing scholarly products is a lack of time (Palmer, 1992, p. 61).

Back to the question: Why should community college faculty members be scholars? One writer goes to the heart of the matter when he states that there is no doubt a faculty member ought to be both teacher and scholar in the broad sense. He asks: "Can a faculty member really be a good teacher unless he continues to take seriously (and gladly) his own learning?" (Nelson, 1981, p. 9). This writer builds a strong case for scholarship as a source of renewal for faculty members. He suggests that scholarship is at the very heart of professional development. He defines scholarly study in a number of ways, including presenting papers on campus or in professional groups, leading professional associations, and engaging in musical performances and theatrical productions. He believes that at some point scholars must place their work before a critical public audience for review and evaluation (Nelson, 1981). Renewal, rewards, and self-satisfaction are some reasons for engaging in scholarly work.

Robert E. Parilla, president of Montgomery College, Maryland, also sees scholarship as an important source of renewal not only for the individual, but for the institution as well. He writes: "I believe that scholarship, the link that energizes the teacher-learner relationship, as well as the college experience generally, must be at the heart of efforts to revitalize the academic environment" (Parilla, 1991, p. 27). Parilla believes that faculty must be actively involved in their disciplines or technical fields if they are to be effective teachers.

Robert Templin, president of Thomas Nelson Community College, Virginia, sees presidential involvement in scholarly activities as an important part of his leadership role. He believes that scholarship keeps the professional in touch with core institutional values, including protecting academic freedom in the pursuit of truth and knowledge. He also sees scholarship as an important source of renewal for all members of the college community (Templin, 1991).

Why engage in scholarly activities? Scholarship is the lifeblood of the academic profession. Without it classroom teachers simply barter information rather than engage in the search for truth, knowledge, and order in their work. The teacher-scholar must make time for scholarship, for scholarship is as much a part of the professional person's life as eating, sleeping, and surviving. Why engage in scholarship? The answer is that if one is to be an effective teacher, one must by definition be a scholar.

ELIMINATING BARRIERS TO SCHOLARSHIP

In making time for scholarship, faculty members need the support of the governing board, the president, and the academic dean. The board can establish policies whereby faculty members are given time off to pursue their scholarly activities. Presidents can see that the policies are followed and that scholarly activities are rewarded. When one thinks of taking time off to pursue scholarly activities, the sabbatical leave often comes to mind, but there are a number of other ways to provide time for scholarship. For example, the faculty member's teaching load may be reduced by one course per semester. This often can be done at very little cost to the institution, since low-cost adjuncts are available in most fields. Institutions can support travel to professional meetings and summer study. If scholarship is to assume a prominent place among community college faculty, the institution must support it and provide rewards. As suggested by Templin (1991), presidents should see scholarship as part of their leadership role and therefore be scholars themselves. One can eliminate many barriers to scholarship on the community college campus if presidents are practicing scholars and thus role models. Presidential support will go a long way toward assuring that scholarship is an important part of the faculty member's role.

Perhaps the major barrier to scholarship on community college campuses is the attitude that no one cares whether faculty engage in scholarship. Apathy on the part of the governing board and president often creates apathy among the faculty. This is especially true when dealing with such ill-defined and misunderstood concepts as scholarship. To have a major impact on faculty, scholarship must become a part of the community college culture. For this to happen the board and president must get excited about scholarship and make it a part of the college culture, including the rewards system.

Finally, a barrier to integrating scholarship into the community college culture is a lack of understanding of what is meant by scholarship in relation to the community college mission and the faculty member's role in fulfilling that mission. Faculty should insist that the institution define what it means by scholarship and reward its faculty for engaging in scholarly activities. The governing board and president should ensure that this definition is in concert with the institutional mission. Faculty members in turn

should ensure that the definition is applied consistently throughout the institution.

ENGAGING IN SCHOLARSHIP: A PRACTICAL GUIDE

Moving from institutional barriers to individual concerns, the
following offers some practical advice for faculty members who
might have trouble placing their scholarly activities within the
context of their professional and personal lives. First, a caveat: I
realize that many community college faculty members are very
fine scholars and that much of the following is elementary to
them. Nevertheless, based on my own practical experience as a
community college president and scholar, I believe that most of us
can profit from what others have learned. With this in mind, I
offer the following as a practical guide for engaging in scholarship.

Pursue a Topic in Which You Have a High Degree of Interest.
While your discipline will normally define the boundaries of your
scholarship, you should nevertheless pursue a topic in which you
have a high degree of interest; otherwise, it is unlikely you will pursue the topic over time. Graduate schools specializing in higher education are infamous for insisting that students engage in quantitative research, regardless of their interest and abilities. It is little
wonder that once students earn their doctorate, many of them
never want to engage in research again. (One is reminded once
again of how important it is to define scholarship in ways that go
well beyond the traditional definition of research.) If you hate statistics it is usually unwise and a waste of time and energy to pursue
a statistical study. Write a short story, a play, or an op-ed piece for
the Sunday supplement based on your discipline and knowledge.

*Recognize that Scholarly Pursuits Must Also Be Tailored to
Your Habits and Lifestyle, at Least Up to a Point.* To paraphrase
the poet John Donne, no person is an island. If you have a family,
little is to be gained by rejecting their needs and wants for the sake
of engaging in scholarly activities. For example, deciding to carve
out that three-hour block on Saturday afternoon when the children have a soccer game or concert will likely result in frustrated

and angry children, a frustrated spouse, and a frustrated, nonproductive scholar. Choose times for your scholarly work that flow with family life. Early mornings on the weekend often find the rest of the family sleeping late; these hours should find the serious scholar at work. If you do not like to work early in the morning, late at night may be the only other logical choice. The point is, set aside some time for scholarship that does not disrupt the flow of family life. If you live alone, the solution to the problem may be more flexible, but the advice remains the same: set aside a time for scholarship that suits your own lifestyle—morning, night, with music, without music, whatever. Take the advice every child has heard since kindergarten: in addition to setting aside time for scholarly work, have a place set aside.

Keep Your Perspective Broad but Your Focus Narrow. A major mistake of many would-be scholars is trying to tackle a subject that is too broad to fit into their schedule or for which resources are unavailable. Nevertheless, it is important that scholarly work fit into a broad perspective. If your discipline is sociology and your interest is in world hunger, it is important that you understand world hunger in its broader perspective. As a full-time faculty member at a community college, it is unlikely that time and resources will be available for a study of world hunger. On the other hand, both time and resources are available to study the topic as it relates to one segment of the population served by the college. Trying to take on too much results in frustration and few results.

Keep Files on a Number of Topics Falling Within Your Broad Perspective and Your Narrow Focus. Once you define the boundaries around your scholarship, it is amazing how many sources you will discover related to your topic. Most of us find it very difficult to keep up with what we find on our topic, much less store it for future use. I find it very useful to keep a number of files on the topic at hand. In the study of hunger, keeping files on the population of the area would be useful, as would files on migration patterns, family income, the area's tax base, and transfer payments. Files allow the whole to quickly exceed the sum of its parts. Moreover, as the files are built, new areas of scholarly interest emerge. Keeping files on the topic permits you to keep your perspective broad and your focus narrow.

Take Notes at Professional Meetings, when Talking with Colleagues, and when Reading the Popular Press. I am amazed at how few individuals take notes while listening to professional presentations. It is as if we feel it might not be "cool" to be seen taking notes, even though much of higher education's effort is devoted to encouraging students to take notes. I witnessed a contrasting example at a rather mundane meeting of college presidents held in Richmond, Virginia, some years ago.

One member of the audience was David Riesman, distinguished Harvard professor and keynote speaker for that evening. I noted that Riesman had a small pad on which he was taking copious notes. I had no idea what he planned to do with them, since I felt the speaker we were hearing brought little that was new to bear on the topic at hand. But in one of Riesman's books, I later recognized a bit of the material covered by that speaker. In Riesman's skillful hands, what appeared to be routine material was used (with proper attribution) to encourage the reader to view the issue from a new perspective. I learned two things from observing Riesman that day (I have learned much more over the years): no matter how distinguished the scholar, he or she can learn from others, no matter how basic the material might appear; and, if a scholar of Riesman's renown felt a need to take notes, there certainly is no need for those of us who have not achieved his success to hesitate to write down the thoughts of others.

Three pieces of advice might make the note taking more valuable. First, immediately upon returning home, or even sooner, distill the notes, pulling out the key points and discarding the rest, for it is unlikely that months later we will be willing to wade through pages of hand-written notes. Second, file the notes in the appropriate file or files described above. And third, be sure to note the time, place, dates, name, and position of the speaker.

Think About Your Scholarly Work While Walking, Driving, Cycling, Lying Awake at Night, or Whenever It Is Convenient and the Mind Is Not Otherwise Occupied. One scholar I know who is viewed as being able to produce large amounts of writing in a short period claims that he is able to transfer his thoughts to writing because he has been thinking about his subject while taking his morning walks. While most individuals probably do not "write" while walking or doing similar things, it is nevertheless very helpful to have one's thoughts organized before beginning to write. As most scholars know, some of the most brilliant thoughts come at the most unexpected times, such as the middle of the night.

Let Your Mind Flow, for Most of Us Are More Creative than We Think. Most scholars are somewhat hesitant to venture beyond what they think is safe territory, especially if they intend to publish the results of their scholarship. While some faculty members, short-story writers and novelists for example, are more likely to use their creativity than the faculty member writing about hunger, it nevertheless behooves community college scholars to push their creativity to the limits of good scholarly practice. The results will often surprise even the most conservative scholar.

Each Time You Prepare a Lecture, Include Some New Material that Is Based Upon Your Scholarly Work. The new material may include only a short introduction, but the point is that you are engaged in perpetual scholarly activity when you regularly add new material to your lectures. The files discussed above should serve as ready sources of new material. Moreover, once the material is included in the lecture, it can be added to the files to become part of your larger scholarly projects.

Each Year, Commit Yourself to a Scholarly Project that Extends Beyond Class Preparation. Professionals keep their commitments. By making extracurricular scholarship one of your goals for the year, you will be more likely to take on projects that you otherwise might ignore. If your discipline is biology, you might commit yourself to doing a newspaper op-ed piece on threats to the local environment. The piece would draw upon your discipline, teaching, experience, and knowledge of the local area. This is an excellent approach for community college faculty members who want an outlet for their scholarship other than professional journals, yet who want their scholarship to receive wider attention than it does in the classroom.

172

Volunteer for Presentations at Faculty Meetings and Professional Meetings on Your Own Campus and with Professional Associations. This suggestion is important for those individuals whose work might not lend itself to the written word. For example, a demonstration on how you plan to stage a drama production in new ways might be of interest to the faculty. The presentation, no matter how esoteric, should include references, the appropriate discussion of theory as well as practice, and other facets that take it out of the "show and tell" category and make it an example of good scholarship.

The above suggestions are meant more as reminders than as answers. Most important, community college faculty members must remember that scholarship is the lifeblood of their chosen profession. All things considered, having time for scholarship is not even the question. The question is how one can engage in scholarship efficiently and effectively.

IF YOU WANT TO PUBLISH YOUR SCHOLARSHIP

Publishing is not a prerequisite to being a scholar. The community college faculty's primary mission must remain teaching and not publishing; to fall into the "publish or perish" syndrome of the university would be a mistake. However, publishing remains the most visible form of scholarship and the one most recognized by much of the higher education community. There are some good reasons why community college faculty members should publish. Among them are pride and satisfaction at seeing your name in print; the opportunity to call attention to your institution within the higher education community; the discipline that is required to prepare a manuscript for publication; and the opportunity to enhance the image of the community college faculty member as a contributing member of the academic profession. The most important reason of all, of course, is the contribution one makes to improving education by advancing knowledge and sharing creative ideas and practices. For those faculty members who wish to publish the results of their scholarship, I offer the follow suggestions.

173

Make Writing for Publication a Part of Your Scholarship. Once scholarship becomes a part of your daily activities, write about some aspect of your area, remembering that publications require thorough documentation.

Think Big, Write Small. It was suggested above that you keep your perspective broad and your focus small. This is good advice for writing for publication. Instead of tackling a book the first time you write for publication, settle for an article. The book can and likely will come later, assuming publication continues to be one of your goals.

Consider Working with a Co-author. Beginning authors can give their careers a big boost by writing with established authors. You may have to settle for second billing, but this will be a temporary situation. Once your name is associated with a well-known person in your field, your credibility will be enhanced and other writing opportunities will become available. Working with a co-author creates many tensions that are not present when working alone, so choose someone with whom you feel you can work. Unfortunately, choosing a co-author is a bit like getting married: you do not know what you have gotten yourself into until the agreement has been consummated.

Choose a Timely Topic. Timing can be very important in getting your scholarly work published. Peters and Waterman's best seller *In Search of Excellence* would not have had the impact in the 1960s that it had in the 1980s, nor would Allan Bloom's *The Closing of the American Mind*. You can increase your chances of being publishled if you go with the flow of what is popular, or better yet if you build a case against what is being written on a topic. Remember to let your imagination flow.

Strive to Make an Original Contribution. You should know what has been written on your topic and not submit something that has been discussed in every conceivable way. While you may not be contributing new knowledge on the subject, show that you are adding to the knowledge base, not simply restating old themes.

Establish Your Credibility. It is important that editors have some idea of why you are writing on the subject covered in your manuscript. You can state your case in a brief cover letter. You might, for example, point out that you have taught English at Mountain Community College for the past ten years and, based upon this experience, you have learned the following, etc.

Have a Thesis, Develop It, and Defend It. Let the reader know from the beginning what you intend to cover; develop your interpretation and defend it, using examples if appropriate; and make it interesting.

Speak to Your Audience. Do not limit your discussion to some specific project that is taking place on your own campus, no matter how good. You can use your campus as an example, but if you do, relate it to your broader theme. If the literature on community colleges is guilty of an unforgiveable sin, it is that too much of it is devoted to "how it's done on our campus."

Become Familiar with the Publication to Which You Are Sending Your Manuscript. Nothing will ensure rejection more quickly than submitting a manuscript to a journal that has no interest in the subject you are discussing. If the journal has a style sheet (most do; even the *National Enquirer* has one) follow it religiously. Follow the guidelines for references, headings, footnotes, and other technical aspects of publishing. If the directions call for the manuscript to be submitted to the managing editor, do not send it to the executive editor. If manuscripts are to be limited to twenty pages, do not send in thirty or forty. You should not make the editor angry before he or she reads your manuscript.

Do Not Fear Rejection. If you lie awake at night worrying about your manuscript being rejected, you will never have one rejected because you will never submit one for publication. Shop around. If your manuscript is rejected by one publication, send it to another. If the rejection letter contains criticisms, take them seriously and make changes before submitting the manuscript to another source.

In the Beginning, Settle for Less. Just as you may have to settle for an article rather than a book, in the beginning you may have to settle for publishing your story or article in the campus literary magazine rather than *Atlantic Monthly* or the *New Yorker.* Instead of having your article published in *Change* or the *Review of*

Higher Education, you may have to settle for a less competitive publication. Remember, as a scholar your objective is to engage in scholarly activities with publishing as only one outlet for these activities.

Have Others Read Your Manucript. Ask someone who knows your subject to read your manuscript; also, select someone who is familiar with the field but is not an expert, for good writing should be coherent to such a person. If you cannot find a Maxwell Perkins waiting in the wings, settle for your office mate. In any event, find someone you respect and heed his or her advice. Incidentally, if you hand someone a thirty-page manuscript and it is returned to you unscathed (with a short note telling you how wonderful it is), you likely need to pass it on to someone else to read, for few of us can produce a perfect manuscript the first, second, or third time around.

Get to Know the Editor. If you are a member of a professional association and wish to publish your work in its journal, get to know the editor. Knowing the editor will not ensure publication, but will give you some insights that may not be available to others. Once you have established your credibility, you may be asked to serve on the editorial board of the publication. If asked, accept.

Learn to Operate the Word Processor. This advice sounds rather mundane in this high-tech age. But if you cannot use the word processor, learn to do so. Using it may increase your creativity, especially for those of us who grew up with the manual or electric typewriter and who were always afraid of trying new words, new sentences, and new ways of describing our subject because the fear of starting the page over never left us. Anyone who has ever had to present "two perfect carbons" of a manuscript will find the word processor the most liberating of all inventions. In addition, learning a new skill such as word processing will give you confidence to try other new things, including submitting a manuscript for publication.

Begin Writing. Borrowing a page from Snoopy's notebook, begin writing even if you begin with "It was a dark and stormy night." Recently, a good friend called to inform me that she felt she had the makings of an outstanding book. Her question to me was how to go about writing it. I could not resist the temptation to reply with the old cliche, "One page at a time."

Write, Re-Write, Re-Write....

If scholarship is to become an important part of the daily life of community college faculty, it must become a part of the institutional culture. Faculty, with administrative and trustee support, can and should integrate scholarship into the institutional culture in ways that ensure that the teacher and scholar are one and the same. The result will be a renewed faculty, improved teaching, a better understanding of the role of community college faculty, a better understanding of the community college, and a new image for these important institutions, which will result in new respect and understanding from members of the higher education community and from the public at large. No investment has the potential for bringing more returns to the community college than a new and vigorous pursuit of scholarship.

REFERENCES

Boyer, Ernest L. *Scholarship Reconsidered: Priorities of the Professoriate*. Princeton, N.J.: Carnegie Foundation for the Advancement of Teaching, 1990.

Brodie, James M. "Faculty Research at Community Colleges Debated." *Community College Week*, April 13, 1992, p. 9.

Commission on the Future of the Community College. *Building Communities: A Vision for a New Century*. Washington, D.C.: American Association of Community Colleges, 1988.

Mooney, Carolyn J. "Critics Within and Without Academe Assail Professors at Research Universities." *Chronicle of Higher Education*, October 28, 1992, pp. 17–19.

Nelson, William C. *Renewal of the Teacher Scholar*. Washington, D.C.: Association of American Colleges, 1981.

Palmer, James C. "The Scholarly Activities of Community College Faculty: Findings of a National Survey." In J.C. Palmer and G.B. Vaughan (Eds.), *Fostering a Climate for Faculty Scholarship at Community Colleges*. Washington, D.C.: American Association of Community Colleges, 1992.

Palmer, James C. and Vaughan, George B. (Eds.). *Fostering a Climate for Faculty Scholarship at Community Colleges*. Washington, D.C.: American Association of Community Colleges, 1992.

Parilla, Robert G. "Scholarship in the Community College: A President's Perspective." In G.B. Vaughan and J.C. Palmer (Eds.), *Enhancing Teaching and Administration Through Scholarship*. New Directions for Community Colleges, no. 76. San Francisco: Jossey-Bass, 1991.

Templin, Robert G., Jr. "Presidential Scholarship and Educational Leadership in the Community College." In G.B. Vaughan and J.C. Palmer (Eds.), *Enhancing Teaching and Administration Through Scholarship*. New Directions for Community Colleges, no. 76. San Francisco: Jossey-Bass, 1991.

Vaughan, George B. "Scholarship in the Community College: The Path to Respect." *Educational Record*, 1988, 69 (2), pp. 26–31.

Vaughan, George B. and James C. Palmer (Eds.). *Enhancing Teaching and Administration Through Scholarship*. New Directions for Community Colleges, no. 76. San Francisco: Jossey-Bass, 1991.

George B. Vaughan is associate director, ACCLAIM, North Carolina State University.

Chapter 10

Enriching Teaching and Learning Through Learning Communities

By Roberta S. Matthews

T he 1988 report *Building Com-
munities: A Vision for a New Century* explores how community
colleges may live up to the implications of their name. The document calls urgently for the creation of learning communities, in
the broadest sense of the term, at all levels and in all areas of activity within the community college. It recommends six interlock-
ing ways for colleges to create community: teacher/student partnerships for learning, curriculum, classroom environment, the
quality of campus life, connections beyond the college, and the
challenges of leadership. Vision depends on the creation of community through an acknowledgment of common goals and the
need for cooperation to achieve them. The report recognizes how
critically community colleges are situated, how large a constituency they serve, and how essential is their contribution to the
common good (Commission on the Future of Community Colleges, 1988).

Because of the concentration of challenges they face and conditions under which they operate, community colleges tend to illustrate, in distilled form, essential issues confronting higher education. Barber (1991) developed the implications of a system of higher education torn by factions, lacking an essential sense of community. Disturbed by the results of such divisiveness, Barber offers an alternative view of education as the vehicle for creating the sense of community necessary for the survival of a democratic society:

> ...[A] far more dialectical model of education [is] one that refuses to prostrate itself, its back to the future, before the ancient gods of the canon, but is equally reluctant to throw itself uncritically, its back to the past, into the future as envisioned by the new gods of the marketplace. This argument suggests...that the university is a civic mission...defined as the rules and conventions that permit a community to facilitate conversation and the kinds of discourse upon which all knowledge depends. On this model, learning is a social activity that can take place only within a discursive community bringing together reflection and experience...knowledge is an evolving communal construction whose legitimacy rests directly on the social process...education is everywhere and always an ineluctably communal enterprise (p. 165).

The community college confronts the split between the canonical and the vocational with each program developed and course created, at every curriculum and faculty senate meeting, and each time personnel and budget are discussed. Although frequently present at senior colleges and universities, the conflict between the canonical and the vocational is literally at the heart of the community college. Given the many missions of the community college and its diverse populations, its faculty, even more than colleagues in other higher education institutions, need to consciously seek ways to integrate curricula and constituencies. At the least, such an effort would provide students with a coherent educational experience; at best, a community college education would contribute to the preparation of an informed and thoughtful citizenry.

As Barber suggests, the quality of discourse outside the walls of academe depends upon the quality of conversation within its walls.

This chapter will focus on a particular kind of learning community—curricular structures that provide coherence by linking courses from different disciplines around a common theme or question. Structured learning communities offer a vital sense of shared inquiry to participating students and faculty. These communities contribute directly to the enrichment of the teacher/student partnerships for learning, curriculum, and classroom environment cited by *Building Communities*. By implication, learning communities enhance the quality of campus life, contribute to the development of connections beyond the college, and help prepare students for the challenges of leadership.

The National Institute of Education's *Involvement in Learning: Realizing the Potential of Higher Education* report recommends the creation of structured learning communities at colleges and universities because they:

- Are usually smaller than most other units
- Have a sense of purpose
- Help overcome the isolation of faculty members from one another and their students
- Encourage faculty members to relate to one another as specialists and as educators
- Encourage continuity and integration in the curriculum
- Help build a sense of group identity, cohesion and "specialness" (National Institute of Education, 1984, p. 33)

Since 1984, when *Involvement in Learning* called for smaller, more manageable, and more humane units of learning, enrollments have soared and budgets have plummeted; it is now even more difficult to welcome students into the academic community. Community colleges face the challenge of providing a sense of community to an extraordinarily diverse group of students, many of whom have families and job responsibilities and no extra time. As commuter institutions, community colleges cannot assume that students will interact with each other in lounges, snack bars, or dorm rooms, but rather that other responsibilities are more than likely to pull them away from college campuses. The classroom is often the only arena for offering students a sense of academic community.

THE SHAPES AND SIZES OF LEARNING COMMUNITIES

Learning communities come in several generic models linking students and teachers in small units that integrate disciplines and coursework. Each model has been modified to local conditions on the campuses where they flourish. Three models—paired courses, course clusters, and coordinated studies—are common in community colleges. They offer developmental, general education, career, and liberal arts courses and combine them either as regular offerings that fulfill program or distribution requirements, or as part of an honors program. Most important, learning communities are cost-efficient: They conform to standard workload requirements and fit into the normal academic operating budgets. Although they require administrative support and coordination, this cost is easily offset by increases in retention, grade point averages, and credits earned.

The simplest and most popular version of the learning community is the linked or paired course, often the vehicle for an academically sound writing-across-the-curriculum program. A composition course is linked with an introductory course in a subject discipline, and the two instructors cooperate so that the discipline shapes much of the content of the writing assignments in the composition course. Based on several years of very positive experience, faculty at Skagit Valley College, Washington, recently decided to link all introductory composition courses with another course. Linked courses are offered in at least three modes: both courses share the same students, class size being set by the limits of the composition course; the composition students are a small subset of a larger lecture course; and instructors team-teach a linked course by doubling the class size. Linking has been used to tie a variety of developmental courses to vocational or general education courses. The College of the Sequoias, California, offers students eight to ten learning communities per term in these modes. At Oakton Community College, Illinois, paired courses have been the core of the honors curriculum for eight years— each semester offers a choice of history-humanities or science-humanities pairs. In all cases of paired courses, the most successful linkages coordinate curriculum so that different course contents reinforce each other.

Course clusters and coordinated studies join more than two curricula and offer students an integrated multi- or interdisciplinary program. Both models give faculty and students large blocks of time and the flexibility to take advantage of field trips, book seminars, and varied groupings of students.

Clusters, which tend to have twenty-five to thirty-five students, usually provide a complete program, although some students may take additional course outside the cluster. However, teachers in the cluster fulfill their workload obligations with a combination of cluster and noncluster courses. The early and ongoing experiences with clusters in the liberal arts and the early business cluster at LaGuardia Community College, New York, continue in a similar positive mode (Matthews, 1986). Liberal arts clusters, introduced there in 1979 and offered each term since, have grown steadily. In fall 1992 seven liberal arts clusters served more than two hundred students. Each cluster contained a composition course, a course in writing the research paper, an integrating seminar, and a combination of philosophy, social science, or humanities courses.

Coordinated studies provide students and faculty with a complete program, and their size is proportionately larger than clusters. A coordinated studies grouping (depending on the number of courses and faculty involved) might contain seventy-five to 100 students. A large coordinated studies program at Seattle Central Community College, Washington, serves approximately 1,200 students per year through eight to ten coordinated studies groupings offered each term. A full range of developmental, general education, and vocational courses are offered in a wide variety of combinations that link three, four, or five disciplines.

Learning communities are not merely block programming, an administrative convenience that facilitates registration and room utilization. Rather they are a conscious intellectual structure created by teachers and participated in by students in order to share a high-quality and enduring educational experience. Unlike block programming, the idea of community is a central and shaping force. Readers who wish to learn more should consult the "Learning Community Models" chapter in *Learning Communities: Creating Connections Among Students, Faculty and Disciplines* (Gabelnick et al., 1990), which provides detailed descriptions of the models and their variations as well as a chart comparing their various elements. There are as many variations on the models of learning communities as there are institutions willing to implement them and faculty willing to participate. All however strive to provide an intense and supportive environment for intellectual growth and development.

THE CONTINUITY AND PURPOSE OF LEARNING COMMUNITIES

Community colleges, by definition, respond to the needs of the surrounding community. The tremendous range of need, however, often results in a fragmented curriculum. Today's community colleges generally offer at least three curricular concentrations. The first is the developmental and English as a Second Language courses where many community college students begin their college careers; the second is required general education and liberal arts courses—the curriculum of transfer programs and the distribution requirements of career programs; third is the array of career courses that prepare community college students to enter the workplace as, for example, computer or allied health technicians or at entry-level business, computer, or accounting positions.

Students careen among these broad categories of courses based in curricula that frequently begin from different sets of assumptions, make conflicting demands, and deliver different messages and grades. They often see little connection between the courses they are taking, even when the skills learned in one might be essential in another. Learning communities, on the other hand, consciously link different contents. The sense of purpose they encourage in students and faculty, and the continuity and integration they encourage in the curriculum, therefore address a second challenge to the community college: how to provide coherence in a curriculum that often consists of disparate elements.

Learning communities explore common problems or themes so that different contents reinforce each other. They help students systematically apply what they learn in one class to others. For example, the theme of "relationships" in a coordinated studies program of developmental reading, writing, and speech helps students enhance language skills in a context where three instructors build on a common curriculum and coordinate instruction to reinforce the simultaneous development of these skills. Mathematical skills and concepts may be applied directly in a linked computer or an electronics or biological chemistry class. Abstract economic concepts find immediate practical application in a business class and an expressive outlet in a composition class when all are clustered. A coordinated studies grouping that brings together art, art history, sociology, history, and literature creates a multicultural discourse exploring the experiences of various ethnic groups in the United States. The exploration of diversity thus becomes a common purpose. In the midst of diversity, learning communities find and define areas of commonality.

Gabelnick et al. (1992, p. 104) note that the "second wave" of general education reform, as reported by such leaders as Astin, 1992; Gaff, 1992; and Gamson, Kantor, and London, 1992; characterizes effective general education as "less a function of content (core vs. non-core, distributive vs. highly elective) than it is of active learning strategies and a purposeful, shared creation of community on campus." All over the country, institutions of higher learning have turned to learning communities that "by their very nature, juxtapose diverse perspectives and diverse disciplines so that teaching and learning inevitably engender social, cultural, and intellectual linkages" (Gabelnick et al., 1992, p.112). This is true of all learning communities that help students and faculty break down the barriers between disciplines and skills and allow them to work together as they must in the real world. Faculty in learning communities recognize that they need to support each other in order to reach their common goal of giving students the best education possible. The process of education thus becomes "a civic mission" because structured learning communities "facilitate conversation and the kinds of discourse upon which all knowledge depends" (Barber, 1991, p. 165). Through participation in learning communities, faculty work to bring unity out of diversity. In the midst of fragmentation, learning communities explore common concerns and issues.

THE IMPACT OF LEARNING COMMUNITIES ON FACULTY

McGrath and Spear (1992) place the need for community building in today's community colleges in the context of faculty needs:

> Improving the academic culture and the quality of teaching and learning will call for new relationships among significant numbers of faculty, partly so that teachers can support, encourage, and sustain one another; but more importantly so that faculty can join together to create a vigorous academic setting for students (p. 157).

Since learning communities "help overcome the isolation of faculty members from one another and their students" and "encourage faculty members to relate to one another both as specialists and as educators," (National Institute of Education, 1984, p. 33) they become change agents, on a number of different levels, for faculty participation in meeting institutional goals.

The act of creating and participating in a learning community is itself a community-building experience for faculty, ullustrating Barber's thesis that "education is everywhere and always an ineluctably communal enterprise" (p. 165). Faculty, administration, and staff must cooperate in order to implement learning communities and coordinate activities more intensely than is necessary with traditional curriculum. The variety of learning communities currently offered at community colleges suggests that as the shared sense of purpose encourages continuity and integration in the curriculum, so too the impact of the learning community experience grows outside its boundaries, affecting teaching and learning throughout the institution.

Colleges have devised ways of involving faculty in the process of creating learning communities. At Collin County Community College, Texas, where the learning community is the primary focus of the honors program, offerings are administered by a faculty task force. Programs and teaching faculty for coordinated studies at Seattle Central Community College, Washington, are chosen by a faculty planning committee. The director of the learning community effort at the Community Colleges of Spokane, Washington, orients faculty and then works closely with them to program their learning communities.

Traditional modes of teaching tend not to facilitate mutual support or encouragement. Some faculty members can expect never to be visited by a colleague (except, perhaps, during formal, judgmental observations) or to engage in sustained conversations about one's discipline or teaching except with an office mate or close friend. Large departmental discussions often address highly charged agenda topics, about which individuals, sometimes disconcerted by colleagues' attitudes, make feeble or watered-down statements designed for public consumption or retreat into silence. Neither the chance conversation nor the large forum lends itself to the thoughtful exploration of different approaches and points of view, and the victim is too often the teacher.

The act of creating a learning community breaks down the isolation of faculty and the essential loneliness of teaching as currently conceived and executed. Participation in a learning community offers a way to colleagueship by creating community among faculty:

My wife kept saying, "You've got to teach this way again; you're a different person this quarter." Subjective and private though this perception is, can one overestimate its significance for a 46-year-old teacher approaching his twentieth year teaching in the same college at the same level? I am exactly the kind of teacher that college administrators shudder at the thought of getting stuck with for another twenty years. I shudder at the thought of getting stuck with myself! (Gabelnick et al., 1990, p. 77).

Participation in a learning community is a faculty development activity. It gives faculty a different lens on their disciplines and facilitates their working with each other—an opportunity many welcome with relief. Such an experience goes a long way toward creating the kind of "strong academic culture" that McGrath and Spear (p. 154) find missing from but essential to the community college and its mission. In addition to providing faculty with the opportunity to reconfigure stale courses and make cross-disciplinary thematic connections, the act of teaching in a learning community has an impact upon the craft of teaching. Feedback from colleagues and from students is inevitable. For one faculty member, participating in a cluster changed the way she worked in her classroom. She became more open to sharing learning with her students and giving them the opportunity to learn from each other: "As a young teacher I felt I needed to be in complete control. I wouldn't have taught in clusters then. I needed to stand up in front of a class with tight control. As I got more confident, I began to loosen up. That's the way it is with most people as they discover collaborative learning" (Gabelnick et al., 1990, p. 83).

Because learning communities offer more opportunities on more levels for teachers to cooperate with each other and their students in the common endeavor of learning, the use of collaborative, active learning is more likely. Group work and peer study sessions happen naturally among students who share a rich educational experience. Group projects are organic to learning communities, and students support each other in their work by, for example, research sharing and peer critiquing. As a result, the quality (and quantity) of student work soars. And the data suggest that students thrive in a small, friendly, intellectually rigorous situation where the demands made upon them are consciously and systematically supported by faculty working together toward shared goals and by peers who are comfortable enough to demand only the best from each other.

THE IMPACT OF LEARNING COMMUNITIES ON STUDENTS

Learning communities, because they "help build the sense of group identity, cohesion, and specialness" (National Institute of Education, 1984, p. 33), have great impact on students. They contribute to the transition into the social and academic communities so essential for retention and success in college (Tinto, 1987). For this reason alone, learning communities should be a central part of the community college experience. Such structures create community among students in at least two ways. Socially, participation in a learning community helps students feel comfortable, make friends, and develop a support network. Academically, the learning community experience facilitates communication between students and faculty and virtually guarantees the establishment of a working relationship with a faculty member around a shared interest. Teacher-student partnerships naturally arise from the learning community experience, and students are initiated into the academic culture through their participation with teachers and peers in a common endeavor. The learning community process, in itself a collaborative activity, facilitates other kinds of collaborative activities to create a special seriousness of shared purpose. The classroom environment is less alien and more inviting than that of individual classes filled with strangers and managed by faculty who neither refer nor relate their content to other subjects students might be taking.

A wealth of national data and experience affirms the value of the learning community experience. The Washington Center for the Improvement of Post-Secondary Education at Evergreen State College is a statewide consortium that has made learning communities a central focus of its work. The center is a clearinghouse providing technical assistance to colleges interested in creating learning communities and implementing collaborative learning. Of the twenty-seven community colleges in the state, nearly all are at least experimenting with learning communities, and nineteen of them are actively engaged.

The fall 1991 *Washington Center News* shares the results of a statewide initiative to assess learning communities and evaluate the center's efforts to support development of these communities. It describes a number of different learning community models and summarizes a variety of assessment projects undertaken around the state to capture the impact of learning communities on the participating students and faculty.

Various surveys cited by the *News* conclude that students who enroll in learning communities are pretty typical of students in general; however, their retention and achievement, especially in community colleges, are significantly higher than those of their counterparts in regular college classes (p. 5). A study of intellectual development in learning communities conducted by Jean Mac-Gregor, involving coordinated studies programs at Evergreen State College and several Washington community colleges, concluded that students in learning communities generally made a significant and unusual leap in intellectual development during their learning community experience. The study used the Measure of Intellectual Development (MID), an essay writing test derived from and scored along William Perry's positions of intellectual development. The study concluded that after their learning community experience, new college students were "significantly more developed than their counterparts...the meanings these learning community students are making of their academic environments are more typical of college juniors and seniors" (pp. 6–7).

A study by Gary Tollefson was specifically designed to identify "faculty perceptions about the impact of learning communities...on general education programs and practices." Responding faculty identified four ways that learning communities enriched general education at their community colleges:

- Learning communities provide more opportunity for student writing and speaking

- They encourage a more complex world view
- They encourage higher-order thinking skills
- They offer more coherent course work in general education (*Washington Center News,* p. 10)

As part of a Title III grant, North Seattle Community College, Washington, was able to expand its learning community offerings and assess their impact. The "Learning Community Enrollment Study" presents data collected between 1986 and 1990. This study, which includes the records of 900 students, further affirms the value of the learning community experience. Similar to other studies conducted in Washington, this one found that students who chose learning communities were otherwise indistinguishable from students who did not enroll in learning communities. Nevertheless students in learning communities had a slightly higher retention rate than those in traditional courses and persisted longer—they re-enrolled, stayed at the college for longer periods of time, and were more apt to complete degrees. Based on grades, student achievement was significantly higher, and students demonstrated correspondingly high affective and cognitive growth resulting from their collaborative learning experiences (Wilkie, 1990). These results support the belief long-held by learning community proponents that these structures serve all students well.

Since 1990 LaGuardia Community College has collected data on the learning communities offered through its Enterprise Center, which focuses on students in business and computer career programs, and also on learning communities developed and offered for the more general student population through a Freshman Year Initiative program.

The Enterprise Center supports academic innovation through the introduction of collaborative learning strategies, including group work and case studies. These practices occur either in thematically linked learning communities or in sections of high-risk courses that are enhanced by student-led study groups. Between 1990 and 1992 over 700 students participated in Enterprise Center offerings. An evaluation of the 1990–91 cohort revealed that in over half of Enterprise Center courses, 10 to 50 percent more students received grades of C or higher than equivalent students in traditionally taught sections of the same courses. Indeed, in Economics I, where over 25 percent of the students normally fail the course, the two sections taught in the Enterprise Center's business cluster (which includes Composition I, introductory business, and introductory economics), had a significantly higher pass rate, and, in addition, over 30 percent more students received C or better than their peers in regular sections. Enterprise students earned over 15 percent more credits than their peers attempted and ended the year with higher cumulative grade point averages than their peers. The learning community experience was especially appreciated, with over 80 percent of the students consistently agreeing that "it was helpful to have courses linked through content and assignments; they like having the same group of students in more than one class; and they gained confidence in their ability to succeed in school" (Sussman, 1991, p. 9).

Results from the 1991–92 evaluation of Enterprise, involving 350 students in a variety of learning communities, echo those of the preceding year. Additionally, Enterprise students had 16 to 26 percent higher retention rates than control cohorts (Sussman, 1992b). Qualitative responses from faculty and students support the value of collaborative approaches. Faculty appreciate the exposure to real-life group situations in the business world and the more advanced cognitive connections students make. They also enjoy the extended professional contact with colleagues from other disciplines: "My experience has been whenever faculty from different disciplines interface on a regular basis, it has a beneficial effect. Furthermore, whenever students can seek the linkages between disciplines it helps in their overall understanding of taking courses out of their majors..." (Sussman, 1991, p. 7).

Students cite increased self-confidence and participation in class and point to the value of exposure to different viewpoints:

This was truly an experience. I have taken other college courses, but the cluster linked each class with the other and made me feel the teachers were close to the students....

Also, travelling with the same students allowed many of us to get close together. This cluster is a wonderful system which helps students function better (Sussman, 1991, p. 3).

Freshman Year Initiative (FYI) data about learning communities offer further corroboration of current findings on learning communities. For example, FYI offered course pairs for computer majors, one linking the second-level developmental math course with a course in computer hardware interfacing and another pairing a precalculus course with Electronics I. In both pairs, the pass rate for students was significantly higher than those in single courses, ranging from 6 percent to a remarkable 33 percent. Veterinary technology students were offered "Comparative Vertebrate Anatomy and Physiology" paired with "Research Animal Technology," resulting in a 6 to 10 percent higher pass rate (Sussman, 1992a).

The nine-year-old Quanta program at Daytona Beach Community College, Florida, which combines psychology, English, and humanities in a thematically linked coordinated studies effort featuring collaborative learning, has recently completed three longitudinal studies. The first, based on data from 1985 through 1991, puts the annual mean retention rate of Quanta students at 93 percent. Students cite increased involvement, the sense of belonging to a group, and the support and encouragement of peers and teachers as significant factors in their completion of the term. Indeed, "many students...believe that had they not been enrolled in a program like Quanta, they would not have made it through their freshman year" (Avens, 1992a).

Since 1988 Quanta has added quantitative questions to its original qualitative form and developed an evaluation consisting of ten objective and five open-ended questions in order to collect comparable data from year to year. Eight of the objective questions attempt to determine which specific outcomes are most important to students. Student most often chose the objectives that said Quanta "helped me realize that there are multiple perspectives with which to view an issue;" "helped me see the relationships between courses;" "gave me the opportunity to learn from other students as well as faculty;" and "was worthwhile because of the 'active learning' methods used" (Avens, 1992b).

One characteristic student comment gives the flavor of Quanta:

> In Quanta, where we get to explore the basic tenets of the individual disciplines and simultaneously discover the 'big picture' of complexity and interconnectedness, I have found a learning experience which is not only worth the effort but is irresistible! My personal learning style has flourished in the setting of looking at subjects from multiple perspectives and interrelating [them]...I have learned that learning is a challenge and I want to continue the quest! (Avens, 1992b).

A final piece of evaluative data is especially interesting because there has been little follow-up nationally on the long-range impact of learning communities. In spring 1990 approximately 350 questionnaires were sent to students who had participated in Quanta from 1984–85 through 1988–89. Fifty-five responses were received, with representation from each of the five years. One open-ended question asked students, "Looking back, what do you think was most beneficial about your Quanta experience?" Often students cited more than one aspect, but the results are quite clear. Close to two-thirds cited some aspect of "community...social interaction, group work, cooperative learning." Students felt that working in groups, learning about their dynamics, and learning how to cooperate were especially valuable. They also valued the friendships often with people they would not have considered "friend material"—and finally, they cited the sense of "belonging to a supportive group" that helped them overcome feelings of alienation. One third of the students felt the interdisciplinary nature of the program was most beneficial, with the development of critical and creative thinking and personal growth cited by more than one-fifth. Alumni comments mirror those of students currently in the program. The advantages perceived while participating in Quanta are sustained in retrospect and suggest that the high rate of retention reflects an initial recognition of a high-quality experience that remains through the completion of undergraduate studies and, in some cases, graduate and professional school (Avens, 1992c).

The data collected about students who participate in learning communities are remarkably consistent—the quality of the experience is a given. Other campuses have conducted studies that further support the importance of learning communities as a delivery system for quality education in the community college. Solano Community College, California, recently received funds to conduct a substantial evaluation of its learning community effort; results will be available in 1994 or 1995. Finally, Vincent Tinto is currently undertaking a longitudinal study to evaluate the impact of collaborative pedagogies and learning communities on student learning and persistence in college, one of the research projects of the National Center on Postsecondary Teaching, Learning, and Assessment. His work will be completed by winter 1993. Seattle Central Community College and LaGuardia Community College are participating in the study.

PRACTICE AND PRACTICAL ADVICE: NOTES FROM THE FIELD

A survey of learning communities in the community college, conducted for the preparation of this chapter, yielded a wealth of practical advice, including recommendations about how to implement and offer learning communities.

In order to succeed, learning communities must have administrative support as well as support from counselors and registration staff. They also require a higher level of faculty involvement. Classroom faculty ordinarily do not work with colleagues, but those who create learning communities report being heartened by the support and good ideas generated by others. However, too much time and energy spent on marketing, recruiting, and registering students may result in faculty burn-out and the demise of a learning community. At best the learning community initiative should be an "institutional change" effort, as broad-based as possible, with curricular and structural changes facilitated by collegewide cooperation—a community-building experience.

Initial forays into the world of learning communities should begin with the best faculty. Once the beginning experiment in learning communities has proven itself, the group must reach out quickly to a broad base of faculty; the alternative is isolation and accusations of elitism or separatism. To avoid an "in group" mentality, colleges offer orientations that introduce new faculty to the learning community experience and invite them to submit learning community proposals to a peer committee. This type of process supports faculty ownership of the learning community and invites broader participation. Faculty need to select their own teams and develop their own curricula together. The "Checklist for Implementing Learning Communities" (Gabelnick et al., 1990, p. 51) offers some useful guidelines for the process of beginning and sustaining these efforts. Most important, faculty leaders must modify general guidelines to respond to local conditions and implement the program at a pace that makes sense given local realities.

Respondents agreed that faculty development is essential to orient instructors to learning communities and is an integral part of teaching in a learning community. Once communities are launched, faculty should be involved in periodic meetings and retreats to share their experiences and refine their understanding of the process. When the honors program began at Frederick Community College, Maryland, the creation of clusters was supported by student and faculty training in group process and course design. At Bellevue Community College, Washington, how-to workshops orient faculty who then submit proposals for learning communities. At Delta College, Michigan, the experience of creating and offering linked courses is viewed by faculty as an effective vehicle for professional growth.

Opinions varied about how to choose teaching teams. One respondent recommended that teachers with experience in the active learning strategies of learning communities be teamed with novices to help counteract the pull of traditional and familiar ways of teaching and to ease the new participant into the role of facilitator. However, another stressed that teachers with different teaching styles and from different disciplines should be involved to expose students to a variety of methodologies, ideas, and ways of knowing.

196

Both positions derive from clear, well-articulated goals for learning communities that shape faculty development efforts as well.

The best learning communities, regardless of their initial assumptions, are staffed by colleagues who are comfortable working with each other and who acknowledge and use their differences to advantage. As there is a need to incorporate time for group process into the learning communities, so too do faculty need time for group process in planning the learning community. This is especially important because the best communities are well-planned (but not over-planned). Teams need to coordinate syllabi, blend ideas, articulate goals, and clarify differences. They also need to be assured that the college will offer their community again, making the first time a learning experience with a purpose.

Several respondents stressed the importance of team teaching—being physically present in each other's classes all or part of the time. Since this may be expensive, different colleges support team teaching in different ways: by adjusting class size to the number of faculty involved to conform to workload requirements; by having faculty teach learning communities as overload (although some respondents thought this was burdensome); or by creative and idiosyncratic arrangements with individual administrators. If team teaching is impossible, faculty depend on constant conversation, occasional "cameos" in each other's classes, and shared trips, assignments, and activities to ensure that links are made. Coordination and cooperation are the keys to a successful learning community.

Course selection is critical to the success of learning communities. For students to participate in a learning community, its offerings must follow their footprints. Particularly in a community college, where students have so many required courses, learning communities should be situated in the mainstream of requirements. They must be offered at times when students are most likely to take them—as attractive schedules and as a reflection of the pattern of program requirements. Alternatively, a learning community may become part of established programs, ranging from developmental through general education to honors. Sometimes, as with the program for returning women at Everett Community College, Washington, special populations thrive in learning communities. But learning communities should be used sparingly in support of exotic electives.

It is important to consider and address financial implications for faculty and students. Although many learning communities begin as grant-funded initiatives, colleges must take steps to ensure that the learning community does not depend completely on outside funding that, when it disappears, will take the learning community with it. In order for students on financial aid to participate easily in learning communities, their special requirements must be met and communities should be planned and modified accordingly. Learning communities must be integrated into the financial realities of an institution and its constituencies.

Finally, feedback from older initiatives suggests that several are reaching the point where faculty who have participated in learning communities for more than five or six years may need some renewal themselves—an opportunity to make major curricular changes or take a new look at teaching. Learning communities, while they address some of the ills of the community college, are also prey to them. Although learning communities facilitate change, they need to change themselves. Sound institutional practice suggests that review and revision need to be built into the equation that keeps learning communities vital.

SMALL REPUBLICS OF THE INTELLECT

If, as Benjamin Barber suggests, "the university is a civic mission," then ultimately, the learning community helps further that mission. Zelda Gamson overtly makes this claim for the learning community experience:

> Schools and higher education even more must recognize that they should be engaged in a mammoth reclamation project: the teaching of the arts and skills of democracy and community.... The key to the social implications of a liberating education lies in what Brann (1979) calls small republics of the intellect, what we have been calling learning communities (1984, pp. 168–169).

Community college students are often the first in their families to go to college and lack role models for the academic culture. Learning communities, however, provide a structured context for students to develop the mental habits essential for academic success. Students stretch to make connections in a supportive and holistic learning environment that insists it is worth the effort to articulate and understand different ways of thinking, learning, and knowing. And it is precisely their participation in small republics of the intellect that helps prepare students to exercise "the arts and skills of democracy and community." The kind of challenging, integrated learning offered in these communities, when combined with the experience of cooperating with a diverse group of fellow students and teachers, helps prepare students for the real world beyond the classroom and beyond the college.

REFERENCES

"Assessment and Learning Communities: Taking Stock After Six Years." *Washington Center News*, 1991, *6* (1).

Astin, A.W. "What Really Matters in General Education: Provocative Findings for a National Study of Student Outcomes." *Perspectives*, 1992, *22* (1), pp. 25–48.

Avens, C. "Quanta Retention Rates." Daytona Beach, Fla.: Daytona Beach Community College, 1992a.

_____ "Student Evaluations of the Quanta Program." Daytona Beach, Fla.: Daytona Beach Community College, 1992b.

_____ "The Quanta Experience in Retrospect: Reflections by Quanta Alumni." Daytona Beach, Fla.: Daytona Beach Community College, 1992c.

Barber, B. "The Civic Mission of the University." In B. Murchland (Ed.), *Higher Education and The Practice of Democratic Politics: A Political Education Reader*. Dayton, Ohio: Kettering Foundation, 1991.

Commission on the Future of Community Colleges. *Building Communities: A Vision for a New Century*. Washington, D.C.: American Association of Community Colleges, 1988.

Gabelnick, F., J. MacGregor, R.S. Matthews, and B.L. Smith. *Learning Communities: Creating Connections Among Students, Faculty and Disciplines*. New Directions in Learning, no. 41. San Francisco: Jossey-Bass, 1990.

_____. "Learning Communities and General Education." *Perspectives*, 1992, 22 (1), pp. 104–120.

Gaff, J. "The Rhetoric and Reality of General Education Reform: An Overview." *Perspectives*, 1992, 22 (1), pp. 49–59.

Gamson, Z.F. and associates. *Liberating Education*. San Francisco: Jossey-Bass, 1984.

Gamson, Z.F., S. Kantor, and H. London. "General Education Reform: Moving Beyond the Rational Mode of Change." *Perspectives*, 1992, 22 (1), pp. 60–70.

McGrath, D. and M.B. Spear. *The Academic Crisis of the Community College*. Albany: SUNY Press, 1992.

Matthews, R.S. "Learning Communities in the Community College" *Community, Technical, and Junior College Journal*, 1986, 57 (2), pp. 44–47.

National Institute of Education. *Involvement in Learning: Realizing the Potential of Higher Education*. Final Report of the Study Group of the Conditions of Excellence in American Higher Education, 1984.

Sussman, M. "Evaluating the Experience of Students and Faculty in Enterprise: An Analysis of the Cohort in the 1990–91 Academic Year." Prepared for the Office for Academic Affairs, LaGuardia Community College, 1991.

_____. "Freshman Year Initiative, 1991–1992: A Review Survey." Prepared for the Central Office for Academic Affairs, City University of New York, 1992a.

_____. "Vocational And Technical Education Act Final Report 1991–1992." Prepared for the New York State Education Department, 1992b.

Tinto, V. *Leaving College: Rethinking the Causes and Cures of Student Attrition*. Chicago: University of Chicago Press, 1987.

Wilkie, G. "Learning Community Enrollment Study." Seattle, Wash.: North Seattle Community College, July 1990.

Roberta S. Matthews is associate dean for academic affairs, La-Guardia Community College, New York.

Chapter 11

Transforming Teaching and Learning Through Technology

By Don Doucette

Perhaps no predicted event in education has been more ballyhooed that the impending transformation of the teaching and learning process by the application of information technology. As a result, perhaps no apparent failure to improve education has generated as much disappointment and skepticism. The jokes abound: "Did you ever wonder why it took twenty years for the overhead projector to make it from the bowling alley to the classroom?" Still, we inevitably insist on including a chapter on the application of technology in a book about teaching and learning in the community college. We seem to persist in the notion that technology will eventually make some profound difference—if we can only figure out what computers have to do with students and teachers.

Extravagant claims for instructional technology have been made by respectable people, and elaborate explanations have been offered for the minor impact that technology has so far had on instructional practice. In a keynote address at the 1991 Leadership 2000 conference, Terrel Bell, former U.S. Secretary of Education, argued that almost no progress had been made in improving our schools since the 1983 publication of *A Nation at Risk*, primarily because teachers were not provided with the tools they needed to make a difference—instructional technology. Technology offered the only hope for real improvement in student learning, he claimed, by helping teachers to individualize instruction and empower students. He noted that no alternative large-scale solution had even been seriously proposed.

In his 1990 keynote address to the Community College and the Computer conference, Bernard R. Gifford, former dean of the graduate school of education at the University of California at Berkeley and former vice president for education at Apple Computer, used historical analogy to explain the lag between the invention of the personal computer and its use to transform education. He noted that soon after the invention of the Gutenberg printing press ushered in the book as a potentially powerful instructional technology, printed notes in a book simply replaced hand-inscribed transcriptions of lectures. It took nearly 100 years to overcome the notion that a book was merely a means of archiving notes and to begin using the technology to make advanced, complex, multidimensional arguments with footnotes, commentaries, retrospective observations, and summaries—the equivalent of modern textbooks. "Old models of learning, passive and imitative, gradually gave way to new models, interactive and generative" (Gifford, 1991).

While a decade of experimenting with computer-related technologies to improve instruction has yielded a thousand points of innovation and initiative, technology has yet to transform teaching and learning in the community college—or anywhere else. So, this chapter focuses on exceptions to still-prevalent traditional instructional practices in community colleges. It reviews examples of how informational technology has been used to improve teaching and learning and attempts to use these examples to illustrate the potential application of technology to increase the quality of student learning and the productivity of the instructional process.

Although technology has admittedly had only limited impact on teaching and learning in community colleges thus far, enough has been learned to predict the technological transformation of the process in the relatively short term. Irresistible economic forces are at work to force the application of technology to improve instructional productivity, and the essential components of a model that will be in widespread use before the end of the decade are already in operation in a number of community colleges across the country. How to transform the teaching and learning process with technology is becoming known, and in the next few years the organizational structures, human resource models, and funding mechanisms necessary to reinvent teaching and learning in community colleges will likely be developed and, with any luck, implemented on a global scale.

INITIAL USES OF COMPUTERS IN INSTRUCTION

The first uses of computers in instruction in community colleges predate by more than a decade the development of the personal computer that today has come to represent what most think of as instructional technology. Bleed (1989) notes that in the 1960s the larger community colleges acquired mainframe computers primarily to provide career training in data processing and other computer-related fields. As the cost of mainframes declined in the 1970s, more colleges acquired these systems, often by using vocational-technical funding sources, to provide training in this increasingly popular field. Later, most colleges tapped the unused capacity of these original machines to support student record systems and other administrative processes, but the precedent was indelibly established that computer use in community colleges was primarily to support student learning. Meeting student needs has always driven computer use in these colleges. In this respect, community colleges use technology in significantly different ways from other segments of higher education.

203

Computers as the Subject of Instruction

These initial uses of computers represent a major category in the way that technology has been used in teaching in community colleges as a subject of instruction. Beginning with instruction in data processing and progressing to computer programming, information systems design and operation, hardware repair, and telecommunications, instruction in computer-related fields has long been a staple of nearly all community colleges' career programs. Advanced applications of computers to perform design functions and to control manufacturing operations have also become career programs in recent years. Colleges have experienced huge enrollments in courses that teach the use of common applications software programs—the most popular word processing, spreadsheet, graphics, and database programs used by businesses and home computer users. As a result, thousands of technicians and millions of ordinary computer users have received computer-related instruction in community colleges.

However, the introduction of computers in education as a subject of instruction has an unfortunate legacy. Too many students and teachers still think of computers as something to be learned, rather than something to use in the learning process. This notion is reinforced by the common placement of computers—for good, pragmatic reasons—in open-access, multipurpose laboratories. Computers are too often not seen as a routine part of a classroom or other learning environment; they are something that one goes down the hall to the lab to learn about. This early pigeonholing of computers as a subject of instruction, largely for "technical types," remains a psychological barrier to their routine integration into the mainstream of instructional practice.

Computers as Tools Used in Instruction

The barrier has, however, been slowly chipped away by the increasingly pervasive use of computers as tools by teachers and students. The conventional wisdom used to be that 90 percent of new users learn to use computers for the purpose of word processing. Curious faculty discovered that they could use word processing programs to easily create nearly error-free and attractive class materials, store them, and have them available for future updating, and that such capabilities greatly increased their productivity.

Writing teachers immediately saw the application of this tool in their classes. Beginning as many as ten years ago, they introduced computers and word processing as tools in English composition classes, primarily because the technology encouraged and simplified students' revision of their own writing. Faculty also discovered that ease of revision removed an unspoken writing-class taboo: when asked to critique each other's papers, students would almost never suggest their peers revise writing that had already been typed—at least partly because they empathized with the problem of having to retype the whole paper to make any substantive change. Suggestions were almost always limited to changes that could be executed on the existing paper. However, once freed from the typing constraint, students became more open to revision not only to improve their own papers, but also to participate in collaborative writing projects. Many introductory writing classes in community colleges actually begin with some basic instruction in the use of word processing tools, for as the tools have become easier to use, it has become more pragmatic to spend a week in a writing class ensuring that all students have requisite word processing skills than to require a full-length course on word processing as a prerequisite to enrollment. In writing classes, then, word processing is only briefly an object of instruction, but becomes an essential tool for models of writing instruction that are either greatly enhanced or virtually impossible to implement without it.

While word processing is probably the most commonplace and straightforward example of using computers as a tool in instruction, there are dozens of others. The use of spreadsheet programs in accounting and other business-related courses follows the word processing model. Instead of hand calculations and endless recalculations of columns and rows when one number changes, spreadsheets allow faculty and students to concentrate on the content of accounting, not the arithmetic that is its base. Spreadsheets also allow "what if" modeling by linking columns and rows of numbers by algebraic formulas. A similar example is the hand-held calculator, which is now a sophisticated computer that replaced the slide rule as the tool for those preparing to be engineers, financial managers, and scientists.

Another major category of computers used as tools in instruction involves the apparatus used in science and applied technology courses. Computers have been built into a range of scientific instruments that students learn to use to observe and make measurements in laboratory-based classes such as biology, physics, and chemistry. Similarly, computer-controlled robots and other such devices carry out manufacturing processes designed by students and conduct analysis and diagnosis of machine functioning in automotive, electrical, and other mechanical arts courses. It is perhaps even a bit ironic that computers have become indispensable tools in disciplines such as commercial art. Not only do artists use computer tools, such as page-layout, image-capturing, and electronic drawing tools to articulate and modify their original designs, but computer-assisted design tools can actually be programmed to create designs. In sum, as computer-based tools have become integrated into the way that individuals and businesses work, these tools have become part of instructional practices in community colleges in ways that mirror usage outside classroom walls.

Computers as a Medium for Providing and Managing Instruction

A final category of computer use in community colleges is a series of applications specific to the instructional process. In fact, using computers as a medium for instruction recalls early efforts at providing computer-assisted instruction (CAI), the first and primary association that many make when thinking about using computers to aid teaching. CAI is a technique for using a computer to make a tutorial presentation of previously prepared text, computer graphics, or video. The computer asks students prepared questions and selects subsequent information based on student responses. Variations of this approach include hypertext, in which words are linked to additional text that elaborates upon the content, and artificial intelligence, which improves upon traditional branching techniques by imitating the decision-making processes used by a well-informed human tutor.

However, it must be admitted that CAI is at least partly responsible for the impression that the computer revolution in education has failed, for in its early incarnations it was widely perceived, with some justification, as little more than unimaginative drill-and-practice exercises. In retrospect the more significant reason that CAI has had little impact on transforming teaching and learning is that it was only a supplement to classroom-based instruction and was usually done in the computer lab down the hall. As an add-on to regular instruction, it had only limited impact, even though experience indicates that students benefit from additional instruction provided in this format.

Updated management systems, however, have been integrated with instructional modules to create computer-based systems that can not only supplement, but also actually replace some classroom-based instruction. Considerable advances in assessment techniques now permit CAI that can assess students' entry-level skills, monitor student progress through a program of study, and certify when students have completed all learning objectives of a course. An increasing number of colleges now employ such systems to support open-entry/open-exit courses that can virtually eliminate traditional classroom-based, student-teacher interaction.

A range of other applications can be catalogued in this broad category of using computers as an instructional medium, including computer-based simulations. The gradual movement from treating computers as objects of instruction to using computer-based tools, and from using tools to operating integrated computer-based instructional systems, represents a movement toward increased complexity—and toward a greater potential for using technology to transform the teaching and learning process.

A TYPOLOGY FOR CURRENT USES OF INSTRUCTIONAL TECHNOLOGY

Another way of categorizing the instructional uses that community colleges make of technology is to divide the applications into two types: those that help faculty and students do better what they already know how to do, and those that actually transform the way faculty teach and students learn. However, as with most typologies, membership in either category is not always so certain. It is relatively easy to identify when technology is used to automate existing processes or to improve the efficiency or effectiveness of current practices in instruction. On the other hand, it is not completely obvious when some applications cross the line between improving existing practice and become those that actually transform the teaching and learning process. The typology is most useful as the basis for exploring how technology can assist in transforming teaching and learning.

MAKING CURRENT PRACTICE BETTER

Faculty use word processing and page-layout programs to prepare higher quality classroom materials; students use similar technologies to produce higher quality written work; and nearly all of the previously cited illustrations of using computer-based tools fall into this category of applying technology to existing processes and tasks to perform them either more effectively or more efficiently. There are many more examples.

Multimedia Presentations

Using multimedia technologies to make high-tech presentations in classes or lectures is clearly an example of using computers to enhance an existing practice, rather than to transform the process—though the proponents of multimedia would probably push for a more exalted characterization of their products. The term "multimedia" is generally used to refer to the combining of several media, including text, graphics, audio, still images, and video, with a controlling device, usually a computer. The excitement surrounding the relatively recent advances in multimedia technology is linked to the technology's ability to support eye-catching presentations with the potential to engage students' attention and demonstrate concepts, especially for visual learners and the Nintendo Generation.

Educators in all segments of the system immediately see the usefulness of presentation-building tools to enhance their efforts to dispense information, and faculty in all disciplines and in most community colleges nationwide have experimented with different levels of sophistication in such presentations. St. Petersburg Junior College, Florida, has developed the concept of the "teaching bunker" to standardize presentation technology for its faculty and thus to overcome one of the most common obstacles to multimedia classroom presentations: the cost and complexity of configuring appropriate equipment, especially for displaying video images to large audiences. The teaching bunker is a presentation station set up in the front of a classroom and contains a built-in Macintosh computer networked to other on-line resources, a videodisc player, a CD-ROM player, a speaker system, and an overhead projection and color computer-projection panel. Its components allow a range of computer-supported presentations, and the standardization of its parts simplifies support requirements and reduces variability for faculty. On the other side of the house, Fred Hofstetter at the University of Delaware developed an MS-DOS/IBM-based multimedia presentation system designed as a mobile unit that can be wheeled into any classroom or lecture hall to make computer-based presentations. He also developed the software system "Podium," which assists faculty in easily making and editing such presentations even as they are used in the classroom. Chemeketa Community College, Oregon, has created the "Textbook Toolbox" to assist faculty with HyperCard-based electronic textbooks and presentations.

Certainly one of the motivating hopes of using multimedia in presentations is that these will be more likely to communicate with a generation of students weaned on highly visual media such as television and video games. There is no comparison between hastily making chalk marks on a blackboard and illustrating scientific concepts with actual video of a phenomenon, with the ability to stop, repeat, bring in alternative examples, and alter the phenomenon by changing its parameters. Still, at their core such applications of multimedia technology amount to improvements on the blackboard and movie projector. More interesting applications with the potential to transform the learning process involve providing multimedia materials directly to students for their own manipulation.

Simulations

Multimedia technology is also the basis of many simulations, another powerful teaching tool. Laboratory-based demonstrations of physical laws have long been an integral part of instruction in the sciences, performed by individual students at laboratory stations and by faculty in front of large lecture halls and classrooms. However, a number of experiments cannot be done because they are too expensive to stage or too dangerous. Computer-based technologies can simulate such experiments inexpensively and safely; in fact the inherent freedom to determine the hypothetical environment allows computer-based demonstrations to illustrate physical laws much more discretely and quickly, without elaborate and time-consuming set-up. Stephanie Caravello-Hibbert at Catonsville Community College, Maryland, uses videodisc-based materials in astronomy to view worlds that would otherwise be beyond the scope of her students. Tom Barnett at Johnson County Community College, Kansas, uses multimedia to simulate chemical reactions that could not be safely controlled in a college science lab.

Simulation also extends into disciplines that do not traditionally use laboratory demonstrations. Software has been developed to allow students to "walk" though France and to encounter and respond to the circumstances of the daily life of a seventeenth-century gentleman as part of a course in history. Monopoly-like games illustrate economic models, and computer-assisted simulations allow allied health workers to prepare for life-threatening emergencies without actually endangering anyone's life. Again, simulations can be viewed as interesting applications of technology to improve existing practice when used to enhance teacher-made presentations, but when put in the hands of students, simulation technologies offer the potential to transform the teaching and learning process more fundamentally.

Computer-Assisted Testing

Testing, for assessment and placement in skill-appropriate courses as well as in support of instruction, has been greatly enhanced by applying information technology to existing practices. Initial applications in this area included using optical scanning equipment to score multiple-choice tests and provide quick feedback to students, and such technologies are in use in community colleges nationwide. The College Board and Educational Testing Service took assessment testing to another level by developing computerized adaptive testing. Students take the computerized placements tests (CPTs) that assess their reading, writing, and mathematics skills on the computer, but rather than answering a prearranged series of questions, the computer generates individualized tests based upon student responses to questions. If a student gets a question correct, the test generates a more difficult question; if wrong, an easier one. Students' skill levels are bracketed by a relatively small number of questions with demonstrated accuracy. By comparing students' responses to as few as twelve questions, the computer actually predicts students' responses to hundreds of other questions. Computer technology, coupled with item-response theory, has revolutionized testing by creating more accurate, easier to administer, and shorter tests.

Central Piedmont Community College, North Carolina, combines CPTs with test management software and administers assessment tests in local high schools as early as the sophomore year. The tests provide students with information about what skills they need to improve in their remaining years in high school if they are to be successful in college. Such applications in environments other than entry-level assessment of students' basic skills begin to improve practice in ways that can have significant implications for teaching and learning.

Custom Publishing

Customized textbook publishing is another example of an application of technology that began as a straightforward improvement of existing practice but has potential for transformation. In recent years publishers have turned to "encyclopedic textbooks" in an attempt to capture the largest possible market with a single text; after all, most faculty use only a portion of a textbook. The major negatives of this approach include the high costs of texts and the length of time it takes to get an up-to-date text to market. In response, McGraw-Hill has developed a publishing system called Primis that counters the trend by providing higher education faculty with examination copies of textbooks on computer discs. Faculty are invited to review the text, delete unwanted material, rearrange chapters, and add material either from a database of supplemental material for which McGraw-Hill has already acquired copyrights or from their own material, including class notes and home-grown exercises. The faculty then return the disc to McGraw-Hill, which produces customized texts for the class in as little as forty-eight hours. This is an improvement in practice to which nearly all faculty can resonate.

However, the implications are nearly as profound for changing the way textbooks are used. If the textbook is provided on disc to the faculty, it could also be provided on disc to students. If a textbook becomes a computer disc, it can include not only text and graphics, but also moving pictures and simulations that can be varied or controlled by students. Students themselves can revise the texts, including their own material and developing their own exercises. Textbooks can become interactive, and there are examples of community college faculty using interactive texts, including the math faculty at West Valley College, California. Even more sophisticated interactive texts are available as educational games on CD-ROM discs for the home market. Clearly the nature of the most venerable of all teaching and learning devices, the textbook, is subject to transformation by the application of information technology.

Electronic Libraries

Another venerable institution, the college library, is perhaps the most affected by advances in information technology. Libraries, especially those that attempt to provide comprehensive support for all disciplines taught at their colleges, have struggled futilely to keep up with the increase in information generated by the popular and scholarly press. However, nothing has increased more rapidly than the amount of stored information in the world, now estimated to double every two or three years. Libraries have already concluded that they cannot afford the high cost of purchasing all of the periodicals and books being published, and they have struggled to identify which other education-related media now produced—including audio and video tapes, audio compact discs, compact-disc interactive, 35 mm slides, and computer software—they should keep in their collections.

Two developments are changing the nature of college libraries. First, all information now published is digitized at some point in the production cycle, thus making it available in computer-readable form. Second, it is possible to share digitized information over electronic networks that link virtually all college libraries. As a result, college libraries can choose to reduce the number of periodicals they carry in hard copy to those most used by faculty and students and can instead provide access to others on demand from electronic services. Libraries have provided interlibrary loan programs for several decades; as libraries carry fewer periodicals and texts in proportion to the number published, these loan programs expand in volume and in kind. Electronic databases now include everything from the Dow Jones daily stock reports to archives of great American music now stored electronically at Syracuse University.

While the possibilities are nearly unlimited, the reality is that college libraries are in turmoil as a result of the information revolution. Those that keep hard copies of periodicals going back a hundred years or more find that their constituents will not let them simply walk away from this massive investment in collections. Librarians trained in using standard reference tools now find themselves confronted with an entirely different array of information processing tools, databases, and on-line collections. Even the standards of their profession are changing as great libraries may be judged not by the number of volumes they hold but by the amount of user access they facilitate.

Community college libraries have not historically invested in massive collections of books and periodicals, so they are in a relatively different situation from research university libraries. These tend not even to be called libraries, but rather learning or information resource centers, terms more descriptive of the nature and function of libraries transformed by information technology. Major issues remaining for community colleges include the role of faculty in guiding students in the use of discipline-related databases and other digitized information resources; the role of information resource centers in collecting and providing access to instructional software, including that developed by faculty; and the economic model by which information resources will be provided. In the past, institutions have traditionally shouldered the burden of providing resources, but user fees are likely to become more common as the range and cost of information services increase. Also, students may opt to purchase not only their own hardware to gain access to resources, but increasingly their own software, and the boundaries between the services provided by college libraries, bookstores, and computer services will become less distinct. While information technology has certainly provided the means for libraries to improve practice, it has already transformed them as institutions, if not their role in the teaching and learning process.

214

TRANSFORMING TEACHING AND LEARNING

While a number of technology applications have potential to transform the teaching and learning process, it seems only those that actually change the nature of the interaction between students and faculty qualify as transformational. The following are examples of technology used in instruction that appear to be actually changing the nature of the process, primarily by giving students more control over their own learning.

Collaborative Writing

Previous examples cited the ways word processing is used in writing classes and how it has made substantive collaboration among students in the writing process possible by simplifying revision. In fact, the use of word processing has come close to transforming writing instruction in a number of community colleges by permitting a process approach to writing that is virtually impossible to execute effectively without word processing tools. The primary focus of a process approach to writing is not the study of examples of good writing crafted by well-known authors; rather the focus is the inner workings of each student's own writing. This approach requires students to work on single pieces of writing for extended periods of time, taking each through recursive stages of prewriting, drafting, revising, editing, receiving feedback, rewriting, and so forth. It depends on developing a sense of audience in writers and thus places a premium on peer feedback. Karen D'Agostino and Sandra Varone at Brookdale Community College, New Jersey, found that in addition to the availability of word processing technology, implementing the approach also involves the appropriate placement of computers and student desks to create public and private spaces where students can work independently or collaboratively. At least in part because instructors using a technology-aided process approach have been able to demonstrate dramatic improvements in the length, quality, and complexity of students' writing (Kozma and Johnston, 1991), the community college writing class is being transformed from a teacher-centered lecture and discussion class into a student-centered, collaborative experience.

The application of technologies that encourage collaboration among students not only outside the classroom, but also from remote locations around the country and the world further transforms community college writing instruction. By providing student access to electronic bulletin boards where they can post their writing and provide feedback on others' work from near or remote locations, information technology actually creates "virtual classrooms"—communities of learners that share the same purpose but not the same physical space. In spring 1992 students at Jackson Community College, Michigan, and St. Petersburg Junior College collaborated with each other in the development of individual and group compositions. Students in writing classes at Phoenix College, Arizona, actively collaborated in the development of their own compositions with students in Israel. The process approach to writing is fundamentally redefining the role of the teacher in the learning of writing. Teachers become the arbiters of taste and standards, but they are not in a position to present model writing or to direct classroom discussion. They add just one of many authoritative voices to the discussion and collaboration. They design and guide students' learning experiences, but the collaborative community of developing writers is what drives the learning process.

Electronic Forums

Essentially the same technology can be used in other disciplines to enhance communication and build alternatives to classroom communities. Glendale Community College, one of the Maricopa County Community Colleges in Phoenix, Arizona, has made the most extensive and systematic use of electronic bulletin boards to supplement classroom discussions. Using a college-developed software application, "The Electronic Forum," the college supports electronic communications among as many as 5,000 student users each semester. Students can use either one of the college's several hundred personal computers located in open-access laboratories to log on to the electronic bulletin board, or their own personal computers and modems to dial into the system through any telephone line. The software is designed to operate with any type of computer, and instructions for logging on and using the system are simple enough to be taught in twenty minutes or contained on a single sheet of paper.

Karen Schwalm, an English faculty member at Glendale who uses the electronic forum to supplement, not replace, classroom discussion, has found that the nature of the electronic conversations are surprisingly different from in-class discussion. Most obviously, they are much less dominated by the teacher, or by the one or two class loudmouths, apple polishers, or articulate students. Instead, shy and quieter students have the opportunity to engage on equal terms in the discussion. Analyzing hundreds of conversations related to a variety of classes, Schwalm has also found that the conversations that take place electronically vary a great deal depending upon whether they are synchronous (carried out in real time) or asynchronous—with comments and responses posted to the bulletin board some time after they are entered. The former electronic conversations are more like classroom discussions, rewarding the quick, witty, and humorous; the latter are more thoughtful and serious, and often richer and more complex than most in-class discussions since Socrates.

The benefits of providing students with the means to enhance classroom discussion are obvious for any commuter institution. The fact that they can be used to build learning communities, either as a supplement for classroom discussion or as a replacement, is particularly important to supporting nontraditional means of instruction, including distance learning. There are less obvious benefits to electronic discussions; for example, such communication among individuals is not influenced by the physical appearance of individuals, nor by race, gender, or physical disability. Electronic communications are blind and can easily be made anonymous if appropriate. Their critical feature, however, remains that they tend to put the teacher in the role as first among learning collaborators, rather than as instructor and leader. Almost invariably, any learning experience that uses electronic bulletin boards or related technology ends up being more learner-centered—which remains the heart of a transformed teaching and learning process.

Independent Learning Systems

Glendale Community College also conducts nearly 30 percent of its credit classes in an open-entry/open-exit mode that is based upon student learning accomplished outside the regular class-room environment using college-provided computer resources. Veteran faculty established the model for computer-assisted independent learning by developing competency-based modules from the objectives of the courses they have taught for years. These materials are made available to students in a laboratory of 400 networked personal computers that is open and staffed around the clock. Students log in to the system, identify themselves and the courses in which they are enrolled, and proceed to work their way through sequenced course modules. The role of the faculty in this environment is vastly different from their role as classroom teachers. Rather than dispense information and lead discussions, faculty are primarily responsible for developing curriculum materials, assisting individual students with questions, and managing a learning environment that also includes a large number of paraprofessional tutors and laboratory assistants—often drawn from the ranks of those who have successfully completed the courses themselves. Students work through the learning objectives at their own pace and receive credit upon satisfactory completion of required material. At its core, this open-entry/open-exit approach is based upon mastery learning. Testimony to the success of the program includes high completion rates, high demand for the courses, strong student preference for the self-paced approach, and increasing numbers of faculty who say they will never go back to classroom-based instruction.

While Glendale houses what is probably the most extensive computer-based learning effort being carried out on a community college campus today, hundreds of other colleges have employed

similar computer-assisted, competency-based instructional programs in a variety of disciplines, including computer science and
business, but also in basic reading, writing, and mathematics
skills. Some programs are developed by commercial vendors and
are used not only as supplemental to the classroom but as primary
means of delivering instruction in basic skills and vocational-technical training. Both commercial and faculty-developed independent learning systems are based on similar principles of competency-based education and mastery learning. Commercial systems
tend to be more highly developed and to integrate systems for
entry-level assessment and diagnosis of student skills, instruction,
and student progress monitoring. The most up-to-date systems
also incorporate multimedia technology into the instructional
modules. Commercial systems also have the advantage of being
developed with broad-based input and consensus regarding learning objectives. Though they are not created locally to the specifi-
cations of individual faculty, some provide a degree of customiza-
tion to specific learning objectives. Of course, commercial
systems are not inexpensive and require up-front capital outlay in
addition to operating costs.

Nonetheless, an increasing number of colleges have found the
movement to independent learning systems positive. St. Philip's
College, Texas, piloted IBM's Academic DeskLab and continues
to enjoy considerable success with underprepared students using
the basic skills system. St. Louis Community College at Mer-
amec, Missouri, uses TICCIT for math instruction with good results. Bakersfield College, California, has had success with a
WICAT/ Jostens Learning Corporation basic skills laboratory.
Anecdotal evidence offered by faculty and academic administrators, some based upon quasi-experimental institutional studies,
generally supports the use of such systems to increase student
learning. Most report comparable or greater student learning and
retention compared to classroom-based instruction. Some also
report initial student disorientation or discomfort with using
computer hardware and software, but most students seem to
overcome this barrier and join the ranks of the computer literate
rather easily.

The two most often-stated objections to computer-based independent learning are that students, especially underprepared students and those with negative academic experiences, require nurturing that is only possible through regular teacher and peer contact, and that the systems cost too much to purchase and operate relative to student learning gains. While both criticisms are valid, both can be overcome by better design. The best uses of computer-based instructional systems do not isolate students but provide opportunities for regular contact with faculty, teaching paraprofessionals, laboratory assistants, and peers. Glendale Community College combines independent learning systems with the electronic forum to encourage students engaged in similar learning experiences to form alternative learning communities to those usually established in classrooms.

The investment in hardware and software and in ongoing operating costs is not insignificant and is a barrier to implementing these systems at many colleges. High costs will be an increasingly difficult barrier if faculty and administrators envision simply supplementing existing classroom instruction with this technology. The best-designed systems solve the problem of cost and actually decrease unit costs by redistributing faculty time over more students and using lower-paid paraprofessional assistants and technicians to provide support. The key to cost-effective implementation is not using technology as an add-on, but redesigning the entire instructional delivery system and the work of those involved in it. Well-designed and properly implemented, independent computer-assisted learning systems are effective in increasing student learning at acceptable costs—but only those systems that transform the teaching and learning process, not those that automate the existing classroom-based paradigm, are likely to accomplish these goals.

Distance Learning

Distance learning is a pragmatic response to a growing phenomenon, the increasing enrollment of adult students who are unable to attend regularly scheduled classes because of family and work responsibilities. These students might once have simply found it impractical to attend college, but increasingly they are pushed by economic pressures to upgrade or learn new employment skills or attempt to move up the socioeconomic ladder. As a result, considerable effort has been made in developing distance learning programs that go well beyond long-used telecourses to provide these adults with active and effective learning experiences. Nearly all use information technology in the delivery system; those that would most fundamentally transform the teaching and learning process use many of the technologies previously discussed in this chapter.

Judy Lever of Miami-Dade Community College, Florida, argues that the essential components of effective distance learning programs are delivery systems that free students from the constraints of time and place and that provide regular and substantive opportunities for interaction among faculty and students (1992). Technologies such as the electronic forum that support remote communication, discussion, and collaboration among students and faculty who might never meet are central to well-designed programs, as are competency-based course materials that make independent learning feasible. Lever combines both in a cost-effective distance learning program at the Homestead Campus of Miami-Dade that does not depend upon such high-cost systems as broadcast television or even cable television. Well-designed materials that can be purchased in the campus bookstore, checked out of the college library, or sent through the mail can be the basis for an effective distance learning program, as can information resource centers with extended hours. The critical component is that faculty-student and student-student interaction be made possible by some means, including an electronic communications system.

The Community College of Maine offers a complete degree program through a statewide distance learning network that provides instruction and student services to learners. Kirkwood Community College, Iowa, broadcasts courses into rural locations across the state, transmitting live and videotaped instruction to homes and remote learning centers. In a national survey of distance learning programs, Lever was able to identify more than 400 community colleges that reported offering credit for courses delivered by alternative means (1993). Clearly, the expansion and re-finement of distance learning programs, generally supported by various information technologies, represents a significant trans-formation of the teaching and learning process. It exemplifies the key elements of any such transformation: movement out of the classroom and placement of the independent adult learner at the center of the teaching and learning process.

THE WAYS TECHNOLOGY CAN HELP

A decade of experimentation has provided the experiential base from which to summarize the essential ways that technology can improve and transform teaching and learning in the commu-nity college. First, powerful and increasingly economical networks can enhance communications between students and faculty, stu-dents and students, and everyone and college resources. There are numerous examples of using electronic communications sys-tems to increase productivity; there are more and more examples of using communications technology to build community and to deepen and broaden the content of intellectual discourse.

Second, related networking technologies can provide access to ever richer sources of information. Digitized data, text, audio, and video can be easily transmitted to any location, no matter how re-mote. Not only information, but tools, human expertise, and other resources can just as easily be shared, thus ensuring greater equal-ity of access to students in rural colleges as well as urban ones, to individuals working or studying in modest institutions as well as to those in wealthy colleges and communities. Information technol-ogy makes it possible for all students to have access to virtually any information they need for their academic and personal develop-ment, and the sharing of resources across a broad base can signif-icantly lower the unit costs of providing them.

The third, and perhaps the most important, way that technol-ogy can help serve students is by providing educational resources tailored to the diversity of learning styles, cultural differences, skill levels, motivations, and educational objectives of an increas-ingly pluralistic student body. Individualized instruction has been the goal of all good teaching for decades, but the fact is that traditional classroom-based methods of delivering instruction make true individualization virtually impossible. New technologies, including interactive multimedia materials, learner-centered instructional management systems, and sophisticated independent learning systems, make real individualization within the reach of all students.

However, the challenge is not primarily a technological one. Rather, the challenge facing all of education is figuring out how it must transform its institutions to take advantage of developments in information technology to meet the needs of students and communities. The task is figuring out how to reinvent these institutions so that the application of technology makes them more productive, not more costly. The discouraging aspect of the current technological revolution is that advances in information technology have not generated corresponding increases in productivity in educational institutions. To date they have successfully applied technology and produced better qualitative results, but almost always at an increased cost per unit. The problem is that when simply automating existing processes, technology is just an add-on cost. To serve more students with no additional resources, colleges and schools must do different things. They must change the classroom-based, faculty-centered paradigm and design and implement a student-centered paradigm that produces more and better outcomes—with no increases in costs—that makes them more productive.

To increase the fundamental productivity of our educational system will require basic changes in the current model, primarily in the way that the system deploys its most precious resources, its professional faculty and staff. The task is to define new roles for this talent, allowing technology to do the hard work that it can do more efficiently than faculty, such as dispensing information, grading student exams and assignments, and monitoring student attendance, behavior, and progress. Rather than perpetuating "the sage on the stage," it is time to develop new learning models that make the best use of faculty expertise as designers of curricula and learning experiences, facilitators of student learning, knowledge navigators and guides in the use of information, and developers of new knowledge.

With the technology problems solved, it is time to get on to the much harder work of transforming community colleges and the roles of the people who work in them. Now that the technology is and will be available for any purpose imaginable, it is time to redesign these institutions with students at their center and get on with the business of assisting them to learn—not with teaching them.

CRUCIBLES OF INNOVATION

Transformation, of course, is not accomplished quickly or without pain, and there are substantial roadblocks to overhauling the fundamental system built so laboriously over time. Even the most adventurous pioneers tend to observe the first rule of wing walking: don't let go of what you have until you have something else to hold on to. However, there are ways to approach change by demonstrating the viability of new models in what might be called crucibles of innovation. With respect to testing models for applying technology to transform teaching and learning, three stand out: teaching underprepared students, ensuring access for students with disabilities, and providing training services to employees of business and industry on a contract basis.

Teaching Underprepared Students

Colleges have experimented with different instructional approaches for underprepared students. Not surprisingly it turns out that the most effective methodology with these or any other students is one-on-one instruction. Since the likelihood that such ratios will ever be funded is zero, a number of colleges have used technology to construct the effect of one-on-one instruction without the cost, and the results are encouraging. Miami-Dade Community College has led a multi-institutional effort to develop a model for using technology to improve the basic skills of underprepared students. Project SYNERGY, directed by Kamala Anandam, has conducted a comprehensive review of over 200 software packages designed for basic skills instruction and has implemented the most promising in electronic classrooms. While the results in student gains have themselves been encouraging, the project has also discovered much about how this population of students interacts with different aspects of the technology and learning environment. With substantial support from both the IBM Corporation and the U.S. Department of Education, Project SYNERGY is developing the next generation of instructional software systems for teaching basic skills. This new system will be designed from the perspective of the student, rather than the instructor, and it will provide students with the ability to manage their own learning.

The implications for the application of technology to teaching and learning with other students are obvious: if it is possible to develop systems that effectively facilitate the learning of the most challenged student populations, then success with students with higher skill levels seems assured.

Ensuring Access for Students with Disabilities

The logic of tackling the most difficult problems first applies not only to teaching underprepared students, but also to ensuring access to programs and services for students with disabilities. While the concern predates the 1992 Americans with Disabilities Act, this broad-based piece of civil rights legislation places a clear burden of proof on all organizations to demonstrate that employment opportunities and access to programs and services are not denied because of an individual's physical disabilities.

The California High Tech Center for Assistive Technologies, located at De Anza College and directed by Carl Brown, has led efforts to examine the nature of obstacles that students with disabilities encounter in pursuit of educational opportunities. The center has focused on identifying and piloting assistive technologies to ensure these students' access to classroom instruction and training; to popular media, including print, radio, television, and film; and to the wealth of information resources made available through technology. In doing so, it has broken tasks and experiences down into component parts and discovered much about how students learn and gain access to information. The center is also at the cutting edge of technology, exploring the implications of virtual reality, not only to assist learning, but to enhance the life experiences of students with disabilities. Again, this crucible for innovative applications of technology has much to offer those who seek models for applying technology to learning for less challenged populations.

Providing Training Services to Employees of Business and Industry

This increasingly important mission for community colleges may create an ideal environment for developing and testing new adult learning models that will invariably include the application of information technology. The training units established by nearly all community colleges to provide services for business, industry, labor, and government employers are usually semi-autonomous and not subject to the rules, regulations, and contracts that govern the mainstream instructional program of the college. As a result, these units are more free to experiment with alternative methods of selecting, using, and compensating faculty and trainers. Similarly, these programs offer the opportunity to implement models for credentialing student learning that are not dependent upon the currently dominant system of credit-for-contact. In important ways, business and industry training provides an ideal environment in which to test the economic feasibility of alternative learning models—not only in the marketplace of ideas, but in the marketplace.

The use of technology to provide training is an expectation of business and industry, where technological applications are pervasive and valued. Businesses understand that investment in technological infrastructure is a cost of competing in a global economy, and they will accept investment in instructional technology if their return on investment can be documented in learning outcomes. Models for providing education and training using distance learning and independent learning systems can be tested with a large number of adult workers whose life responsibilities require the use of these alternative delivery systems. In fact the workplace will become the equivalent of the classroom for many adults, and models for developing and sustaining alternative learning communities can be piloted there.

As with underprepared and disabled students, serving the needs of working adults and the national economy they support is as noble and important a task as any undertaken by higher education. While some may rue the passing of an era in which scholarship and higher learning were the main purposes of colleges and universities, the challenge facing community colleges, as well as the rest of higher education, has never been more high-minded: to provide universal access to lifelong education. The key to success in this endeavor will ultimately be the successful transformation of the teaching and learning process by the application of information technology. We live in a new world and time. Let us embrace it.

REFERENCES

Bell, Terrel H. "A Nation at Risk: Update for the 1990s." Speech delivered at the Leadership 2000 conference, Chicago, July 7, 1991.

Bleed, Ronald D. "Innovative Management Through the Use of Communications Technology." In Terry O'Banion (Ed.), *Innovation in the Community College*. New York: ACE/Macmillan, 1989.

Gifford, Bernard R. "Delivering the Promises of Technology Today." *Leadership Abstracts*, 1991, *4* (1).

Kozma, Robert B. and Jerome Johnston. "The Technological Revolution Comes to the Classroom." *Change*, 1991, *23* (1).

Lever, Judy C. "Meeting Increasing Demand Using Distance Education." *Leadership Abstracts*, February 1992, 5 (2).

_____. *Distance Education Resource Guide*. Mission Viejo, Calif.: League for Innovation in the Community College, 1993.

Don Doucette is vice chancellor of educational services/instructional technology, the Metropolitan Community Colleges, Missouri.

Chapter 12

A Contemporary View of Teaching and Learning Centers for Faculty

By Kurt Lauridsen

The community college teaching and learning center is a tangible expression of the heightened interest in instruction and student academic success. These centers bring together a body of activities designed to highlight and reinforce teaching and learning. For purposes of this chapter, they are defined as any identifiable offices or programs that strengthen the teaching and learning missions of the campus by providing programs, resources, and services for faculty. The word "center" implies a degree of concentrated activity that is not present in the more typical faculty development committee structure.

While virtually every community college has some activity that might be called faculty development, the programs undertaken vary widely in type and in resource base. On some campuses, administrative offices commit modest amounts of money rather haphazardly for faculty travel and research, while others have mature, well-organized, and comprehensive organizations or centers. The title "teaching and learning center" (TLC) in this chapter has merely been adopted as the clearest phrase to describe a higher level of intensified campus activity in the specific areas of instruction and student comprehension. Program titles, organizations, and budgets are less important than achieving the kind of critical mass of activity that comes when the line is crossed from sporadic activities and concerns for teaching and learning to concerted action in planning, regular meetings, and in ongoing involvement by faculty. Typically, a TLC is coordinated by a part- or full-time faculty member or less often by a project committee. There is some clerical assistance and a dedicated facility (office, library, conference space) that may be located in one place.

THE SURVEY

This chapter looks at the current status of TLCs: their purposes, organizations, funding, staffing, evaluations, programs, and services. In this context, the advantages and disadvantages of establishing centers will be reviewed. Much of the discussion presented here is based on interviews with TLC staff and faculty and on knowledge gained from a survey conducted in October and November 1992. In the latter case, a random sample of 100 community colleges in California, Florida, Illinois, New York, and Texas provided timely and useful information on the existence, location, and development of TLCs. One-half of the campuses surveyed responded to the questionnaire, and 42 percent of these (21) believed they had TLC programs as defined in the survey. The general response rate of community colleges by state was California, 40 percent; Florida, 42 percent; Illinois, 58 percent; New York, 57 percent; and Texas, 52 percent. The percent of respondents claiming TLCs by state was California, 44 percent; Florida, 45 percent; Illinois, 45 percent; New York, 60 percent; and Texas, 28 percent.

There is no rigid formula for a TLC. Campuses are more notable for their experimentation, creative efforts, and uniqueness of services. Campus size does not appear to predict either the comprehensiveness or activity levels of a center. Nor is there a clear-cut pattern of services based on size or location. The percentage of faculty use is independent of faculty size, although the gross number of faculty participants is, as might be expected, higher at larger campuses. Other factors, such as the commitment of senior administrators, budget, and faculty leadership and interest, are more important in determining success as measured by the level of participation and activity.

A small to mid-sized campus like Central Florida Community College, with 250 faculty, offers a wide range of services including endowed chairs "on the way" and claims that almost 100 percent of its faculty is involved. With a faculty over twice the size of Central Florida, Fresno City College, California, offers similar activities with its own unique emphasis on mini-grants for teaching improvement, teacher exchanges, and team teaching programs.

Fresno City has a budget four times that of Central Florida, but focuses special attention on a large part-time faculty population. An even larger campus, El Paso Community College, Texas, with more than 1,000 faculty, states that almost all faculty participate in one or more elements of the Office of Faculty Development. In addition to the usual services, El Paso's unique offerings are found in annual faculty retreats, sponsorship of a regional seminar, wellness weekends, and health and environmental awareness activities—all accomplished with a budget less than Fresno City College's and comparable to that of much smaller Central Florida Community College.

HISTORY AND ORGANIZATION OF TEACHING AND LEARNING CENTERS

TLCs represent a fairly recent phenomena in community colleges. A few centers were part of the original design of community college campuses, with the earliest such center identified in this survey established in 1965. But most TLCs are a product of the 1980s, their creation presumably influenced by a synthesis of the themes discussed in this book, which characterize the current climate in higher education: the recent educational reform movement, political and social forces, and innovations in educational theory and practice as well as in educational technology.

It is more the exception than the rule for all faculty development activities to be gathered under one roof. Often, faculty development committees sponsor certain events alongside a TLC. In some cases faculty development committees are connected to centers as advisory groups; in others, both groups function independently. Mohawk Valley Community College, New York, is a comparatively small college with 167 full-time faculty and 213 adjuncts. Yet this campus has three separate programs for faculty under three different professors.

At Mohawk Valley, the Staff Development Committee, with a separate budget, provides workshops for faculty, a teacher exchange program, outreach to four-year institutions and high schools, a newsletter, and travel funds for attending conferences and workshops. The Adjunct Faculty/Staff Development Program sponsors orientations and workshops for part-time faculty. Established more recently, the Teaching/Learning Project has a separate committee and budget concentrating on classroom research and team teaching.

Many community college faculty, staff, and administrators have devoted considerable time and energy to improving teaching and learning. The current climate in higher education and the particular characteristics of each community college setting determine the kind of faculty development undertaken on each campus and, therefore, the existence of TLCs. Not all campuses, however, believe that a "center" is the appropriate way to reinforce good instruction and student learning. As one college president put it: "We have a strong program of continuous strengthening of the teaching-learning mission, and it is *everybody's* responsibility. Teaching-learning is a major item of emphasis on every administrator's and staff member's job description. The dean of instruction has primary responsibility for promoting and monitoring campuswide activities."

This observation raises a major issue going to the heart of the movement to create TLCs. Ideally, the primacy of the teaching and learning mission in community colleges dictates that these activities are everybody's responsibility. In reality, other challenges may produce a different result.

There is a fair amount of tension today on many community college campuses resulting from the desire to strengthen and improve teaching and learning on one hand, and tight budgets and disengaged faculty and staff on the other. These conflicting forces have undoubtedly influenced the extent to which campuses can and will act to create programs and services in support of teaching and learning. Virtually every respondent to the survey listed budget problems as the greatest challenge to the development of TLCs, and almost half cited lack of faculty responsiveness as a major impediment.

From a survey respondent in Illinois came the lament, "If we had the money we might be able to do something...but we're struggling with the basics of having enough faculty to fill sections." From Florida was the observation that the state "formerly dedicated 2 percent of its state funding (by law) to staff and program development. That has been rescinded during the current economic slump." A respondent from New York wrote, "The college recognizes the need and potential for such a center. Budget concerns and reduced funding from all levels have required a focus on maintaining the status quo." It makes sense to assume that in this current era of recession and declining state budgets, these responses represent a fair expression of sentiment on community college campuses.

Faculty attitudes are also a major challenge for TLCs. Virtually every campus has a core of faculty and administrators who are vigorous in their efforts to strengthen the teaching and learning missions of the college. But the second most common challenge (topped only by budget) cited by those involved in TLCs was "lack of faculty response." Apathy and the stand-off attitude of many faculty were often mentioned as problems by survey respondents. Senior faculty approaching retirement, overcommitted faculty, and part-time faculty with a lesser stake in the campus are also difficult to involve.

Campuses indicated program use ranging from 5 percent to 100 percent of the entire faculty. The great discrepancy in these figures is likely a result of some campuses tabulating only unduplicated regular users, while others are counting heads at every event, including such large, one-shot activities as early fall faculty receptions.

For the most part, participation in TLC activities is voluntary. However, about a quarter of the campuses with well-developed programs require attendance at activities such as orientations and for groups such as adjunct and new faculty. McHenry County College, Illinois, has such a program aimed at part-time faculty, coordinated by the personnel director and the staff development committee.

Respondents divided equally on the question of compensation for involvement in TLC activities. Release time and intrinsic rewards were most frequently mentioned, with stipends indicated as the next most important benefit. Few campuses use participation in staff development activities directly in evaluation for tenure, though many note the indirect connection to teaching evaluations and "service." It appears that midcareer tenured faculty members are the mainstay for involvement with the TLC. Tenured faculty use centers the most; part-time faculty and "older" tenured faculty about to retire were the groups mentioned most often as representing the greatest challenge for participation.

The level of commitment of part-time faculty to teaching and learning activities is likely an attitudinal and a situational problem. Many part-time faculty do not have the same sense of belonging to a campus as full-time faculty. Employment elsewhere also complicates the participation of part-time faculty. As a result, some campuses have special activities for this faculty group. Mohawk Valley Community College's Adjunct Faculty/Staff Development Program pays participants for their involvement at the completion of a six-session program. This activity includes workshops on student learning styles and classroom research, mentoring by senior faculty, lectures by "great" teachers, and teleconferences.

The act of centralizing teaching and learning support activities in order to form an inclusive unit serving the entire campus raises a host of issues. Administrators may hope that everyone understands the importance of the teaching and learning mission and may legitimately worry that the centralization of these activities will create yet another program with the usual constituency who demand ever-increasing budgets. Equally plausible is the concern that the creation of one organization committed to such activity will let everyone else off the hook with the accompanying attitudes of "That's not my job" and "Let the center worry about it!" Such views hinder more than help achieve the desired result of raising concern for good teaching among all faculty.

Conversely many teachers and administrators feel public and legislative pressure that community colleges make good on the promise of offering an outstanding teaching and learning environment for a diverse population. They understand that one of the most visible and immediate responses to such pressure is the development of a TLC to spearhead and support the teaching and learning missions. There is additional and more substantive wisdom behind the choice to develop such a center, however, including more effective service delivery, the encouragement of accountability and creativity, and the discouragement of program duplication.

Whatever the argument about the value of establishing TLCs and despite the issues of budget, faculty interest, and administrative policy, the current trend appears to be toward the consolidation of older services and the creation of new activities in support of the teaching and learning mission. Over 40 percent of respondents stated that they had a center as defined in the survey. About half as many campuses were in various stages of planning such an organization or expressed an interest in doing so. Most of the remainder had faculty development committees operating with different degrees of enthusiasm or at least administrative offices (the Office of the President, Personnel Office, etc.) that manage some funds to support broadly defined faculty development.

PROGRAM TITLE AND PURPOSE

According to the survey, the words used to describe centers in addition to "teaching and learning" most frequently include "development" preceded by "faculty," "staff," and "professional." Another rather common title is "faculty resource center." The terms "growth," "innovation," and "excellence" are not uncommon in center titles.

The campus adminstration is credited with initiating most TLCs, then faculty, and finally staff. Many campuses indicated that all of these constituencies were equal in their support.

The most frequently mentioned purpose for TLCs in the mission statement is to improve teaching, then to encourage faculty development, and last to improve learning. Other purposes, less frequently indicated, are developing academic programs, promoting staff and student diversity, and supporting the quality of faculty life.

CENTER LEADERSHIP AND FACULTY

The role and title of the senior administrator who oversees the TLC provides insight into the priority given to the activity. But program assignment to particular senior administrators is determined as much by personalities as by organizational logic. Any survey that attempts to read too much into "reporting lines" must be sensitive to this. Nonetheless, the reporting line most frequently represented is, as might be expected, to the dean or vice president of instruction (or other senior academic affairs officer). A few organizations place the TLC directly under the president, an encouraging sign of the importance placed on this activity at those campuses. In response to a question designed to gain an understanding of "ownership," respondents were equally divided over whether their centers were considered academic or administrative units. Several center directors stated that they report to faculty development committees. But this requires interpretation, in that most committees have some kind of administrative coordination, at least on budget matters.

The majority of centers had part-time directors and coordinators with part-time clerical assistance, although one-fourth of the respondents with centers indicated they had full-time managers with one full-time clerical staff member. Several reported having two part-time faculty in coordinating roles. Clearly, the pattern is to involve only a few permanent career staff, who coordinate volunteers from the faculty, outside speakers, and other campus services such as educational technology offices and student learning centers. It appears that organizational philosophy, as often as budget constraints, dictates minimizing the development of a large, entrenched, and permanent administrative structure to run such programs. Wisely, there is an attempt to build in maximum participation of faculty at all operational levels.

While many campuses have staff development committees, the difference between a "committee" and a "center" in the context of this paper is when teaching and learning activities for faculty become numerous and ongoing, requiring some administrative structure that is usually a part-time faculty member. However, a very active project steering committee sometimes coordinates the program.

Such centers often have a place for offices, a resource library and conference space. For example, Broward Community College, Florida, has a comparatively new but nonetheless comprehensive TLC offering many services. It is run by a very active committee of six faculty members who are given release time to meet on a weekly basis to plan and carry out all activities. An administrator, the director of institutional planning and effectiveness, describes her role as merely "signing the paperwork."

American River College, California, strengthens faculty participation and ownership in another way. This center has developed a system of rotating its program director's part-time position to provide the broadest possible inclusion of faculty. Each year the current Teaching Resources Center director develops a list of active Advisory Committee members as potential nominees for the director's position. Committee members are asked to review the list of nominees and submit recommendations for next year's faculty director. The Resource Committee receives these suggestions, searches for a consensus, interviews the candidates and submits a recommendation to the campus president, who makes the appointment for the following year. Directors normally serve only one year with some release time.

The role of the faculty director at American River College is also rather typical. The director supervises the Resource Center assistant, who is a full-time staff member responsible for day-to-day coordination of the center's programs, library publications, meetings, student helpers, and clients. The director appoints members of the Advisory Committee and chairs regular meetings. He or she also represents the programs to campus groups and outsiders, consults with individual faculty members, reports to and corresponds with the faculty, and remains an ex officio member of related committees for three years after his or her tenure as director. Thus faculty directors continually rotate, but come on board with experience from prior service on advisory committees and lend continuity thereafter as continuing members of these groups.

ADVISORY COMMITTEES

Typically TLCs have advisory committees actively involved with the program. Most reported holding regularly scheduled meetings, usually each month, though a sizeable minority held meetings as needed. Given the major goal of involving the faculty in the process, the creation of an advisory committee seems an obvious step. Yet it is surprising that several programs did not have such committees or reported that committees were convened only for such limited roles as mediating disputes. More often, faculty advisory committees for TLCs were described as providing direction, approving expenditures, reviewing, recommending, and evaluating. Ordinarily, in programs largely funded through the Title III program (a federally funded campuswide support program for small and medium-sized developing institutions), the overall project steering committee plays the role of the faculty advisory committee.

A major justification for TLCs is to benefit student academic achievement. But there is surprisingly little evidence of direct student input into the formation of center policy or practice. Students are seen more as the product rather than a part of the process. Not one center reported having students on its advisory committee. A trace of student participation is found in the Teaching Resources Center *News*, a publication of American River College that carries a feature titled "Student Involvement Corner." This column reports that ideas were solicited from students for a forthcoming publication titled *The Student Involvement Handbook for Faculty.*

LOCATION

The majority of TLCs have a designated place or places on campus where support activities are offered. Half of these centers are located in one place, while the rest are spread throughout the campus. About half of the centers are in a neutral place such as a library and do not appear to be an adjunct to the administration or any one academic department or division.

FUNDING

In these difficult fiscal times, it is not surprising that the majority of respondents complained about budget problems. But two-thirds did say that their funding was adequate for their current stated program purpose. This apparent contradiction may be resolved by frequent comments that some program participants wanted to do more and felt constrained by the current financial squeeze. An observation from Texas is typical: "Current budget tightening is hampering our ability to expand much-needed programs in the area of faculty mentoring/feedback projects designed to enhance the quality of classroom instruction." About 20 percent of the programs reported that their financial support had been cut. Funding for TLCs range from a low of $4,000 to over half a million dollars. Some states allocate special funding to community colleges that requires services for faculty development.

Federal Title III funding plays a consequential role in supporting and encouraging the creation of some centers. In Texas, Paris Junior College, with 80 full-time and 20 part-time faculty and an enrollment of approximately 2,400 credit students and 5,000 non-credit students, reported that it is preparing a Title III proposal that includes a TLC. Niagara County Community College, New York, is ending a five-year term under Title III funding during which it developed a comprehensive Faculty Resource Center for Academic Excellence. Niagara's center has a full-time director and clerical support and is located in a central place. Its comprehensive program includes faculty workshops, lectures by outstanding teachers, mentoring by senior faculty, mini-grants for teaching improvement, a videotape library, and a newsletter. Oxnard College, California, a campus of comparable size with about 300 faculty and 7,000 students, committed a significant portion of its recent Title III grant to a TLC. Oxnard already has a variety of faculty workshops and other services, including an orientation program for new faculty.

SERVICES

The great diversity of programs, resources, and special services provided for faculty by TLCs attests to an impressive range of creativity and thought. In addition to directly influencing teaching styles, these activities focus on new ways to stimulate student interest, achieve insight into student learning styles, gain appreciation by students for various disciplines, and encourage the development and use of higher-level thinking skills.

Survey respondents were offered a list of twenty-five services and asked to indicate which of these were available at their centers. They could add services not on the list. They named an impressive variety of programs, including lectures, seminars, and workshops on an endless list of topics designed to improve teaching and learning. A key ingredient of these activities is faculty sharing experiences, and a relatively common practice is to host seminars by "great teachers" as models for others.

A majority of centers sponsor workshops on computer-assisted instruction, the use of audio/visual aids in the classroom, instructional theory and methodology, and courses across the disciplines. Typically one of the first activities coordinated by a new center is an orientation program for new faculty. These programs vary from short receptions to meet the administration and faculty, to full-day sessions on the philosophy of teaching, expectations of the faculty and administration, specific departmental requirements, a review of campus resources for faculty, grading policies, and so forth. A smaller number of centers offer special programs on student

240

learning styles and learning disabilities, and comments indicated that interest is growing in these areas as well as in classroom research and collaborative learning. Despite budget problems, very few centers give workshops on grant writing.

Resources that centers typically make available to faculty include individual consultation with senior faculty and the center coordinator or director. Several centers make staff available to assess instructional materials for readability and tests for reliability. About a third of the centers provide for videotaped feedback on faculty classroom performance with a follow-up private review by the teacher or in conjunction with a specialist. Larger centers with greater budget flexibility assist the administration in filling endowed chairs on teaching and learning. In addition, many centers offer mini-grants for teaching improvement, often through a competitive process. Where funding is available, stipends are provided for travel to relevant conferences, and compensation often accompanies outstanding teaching awards.

A usual core resource for a TLC with a specific location is a library, which often contains computer software, home-grown and professionally prepared audio and videotapes on teaching and learning, and printed material. A few of these libraries serve as clearinghouses for information on funding opportunities.

Respondents listed a variety of special services that are unique to various campuses but noteworthy for their originality. Included are activities ranging from retraining programs for teaching in new disciplines to loaner computers for notetaking at conferences away from campus. Some of these special programs are more important for their effort to build a sense of community among the faculty than for their immediate impact on teaching and learning. Included in this category are retreats, wellness weekends, and health and environmental awareness activities.

NEWSLETTERS

Half of the centers reported that they produced a newsletter. The major purpose of this publication is to inform the faculty audience about teaching and learning issues. High priority is given to reporting on center activities and encouraging participation. Thus it is common to find announcements about seminars, panels, individual presentations, and the like.

The means of engaging faculty interest are quite imaginative. Newsletters often feature faculty colleagues who achieve special awards, complete publications and research projects, and teach special courses. Indeed, almost anything that might capture the interest of faculty is included in center publications, including in one case the menu in the faculty dining room. The newsletter, with a wide range of articles designed to engage faculty attention, appears to be a common service offered by well-developed centers throughout the country. *Teaching and Learning: A Forum on Practice by and for Educators*, a newsletter published in fall 1990 by Massachusetts Bay Community College, featured an article on conservation with recycling ideas and money-saving practices. The September 1989 issue of *Update*, the newsletter of the Center for Teaching Excellence at County College of Morris, New Jersey, provided a preview of activities for the coming year and an announcement of graduate courses leading to the M.Ed. and the Ed.D. to be given on campus by Rutgers University. A faculty member reported on a conference on "Student Learning Styles," and grant information is also provided. A regular feature of this newsletter is an abstract of a faculty member's research.

EVALUATION

Virtually every center claims to evaluate its program's effectiveness in some way. A few study their programs annually, but most evaluate as the need arises or at the time of various separate events, programs, or projects. In the latter case the typical approach is to record faculty use and satisfaction by survey forms. Only a quarter of the centers try to assess student satisfaction with classroom innovations that result from faculty using their services or the impact on student learning that may result from such projects. In these cases, center staff may conduct interviews with students to evaluate effects and share the results confidentially with faculty. The outcomes may also be used as feedback for improving center programs. Some centers also provide model student-evaluation forms that teachers can use for their own classroom surveys and to provide information back to the TLC about the effectiveness of certain techniques that have been tried in the classroom.

But program evaluation is conducted largely through survey instruments filled out by faculty who participate in TLC activities. For the majority of centers it appears that sophistication in program evaluation has not progressed very far beyond this approach. While the results of these faculty satisfaction surveys may provide some important information for program planners, administrators, and others, it seems clear that more rigorous program assessment of TLCs' impact on student learning and satisfaction may be required in this period of budget constraint in order to sustain ongoing campus support.

FOSTERING EXCITEMENT FOR TEACHING

The critical goal in the mission of TLCs is to capture the interest and gain the involvement of faculty in the process of strengthening instruction and student academic achievement. Undoubtedly this can be achieved in many ways. Whether a center is established to lead this effort depends on many factors. Each community college campus has its own unique characteristics and attitudes. A campus with an active and involved faculty and a well-functioning committee structure may find that a more decentralized approach will more effectively accomplish the task. Evidence in this survey indicates that a newer campus with an immature faculty committee system will often establish a TLC to assure primacy for the teaching and learning mission. Older campuses with a governing style that is traditionally top-down may expect any initiative for faculty development to come from the president's office, perhaps through a variety of unconnected projects such as grants, stipends, and outstanding teaching awards.

The proliferation of TLCs for the faculty in the 1980s was not unlike the movement in the 1970s to establish college learning centers that provide academic support for students. But "treating" the students alone is not enough. Colleges, then as now, are faced with high expectations from the public and state legislatures. It is assumed they will accomplish their mission of providing access as well as success for growing numbers of underprepared and culturally diverse students by offering good teaching. It follows that many campuses are now searching for new ways to educate, support, and encourage faculty in this important area.

Growing numbers of community college campuses are finding that concentrating and intensifying faculty development activities through the formation of TLCs can be an efficient and effective way to take advantage of new opportunities offered by advances in understanding different learning styles and innovations in educational theory, practice, and educational technology. This effort is too important to be left to happen sporadically and by chance with a few motivated faculty hidden in the corners of various departments and programs. It must come to characterize the practice of an entire campus.

Whether a teaching and learning center plays a role during the establishment of a new community college campus, at a later date to better organize faculty development activities, or as a stimulus to mobilize and involve uninterested faculty, the ultimate goal of the whole enterprise is to foster a sense of excitement and opportunity about the possibilities of teaching and learning for faculty as well as students. There is no better guarantee of success in educating a new and diverse community college student population as this century draws to a close.

Kurt Lauridsen is assistant to the vice chancellor for undergraduate affairs, University of California at Berkeley.

Chapter 13

The Miami-Dade Community College Teaching/Learning Project

BY MARDEE JENRETTE AND VINCE NAPOLI

T he Teaching/Learning Project at Miami-Dade Community College, Florida, is the manifestation of one college's commitment to fully examine its practices, undertake fundamental reform, and utilize all necessary resources in addressing issues of teaching and learning. The project was initiated in 1986 to address a set of problems that were about to have substantial impact on the institution. While specific solutions were, by necessity, designed to respond to the needs of Miami-Dade, other community colleges should find elements applicable and appropriate to their own settings. Additionally, the processes to resolve issues and build support for recommendations are transportable, along with many of the outcomes themselves. A description of the program should thus be valuable to institutions with similar concerns.

An understanding of the Teaching/Learning Project can be gained though a review of its origin, goals, progress, and significant products.

BACKGROUND CONDITIONS

The major issues confronting higher education in 1986, when the idea for the Teaching/Learning Project was just forming, still exist today. First, like many institutions, Miami-Dade was projecting large numbers of faculty retirements in the 1990s. The college had many excellent faculty members, a significant percentage of whom joined Miami-Dade in the 1960s and spent virtually their entire careers in its classrooms. How would the college find, attract, and retain high-caliber personnel to continue the good work accomplished by retiring faculty? How would the institution's mission and values be communicated to them? Would it be possible to preserve the strengths, skills, and expertise of outgoing veterans? Could these qualities be shared with new faculty to help them meet the needs of Miami-Dade students better than might ordinarily be expected of novices?

The second issue related to the implications of diversity and the entry of a new type of student into higher education, a student who was predicted to redefine the phrase "traditional student" for the twenty-first century. By 1986 the college's White Anglo majority population had already been supplanted by a wave of Cuban and other Latin American refugees. Its classrooms were being further enriched by a large African American population. More foreign students were selecting Miami-Dade than any other college or university in the United States, and over 50 percent of Miami-Dade students were reporting English as their second language. Would the learning environment thus need to be reexamined to ensure that these students received a quality education?

A third factor of great importance to Miami-Dade was the growing volume of information on adult learning, learning styles, and cultural influences on learning preferences. Were there implications for the particular ways Miami-Dade instructors teach so that their students can learn? How could the research on teaching be actively connected to teachers? With educational technology available at increasingly affordable prices, could technology become an effective component of the Miami-Dade teaching/learning process?

In March 1986 Miami-Dade President Robert McCabe returned from an American Association for Higher Education national conference, at which he heard K. Patricia Cross speak about her concept of classroom research. The presentation made a deep impression and crystallized for McCabe a method of integrating the issues of teacher retirement, nontraditional students, technology, and research on teaching and learning. Cross suggested that college-level teaching and learning would be enhanced if teachers were trained to conduct systematic classroom research on the effects of their teaching. By reflecting on the data collected through classroom research, teachers could make appropriate adjustments in strategies and techniques so that student learning would improve. McCabe recognized that having teachers actively engaged in assessing their own work and the work of their students is a way to begin a dialogue to improve college teaching and learning. Once the dialogue began, many other doors would open. On the flight home, McCabe began to formulate plans for what would become Miami-Dade's Teaching/Learning Project.

THE GOALS OF THE MIAMI-DADE PROJECT

An effort with the planned magnitude of the Teaching/Learning Project is not entered into lightly, nor is the commitment made in a single step. The decision to embark evolved through a series of realizations:

- The issues facing Miami-Dade were making "business as usual" no longer a viable college option. If the indicators were correct and the twenty-first century was to be radically different from the current one, then making minor modifications to existing practices would be totally inadequate.
- While the teaching/learning relationship reaches fruition in the classroom, support for teaching and learning is an institutionwide responsibility. What happens in Miami-Dade classrooms would clearly have to be a major focus of the

247

planned project; however, the entire institution would also have to subject itself to scrutiny.

- Those who do the work of teaching and learning, and thus possess the most relevant knowledge and expertise, have a right to be involved in determining what changes will be made. They also have a responsibility to become involved in the change process.

- Most important: A basic part of the college's culture is a strong and pervasive institutional belief that whatever has to be done can be accomplished at Miami-Dade.

Three goals were conceived for the project. They were interrelated and addressed the issues of fundamental importance to the college. The first and in many respects overarching goal was to improve teaching and learning. Achieving this would require the college to focus on the increasing numbers and needs of nontraditional students. It would also help Miami-Dade do what every educational institution must—provide students with a high-quality education.

A second goal was to make teaching at the college a professionally rewarding career. Achieving this goal would help address the issue of replacing retirees with high-caliber personnel who, like their predecessors, would choose to remain at Miami-Dade for significant portions of their careers. To achieve this it was clear that performance standards would have to be high in order to challenge faculty and enable them to take pride in their accomplishments. Valued performance and achievement would have to be recognized and rewarded, and these rewards would have to be substantial and meaningful to faculty.

The third goal was to make teaching and learning the focal point of Miami-Dade's activities and decision-making processes. When allocating scarce resources, for example, college personnel would be obligated to first consider the question, "What impact will this decision have on teaching and learning?" This goal ensured that the project's arena for action would extend beyond the classroom and sent the message that establishing and maintaining a sound environment in which teaching and learning can flourish is the responsibility of each member of the faculty and staff.

PROGRESS AND PRODUCTS OF THE
TEACHING/LEARNING PROJECT

While it is difficult to pinpoint an actual starting place, the project began with a series of activities designed to allow members of the institution to catch up with McCabe's ideas on teaching and learning, i.e., to understand his rationale for the need to make changes; to measure their own ideas against his; and to extend his concept and add flesh to his skeletal proposal. This catch-up period extended for several months during the summer and early fall of 1986, while McCabe solicited reactions to his proposal and used them to enhance and modify his original concept.

In late fall, a day-long "conversation" on teaching and learning proved pivotal in establishing the scope of the project and ensuring participation by institutional personnel. Participants included thirty administrative and faculty leaders and five invited guests from outside the college. The day began with a single question posed to the group: "What should we do to improve teaching and learning at this institution?" As might be expected, initial responses to this question focused heavily on faculty, students, and their interactions in the classroom.

However, anyone who thought that only teachers would feel the impact of the proposed project had the idea quickly dispelled after an observation by one of the campus presidents. He related several recent encounters with faculty in which they decried the physical conditions of their classrooms: burned-out light bulbs that went unreplaced; broken chairs that sat for months in the corners of rooms; no chalk for the boards. "I wonder what message that sends to teachers and their students about the importance of teaching and learning to this college?" they challenged him. That painful illustration opened the discussion to examine the vital role administrators and all support services play in creating an environment conducive to effective teaching and learning. That the project would be more complex, more comprehensive, more time- and energy-consuming, and more expensive than McCabe originally anticipated was becoming clear. It was also even clearer how critically important it was to take on the project.

By the end of 1986, a full-time project director and a twenty-two-member collegewide steering committee of faculty and administrators were appointed. McCabe pledged that time would be given to do the job well and set aside a liberal budget for development. The project was officially under way. An early challenge for the steering committee was determining how to manage the direction and activities of such a monumental endeavor, one that could legitimately address all aspects of the institution. At its first series of meetings in 1987, the committee agreed on four conceptual areas to begin the work of the project: institutional values, faculty excellence, the teaching/learning environment, and new faculty. It further determined that the work would be carried out by subcommittees, each created as needed and commissioned to focus on a single issue. Subcommittee membership would consist of faculty and administrators and would include others outside of the steering committee to broaden the opportunity for direct involvement of additional personnel.

The first area to be addressed was that of institutional values related to teaching and learning. It was particularly important because a clear delineation of the college's values would serve as a basic foundation for the whole project. Since its work was so significant to all that would come later, the Teaching/Learning Values Subcommittee immediately began an intensive review of college-produced documents, self-studies, and material written about Miami-Dade. From this survey it derived implicit values, then made them explicit through a survey sent to all college personnel and a sampling of students and community members. Several cycles of activity followed, including refining data, obtaining additional input, and providing additional feedback.

By December 1987 a set of seven institutional values related to teaching and learning was agreed upon. Accompanying each value was a series of statements designed to illustrate how the college makes that value operational. This values document then became part of the bedrock of the entire project. It provided not only a sense of direction, but also a sense of boundaries, an essential context within which ideas and actions would be debated by all working subcommittees.

The second conceptual area, that of faculty excellence, would also provide part of the base for the rest of the project. In order to move toward fostering and rewarding excellence, a common understanding of the term would be required. Therefore, the goal was to identify a set of qualities and characteristic behaviors that constitute excellence in Miami-Dade faculty in their service to students. Criteria could then be derived to assess prospective faculty, to review the ongoing performance of faculty, and to make decisions about tenure and promotion.

The Faculty Excellence Subcommittee began with current research on principles of learning, then extrapolated a set of indicators of good teaching. Turning its findings into a survey format, the subcommittee used a process of incorporating continual feedback from small groups of colleagues and responses to mailed surveys to revise and refine its work. The resultant twenty-nine-item "Statement of Faculty Excellence," first published in 1988, reflects contributions from faculty, administrators, and students and meshes with the institutional values. It provides the reader an understanding of excellence as it applies to Miami-Dade faculty. So successful was the "Statement of Faculty Excellence" as a basis for institutional agreements that processes to develop similar statements of excellence for support staff personnel, administrators, and department chairpersons were initiated. When all are completed and adopted by the District Board of Trustees, Miami-Dade will have vivid and distinct conceptions of the qualities it values in employees throughout the organization, as defined by the employees themselves. Further, those qualities will all flow from a focus on teaching and learning, and thus will provide a unifying mandate for the separate constituencies of the college.

The third conceptual area chosen for early development was the teaching/learning environment. While highly skilled teachers and willing learners are required for excellent teaching and learning, so are high-quality support services. The physical plant must be properly maintained; appropriate supplies, together with equipment that is in good working condition, must be readily available; and audiovisual, clerical, and custodial services must be efficiently rendered. In short the commitment to excellence must be shared by all personnel whose efforts support the teaching/learning process, even in the most indirect way.

The Teaching/Learning Environment Subcommittee recommended processes to ensure that support of the teaching/learning relationship would become part of the operational practice of all service areas. It suggested that user feedback be solicited; that faculty be regularly invited to interact with service providers; that annual objectives be established and include recognition of each area's importance to the college's teaching/learning mission; and that items relating to those objectives be included in the annual performance reviews of all service area personnel.

Although the subcommittee completed its work in 1988, the implementation of its recommendations was neither immediate nor uniform in service areas across the college. Areas directly serving the classroom found it easiest to scrutinize their practices vis-a-vis teaching and learning. The bookstores, libraries, and audiovisual services fall into this category. As contrasting examples, the purchasing, budget, and personnel offices, while just as vital, are further removed and therefore had to understand more clearly their relationship to the teaching/learning process before they could respond.

The remaining initial conceptual area focused on new faculty. Principles and practices for recruiting, hiring, and enculturating new faculty were reviewed, and many fruitful discussions emerged as the New Faculty Subcommittee tackled its charge. Groups were convened to discuss and identify the needs of new faculty, as well as the needs of the institution relative to new hires. Recent hires and twenty-year veterans shared their diverse perspectives as they responded to questions such as, "What did Miami-Dade do that was especially helpful as you began your career here? What would have been helpful that was not done?"

The subcommittee recommended that the new values document and the "Statement of Faculty Excellence" be used as recruitment tools. Taken together they would inform prospective applicants about the sort of institution Miami-Dade is and what would be expected of them as employees. After all, just as an institution selects a candidate, so should a candidate carefully measure an institution. These documents would provide ample data to help applicants decide whether to go forward. The subcommittee further recommended that screening committees use the documents to design an interview protocol to elicit information about those critical aspects of the faculty role that a transcript cannot provide. In other words, a strategy was designed to focus on the central questions of does the applicant know the subject, and will he or she be able to effectively teach it to Miami-Dade students?

For a new hire, there are many facets to becoming an effective Miami-Dade faculty member. One of the more helpful creations has been a preservice new faculty orientation program. New faculty report one week before veteran faculty in the fall and are introduced to district and campus operations through workshops, presentations, and meetings. They are given separate contracts, including pay, to cover this preservice period. Follow-up orientation activities continue throughout the faculty members' first year on campus.

A second phase of orientation for new faculty consists of a mentoring program. The program is designed to improve and accelerate the process by which new faculty become knowledgeable about the college, effective in their positions, and comfortable as members of the faculty. Each new hire is paired with a veteran faculty member; mentor and neophyte meet regularly for a year, refining the scope of their relationship as needs emerge.

POLICIES AND PRACTICES FOR FACULTY ADVANCEMENT

As developmental work with the four initial areas was completed, second-tier issues took their place. Once teaching/learning values and the "Statement of Faculty Excellence" were adopted as official college documents, logic dictated a review of existing personnel policies related to faculty. College policies and procedures had to encourage faculty development and reward those whose performance reflects excellence as defined by the values and excellence statement. The comprehensive set of policies and procedures eventually adopted became known as "Faculty Advancement"; it encompasses the annual performance review and the awarding of tenure, promotions, and endowed chairs to faculty members. The system governed by these policies and procedures rests upon three philosophical principles:

- The system should be supportive and developmental in nature. Continuous monitoring of performance provides ongoing opportunity for reinforcement of positive efforts. It also encourages prescriptive intervention long before negative personnel action would normally be taken in cases where performance is below acceptable standards.
- Important personnel decisions should be based on information obtained systematically and from multiple sources. Supervisors, students, and faculty members are in the position to make valuable commentary on faculty advancement decisions. Commentary from peers and other sources will often be relevant as well.
- Individual faculty members should be responsible for their own advancement. Whether seeking tenure, promotion, or an endowed chair, an individual should provide evidence of professional growth and accomplishments. The teaching/ learning values and the "Statement of Faculty Excellence" provide all individuals in the decision-making process with a common standard from which criteria can be drawn.

As these principles emerged, it became evident that the college would require a greatly expanded staff and program development function. Centers for teaching and learning were established on the four large campuses, each with a full-time director, support staff personnel, and a substantial budget. The Support for Faculty Subcommittee was created to review the work of previous subcommittees and to make recommendations regarding the role and program focus of the new centers. Along with more traditional activities (such as funding travel to professional conferences and providing workshops and mini-grants to faculty to help update subject area knowledge and enhance teaching skills), the subcommittee recommended implementation of the following: a technical component to the centers with computer hardware and software, and instructional personnel to help faculty use technology to improve their teaching; program elements for all personnel, including staff, administrators, and faculty, since supporting teaching and learning is everyone's responsibility; and a common, collegewide core of workshops and consultations to assist appropriate personnel in accessing Faculty Advancement.

The project subcommittees, in collaboration with faculty from the University of Miami, developed two graduate-level courses. "Assessing Learning in the Community College" teaches the collection and effective use of data obtained through classroom feedback and research techniques. "Effective Teaching and Learning in the Community College" explores, among other topics, the impact of learning style and cultural background on student academic performance and the teaching of critical thinking skills, and the course helps faculty broaden their repertoire of teaching strategies. Under the tenure policy of the Faculty Advancement system, both courses are required of new full-time faculty as a condition of continuing employment. They are also made available to all other faculty as elective, developmental learning experiences. Since individuals take these courses while they are teaching, they have ongoing laboratories for experimentation, as well as help and encouragement from supportive peers who are their fellow students. The college pays the cost of tuition, and the University of Miami accepts course credits as part of a doctoral program. It is the responsibility of the teaching/learning centers to enroll faculty and schedule course sections.

In addition, the centers facilitate continuation of the dialogue between new and veteran faculty that begins in the classroom. Lead faculty hold periodic "brown bag" get-togethers, informal meetings in which faculty can share their efforts to enhance student learning. Some centers publish newsletters and sponsor sessions, which permit sharing of selected strategies with a larger faculty audience.

Other integral components of the new Faculty Advancement policies and procedures include the documentation of professional growth and development and the attainment of standards for tenure and promotion through a performance portfolio. It is the responsibility of the teaching/learning centers to train and assist faculty in portfolio construction and train tenure and promotion committees in the evaluation of portfolios against established standards and according to published criteria.

The Endowed Chair Program is considered by many to be the capstone of Faculty Advancement. As the Teaching/Learning Project began, McCabe instructed the Miami-Dade Community College Foundation to raise an endowment large enough to support 100 teaching chairs. By 1993 more than seventy chairs had been endowed. Unlike chairs in a traditional university setting, these would be awarded to full-time faculty who had become outstanding in their service to Miami-Dade students in Miami-Dade classrooms. Criteria for awarding endowed chairs were derived from the "Statement of Faculty Excellence." Faculty who wish to be considered for a chair must present a performance portfolio to the Endowed Chair Committee for evaluation. Help in preparing an endowed chair portfolio is available to faculty through each campus Center for Teaching and Learning.

In spring 1992 the first twenty-five chairs were awarded, consistent with the plan to award approximately one-third of the total each year. Endowed chair committees on each campus accepted portfolios from their peers and determined eligibility based on criteria drawn from the "Statement of Faculty Excellence" and evidence of substantive involvement in and contributions made to the discipline or to teaching and learning. A single collegewide committee received those portfolios deemed by the campus committees to be of chair quality and awarded discipline-restricted, campus-restricted, and collegewide chairs after ranking the finalists. At the end of three years, each chair reopens. The current chair holder may again apply and will be evaluated anew along with colleagues applying for the first time.

Beyond high honor, the perks of an endowed chair holder are considerable. Each recipient receives an annual salary supplement of $5,000 and $2,500 to spend on professional-related expenses.

An additional component of Faculty Advancement with implications for teaching/learning centers is a collegewide student feedback program, currently in pilot phase. At the three-quarters point of each major semester, students are invited to give feedback to their teachers via an instrument based on those qualities from the "Statement of Faculty Excellence" that students are in a position to judge. Faculty use feedback data in their portfolios as one source of evidence that they have met required criteria. Chairpersons discuss feedback with faculty as part of the annual performance review. Faculty may consult with the director of their teaching/learning center as they discover skill areas they wish to develop.

The new Faculty Advancement system constitutes a radical departure from business as usual, and thus it became evident that it would need to be monitored and periodically reviewed for effectiveness. The Faculty Advancement Committee recommended the creation of a standing Monitoring and Review Committee composed of faculty and administrators. Its charge would be to ensure consistent and equitable application of Faculty Advancement policies and procedures by overseeing their application and reporting findings annually to appropriate bodies within the college's governance structure. It would also review the effectiveness of Faculty Advancement procedures and, once every three years, make recommendations for changes to those procedures. Hence a built-in self-correcting mechanism for Faculty Advancement procedures will tend to institutionalize change and extend indefinitely the positive effects of the project.

Faculty Advancement, as a concept, has turned out to be such a viable and potentially powerful tool to improve teaching and learning and recognize professional activities of faculty that it is being adapted for all college personnel. A performance review program including feedback from faculty has been piloted for chairpersons and administrators, and a reward system built on excellence is on the drawing board for administrators and support staff. The Support Staff Advancement Subcommittee and the Administrator Advancement Subcommittee have adopted the same philosophical principles that guide faculty advancement: there should be a supportive, developmental system; important personnel decisions should be based on information obtained systematically from multiple sources; and individuals should be responsible for their own advancement.

As the work on Faculty Advancement unfolded, the special needs of nonclassroom faculty (counselors and librarians) and adjunct faculty became clear. The extra responsibilities thrust on department chairpersons, and the pressure on them to become faculty coaches and developers rather than evaluators, caused concern and prompted the commission of the Department Chairperson Compensation/Support Committee. Join these new subcommittees with those already in operation, and it is clear why President McCabe began to refer to the Teaching/Learning Project as "The Project that Ate Miami-Dade."

PROJECT IMPACT

What began as an idea to focus on classroom teaching and learning has evolved into a project that affects all college personnel, including full-time and adjunct classroom faculty, nonclassroom faculty, staff and administrators, and students. The project also affects all college operations, from budgeting to plant maintenance and construction. It represents a completely new way for Miami-Dade to do business and, as such, is certainly the most far-reaching and important set of reforms ever undertaken by the college.

While individuals must often struggle to redefine their personal roles in an institution making major changes, collateral benefits may emerge. At Miami-Dade, bonds are being formed among colleagues who previously thought their roles and responsibilities were very different. A focus on teaching and learning offers a common topic of discussion. While not yet widespread at this writing, faculty, staff, and administrators can be found discussing the college's teaching/learning mission instead of their working conditions. Also becoming apparent is a developing climate of revitalization, a sense of shared purpose in an important endeavor. Even those individuals furthest removed from the happenings in the classroom are able to take pride in the accomplishments of students, a perk usually reserved for faculty and an occasional administrator.

Mardee Jenrette is director, Teaching/Learning Project, Miami-Dade Community College District, Florida. Vince Napoli is chairperson, sociology, anthropology, and social science, Miami-Dade Community College-Kendall Campus.

PART THREE:

The Outcomes

Chapter 14

Measuring Teaching Effectiveness

By Richard L. Alfred

Powerful forces inside and outside of community colleges are changing the art and craft of teaching. Advancing technology, increasing pressure for assessment, declining resources, changing employer needs, aging faculty, and increasing learner diversity are but a few of the factors bringing new meaning to what is "effective" and "ineffective" in teaching. Yet the more these factors loom as forces for change, the more emphasis falls on the importance of "soft arts" in teaching—motivation, interpersonal dynamics, empathy—which bring teachers and students together in learning communities. In other words, the more outside forces reshape the context for teaching, the more important nonquantifiable concepts of effectiveness seem to be. As Parker Palmer puts it, "Good teaching cannot be equated with technique. It comes from the instructor's relation to subject and students; from the capricious chemistry of it all" (1990, p. 11).

263

The art of effective teaching is captured by Whitman, Spendlove, and Clark (1986, p.5):

> In defining the relationship between teaching and learning, some question exists as to whether, in the absence of learning, "teaching" describes the professor's behaviors or actions. One can agree or disagree with the statement that "If the learner didn't learn, then the teacher didn't teach!" Those educators who agree believe that, if no learning occurred, then no teaching occurred either (Meeth, 1976). According to this view, "teaching" is analogous to "giving," and by definition, when something is given, something has been received. The teacher thus breathes a soul into the clod.
>
> Other educators disagree, believing that teaching is anything an instructor does that intentionally promotes learning, regardless of whether learning actually occurred (Donald and Shore, 1977). According to this view, "teaching" is analogous to "offering." When something is offered, it may or may not be received. In this case, the teacher sows seeds that sometimes fall on fertile soil, sometimes on barren soil.
>
> Both views are valuable. On one hand, it is helpful to use students' achievement as a measure of teaching because what students learn is the basic criterion of educational effectiveness (Biddle, 1964; O'Hanlon and Mortensen, 1977). In fact, when only the process of teaching is used as a measure of teaching, only half the educational process has been evaluated (Mark, 1977).

On reflection, this paradox isn't so surprising. Teachers understand the capriciousness of individual learning needs and styles among students, the effects of different teaching methods, and the inability of any objective measure to accurately reflect effective teaching. But the world that most instructors currently inhabit is rapidly changing—reshaped by advancing technology and changing customer needs. Not so long ago instructors were the agents of what was taught and how it was taught. But that was before microcomputers and employers competing in global markets arrived on the scene. Yesterday's instructional manager is today's nonadaptive teacher, and community colleges face the painful task of measuring teaching effectiveness in a radically changed competitive environment.

ELEMENTS OF EFFECTIVE TEACHING

At the center of any effort to measure teaching effectiveness is the assumption that performing in the classroom—like assembling automobile engines, repairing computers, and writing book chapters—is a highly definable process that can be measured by identifying and analyzing performance characteristics. This premise translates into several elements that must be present to determine whether teaching is effective: knowledge of student needs and expectations; evidence of student growth and development; satisfaction ratings of "external and internal customers" (employers and college instructors); student feedback; insights into organizational culture; and rewards associated with teaching. Effective teaching reflects the interaction of these elements, with each contributing a unique set of measures for making judgments about teaching.

The first element, *knowledge of student needs and expectations*, can be combined with student outcomes to evaluate the value-addedness of teaching. Student needs and expectations contribute to effective teaching by setting parameters for instructor effort—what a teacher must do to help students achieve important goals. As such they are the driving force of the entire effectiveness measurement process. In this respect effectiveness follows from student needs. The outcomes of teaching, expressed in measures of student achievement and affective and cognitive skill development, are only tools for determining the extent to which teaching has met, fallen short of, or exceeded student needs.

If student needs and expectations are the foundation for measuring teaching effectiveness, then facilitating and constraining aspects of the *organizational culture* define the opportunities for effective teaching. Any instructor's goals for teaching are profoundly shaped by the organizational climate for realizing them. For example, while the student population and instructional staff

265

at any two community colleges may be matched on important characteristics, their organizational cultures may be entirely different, one facilitating and the other constraining faculty teaching performance. A key to maintaining faculty productivity is maintaining morale. Organizational cultures that promote high morale have identifiable features such as a sensitive, sympathetic administration, responsiveness to faculty needs, and a capacity to engender instructors' feelings of autonomy and control over their work. Additionally these cultures encourage peer support and stimulation from colleagues as essential to a sense of well-being (Baldwin and Krotseng, 1985). Rewards and values are clearly linked, so that if improvement in teaching is desired, its achievement is rewarded (Altschuler and Richter, 1985).

At campuses where the organizational culture promotes involvement, innovation and experimentation are the name of the game for instructors. They experience feelings of security, ownership, and pride in the curriculum, and they take responsibility for the results of teaching.

When student needs and expectations combine with an organizational culture that promotes innovation in teaching, the result is often *satisfied customers*. As the third key element associated with effective teaching, satisfaction is the subjective evidence that instructors and administrators have concerning the effects of teaching. The feelings of satisfaction or dissatisfaction that internal and external customers have with instruction are an important and not easily understood dimension of effective teaching. Different groups carry different expectations for the outcomes of teaching. Instructors look for evidence of learning and skill acquisition through tests, demonstrations, and written work. Employers look for work habits and technical skills that get the job done; elected officials and accrediting agencies look for added value in the form of degrees and learning outcomes that can be readily quantified using conventional measures. This diversity of expectations can lead to difficulty in assessing teaching effectiveness when instructors try to develop coherent goals for teaching outcomes.

Although it is possible to measure teaching effectiveness without evidence of student outcomes, few would want to do it. Evidence of *student growth and development* is the collateral by which teaching effectiveness is measured. To understand the role that outcomes play in effectiveness assessment, we need only ask the question, "What changes or effects is teaching supposed to produce in students in both the short term and the long term?" The obvious answer is, "Make sure that desired knowledge or skills are obtained." This answer is correct but simplistic. When we talk about the outcomes of teaching, we are referring to three distinct things. The first is objective information about knowledge and skill development—cognitive skills, content knowledge, and technical proficiency. The second is feedback or information that can be used to determine the extent to which student goals are attained. Finally, there is information about the extent to which the outcomes of teaching satisfy or fail to satisfy important groups.

MEASUREMENT DYNAMICS

In coming to understand the dynamics of effective teaching and how it can be measured, it is useful to consider measurement approaches in the framework discussed above. These elements compose the dynamics of an integrated approach for measuring teaching effectiveness, one that builds on but enlarges other approaches, one that can point out problems and guide new approaches. Student needs and expectations, organizational culture, customer satisfaction, and student outcomes have the potential to explain much of what happens in community college teaching. They represent a link between the overall organizational context—not just a class, or students, or the instructor, but the overarching culture of the institution—and the outcomes of teaching.

Student Needs and Expectations

Needs and expectations impel students into classes to serve particular ends. The structure of needs—of goals and expectations—is determined by such matters as educational and career goals, academic background and aptitudes, external supports for education, access to resources, and each student's motivation relative to other students. On the basis of current approaches to assessment, we can propose that community colleges need to know the following about student needs, circumstances, and expectations to assess teaching effectiveness:

- Short- and long-term educational goals
- Career goals, both immediate and long-range
- Needs and characteristics that facilitate or impede learning
  - Cognitive and learning styles
  - Study skills
  - Basic skill proficiencies
  - External supports for education in home and work
  - Personal interest in courses, curricula, and college study
- Self-esteem and confidence in academic abilities
- Motivation to succeed in academic work
- Time and resources for college study
- Student needs for general education competencies
- Technical skill needs (for job entry and advancement)

There is a remarkable consistency among and within community colleges in the information they collect from students. They routinely gather data about educational and career goals, basic skills proficiency, and prior educational achievement (Alfred, Peterson, and White, 1992). However, they do not gather information describing characteristics that facilitate or impede learning beyond those related to educational and career goals. For example, they know little about the academic and social preparation of students for college, their needs for support services, and the nature of external supports for learning (financial assets, family support, work environment, etc.). Easy access is most important. Anything that complicates or obstructs enrollment in programs and courses is avoided. The idea is to make access as efficient as possible, and efficiency is best served by collecting only the most essential information.

In general, community colleges are locked into an outdated methodology of identifying and serving student needs. Instructors and advisers wait for students to come in for appointments. The students say, "I have this problem or need," and the staff member provides the service. Students are in a hurry to leave campus for work and other obligations. Staff, feeling the pressure of their own work day, hurry to deliver needed services. Little if any time is spent helping students plan their academic careers or cope with the academic demands of college (Alfred, Peterson, and White, 1992, p. 15).

This methodology of "waiting," or lack of effort in gathering information, poses a major obstacle for measuring teaching effectiveness. It removes from consideration information about student needs that could serve as a benchmark for value-added assessment in courses and curricula. Further, it may communicate a passive and uncaring environment for learning, which colors students' perceptions of the quality of their education. Students will likely be impressed by an institution that develops and maintains a comprehensive information system about their needs, expectations, and goals and can use this information to modify courses, services, and teaching techniques. Conversely, a less aggressive system may be perceived by students to be related to the interest of instructors in teaching, and this negative association may impact motivation and performance.

Organizational Culture

Organizational culture refers to the unique patterns of practice, behaviors, and expressions that influence how students and teachers interact. The effect of organizational culture on teaching is determined by formal policies and procedures and by informal practices. Factors that colleges need to consider about organizational culture in measuring teaching effectiveness are

- Faculty and administrative roles in strategic decisions concerning programs, courses, and curricula
- Faculty involvement in governance
- Provisions and rewards for faculty involvement in planning and evaluation
- Resources and institutional policies supporting professional development
- Administrative policies governing faculty workload

269

- Resources available for instructional innovation
- Collegial relationships among faculty and administrators that support instructional innovation
- Faculty satisfaction with work and commitment to the institution

Regardless of the make-up of a college and its faculty, staff, and students, culture plays an important role in teaching. How basic beliefs and values are enacted in making decisions—about courses and pedagogy, in planning and evaluating curricula, and in the everyday behavior of faculty in relationships with students and administrators—affects teaching. While being uninvolved in program planning and evaluation may not affect how an instructor teaches an introductory math or technology class, it might affect teaching quality as measured by employer satisfaction with the transfer of job skills.

With the exception of an analysis of literature on organizational culture by Peterson et al. (1986), there has been little in the way of systematic research on organizational culture and its effect on teaching. The research that is available shows that faculty satisfaction and identification with their institution is critical to the climate and culture of an institution and also impacts student outcomes through the quality and quantity of teaching undertaken (Cameron, 1982). The observed outcomes of a contented faculty are improvement in teaching, higher morale, greater commitment and involvement, and greater acceptance of developmental and evaluative efforts (Peterson et al., 1986).

The opposite case, that of faculty dissatisfaction, can lead to increased student attrition, negative performance outcomes, and negative student perceptions of teaching quality. Instructors bring more to teacher-student relationship than knowledge; they bring an awareness that teaching is basically a delicate transaction requiring skill and sensitivity in human relations (Bradford, 1958). Furthermore, the relationships between instructors and learners are precarious because of the anxieties of the learner, the threat of the instructor as a judge and expert, and mixed feelings about the values and motives of the instructor. Instructors who are not

270

meaningfully connected to the institution through its culture cannot be expected to bring enthusiasm to the craft of teaching.

Customer Satisfaction

This element refers to the feelings of satisfaction or dissatisfaction that internal and external customers have with teaching. Satisfaction ratings, in the form of student evaluation of instructors, encompass the vast majority of efforts to measure teaching effectiveness in community colleges. The literature is replete with references to the need for and characteristics of comprehensive faculty evaluation systems (Aleamoni, 1980; Ratcliff, 1984; Andrews, 1985; Boggs, 1984; and Andrews and Licata, 1989). Descriptive summaries of existing programs for faculty evaluation are also abundant, including discussion of faculty behaviors and roles that should be evaluated, process considerations, and techniques for improving teaching (Saunders, 1981; Walker, 1982; Kocher and Houston, 1983; Romanik, 1986; Tobias, 1986; Johnson, 1988; Eggers, 1990; Altieri, 1991; and Olp et al., 1991). Figure 1 presents a capsule summary of the key elements of faculty evaluation systems on community college campuses. The emphasis is on roles, activities, and sources of information that can be used to determine internal customers' satisfaction with teaching.

An extensive literature exists on what makes good teachers, focusing on their characteristics, their behaviors in the classroom, and the effects they have on their students. This literature points to three groups as being currently involved in defining good teachers: students, who as research demonstrates are capable of describing the characteristics and behaviors of good teachers; external judges assessing student outcomes as the measure of educational effectiveness; and educational researchers, who through their counting, observing, experimenting, and surveying attempt to provide generalizable definitions and criteria for teaching effectiveness. According to Cross (1986), the literature on criteria for instructional evaluation is deficient in several areas, lacking good discussion of what teachers are trying to accomplish, a constructive approach to applying research to the improvement of

---

FIGURE 1
Key Elements of Faculty Evaluation in Community Colleges

Instructor Roles and Responsibilities	Activities	Sources of Information
Classroom instruction	• Knowledge of subject area • Teaching methods • Course content • Classroom management • Instructional materials • Instructional delivery	Student evaluations Peer evaluations Self-evaluation and documentation
Student advising and counseling	• Academic advising • Special counseling activities	Supervisor observations and assessment
Professional activities in subject field	• Curriculum and course development • Publications • Grant activity	Mutual goal setting Student grade distributions
Service to college	• Involvement in institutional service • Task force and committee work • Special assignments	Attrition statistics Employer satisfaction studies
Professional development	• Self-instruction programs • Participation in professional organizations • Formal coursework • Attendance at seminars, conferences, and workshops • In-service training • Travel	Artifact collections Student performance in sequential courses and standardized examinations
Community and public service	• Creative exhibits or performances • Civic activities	Evaluation conferences

practice, or a body of information on how to conduct classroom research. The most useful approach to filling these gaps in the literature while improving undergraduate instruction involves teachers doing research in their own classrooms and learning laboratories to evaluate their effectiveness while fostering intellectual stimulation and professional renewal (Cross, 1986). Examples of possible classroom research projects include investigations of the dropout problem; whether review sessions before exams promote long-term retention; or whether particular teaching methods are effective. While these kinds of projects do not generally call for complicated research methods, they should use acceptable standards of research practice if they are to have value in improving classroom teaching.

Research on internal customer satisfaction points to a number of faculty characteristics important in effective teaching (Watkins, 1981; Richards, 1982; Cross, 1986; and Smick and Crunkilton, 1989). Faculty viewed as effective teachers are enthusiastic about their work, set challenging individual and collective performance goals for themselves and their students, are committed to education as a profession, project a positive attitude about students' ability to learn, and display ethical professional behavior. In terms of their interpersonal skills, excellent faculty treat all individuals with respect, appreciate diverse talents, work collaboratively with colleagues, are available to students and listen attentively to what they say, are responsive to student needs, are fair in their evaluation of student progress, present ideas clearly, and create a climate conducive to learning. These faculty are knowledgeable about their profession, their disciplines, and their learning processes; they integrate current subject matter into their work, respect diverse views, and are well-prepared and well-organized. And with respect to applying their knowledge, excellent faculty provide students with alternative ways of learning, stimulate intellectual curiosity, encourage independent thinking and analytical listening, provide cooperative learning opportunities, give prompt and constructive feedback, attend to feedback from students and others, and provide clear and substantial evidence that students have learned.

273

Student Outcomes

Student outcomes are the material evidence of effective teaching. Through demonstrated associations between teaching methods and student growth and development, correlates of effective teaching can be identified. Feedback loops in the form of faculty evaluation, follow-up studies, and student performance in sequential courses connect student outcomes and teaching, thereby inducing instructors to employ teaching methods that elicit favorable outcomes, which in turn produce further inducement to employ these methods. Effective teachers become more effective as they forge repeated connections between student outcomes and teaching. Outcomes information can stimulate faculty to become better teachers, or can frustrate them when marginal teaching is confirmed by student outcomes that do not meet expectations.

Community college instructors need to know the following about student outcomes in order to measure teaching effectiveness:

Outcomes During College
• Persistence/nonpersistence in courses
• GPA in courses and curricula
• Persistence in college
• Performance in sequential courses
• Change in educational or career goal

Outcomes at Exit from College
• Cognitive skill development
• General education knowledge
• Technical skill proficiency
• Completion of certificate or degree
• Length of time to degree completion
• Four-year college transfer
• Relationship of job to curriculum
• Entry salary/first job

Longer-Term Outcomes Following College
• GPA at four-year college

- Attainment of baccalaureate degree
- Job promotion and advancement
- Changes in salary
- Performance on licensing, certification, and standardized examinations

If instructors are to achieve maximum success with students through teaching, student outcomes will need to be assessed at regular intervals during and after college. Assessment will need to be carried out not only with students, the direct beneficiaries of teaching, but also with external groups such as business and industry employers, who receive secondary benefits from education.

FORCES OF INEFFECTIVENESS

As complex and demanding as the work of teaching is, we know little below the surface about forces in the work life of community college faculty that constrain effective teaching. We know a lot about faculty workload and how students see instructors, but we can only speculate how the demands inherent in the faculty role and institutional culture contribute to effectiveness and ineffectiveness in teaching. Researchers have identified several prominent features of the organizational culture in community colleges that hamper effective teaching:

- A lack of clarity and understanding concerning faculty and administrative roles
- A fragmented faculty divided along lines of gender, age, teaching area, background experience, and part-time/full-time status
- A growing frustration with a diverse student body that does not readily respond to traditional pedagogical techniques
- A lack of involvement in strategic decisions that affect programs and curricula
- An inability to move from one institution to another, or between programs in the same institution, without economic consequences

These attributes may contribute to a condition of malaise or disengagement from the work of teaching. Disengagement for community college faculty can take many forms, some of which I documented in a 1985 publication. It is worth repeating them here to illustrate how alienation manifests itself among faculty and what can be done to avert the problem or to ameliorate its deleterious effects on teaching.

Powerlessness: a feeling or belief shared by faculty that their behavior cannot determine the occurrence of specific learning outcomes or reinforcements sought with students. Faculty feel they lack the capacity to link student needs with outcomes. This condition of powerlessness is sustained through insufficient research evidence about long- and short-term student outcomes. When information documenting the outcomes of teaching is absent over an extended period of time, faculty satisfaction cannot be nurtured through the reward of positive feedback.

Meaninglessness: a low level of expectancy among instructors that meaningful predictions about future plans and resources can be made. When faculty are uncertain of resource conditions, of what they ought to believe about administrative plans for programs, or of interrelationships between resources and program decisions, minimal standards for clarity in decision making will not be met. Without information, instructors cannot choose appropriately among alternative plans for courses and curricula.

Normlessness: the expectation among faculty that institutionally unapproved behavior is required to achieve important goals. Normlessness develops when commonly held values—academic standards, collegiality, job security, etc.—are submerged in a welter of competing administrative interests. An important function of management is to provide a basis for predictability and regularity in decisions. In the absence of such predictability, faculty attention is focused on survival—a condition that may inhibit effective teaching.

Isolation: the process of detachment whereby faculty assign a low reward value to goals and beliefs that are highly valued by administrators. Some indicators of isolation are:

- Administrative value orientations that favor efficiency in decision making in contrast to faculty values, which favor input.
- Administrative interests in classroom instruction that focus on productivity and student retention in contrast to faculty interests, which focus on academic quality.

Self-estrangement: a form of alienation that concerns the degree of faculty dependence upon rewards that lie outside of teaching. The instructor who works merely for salary and job security and who assigns passing grades to students only for their effect on retention will experience self-estrangement. Self-estrangement refers to the inability of faculty to experience teaching as a self-rewarding activity that engages them. When this happens, teaching is not valued in itself, nor is learning—it is only valued in terms of the security it generates, enabling instructors to pursue other interests.

Inherent in the work of teaching are properties that promote faculty isolation and individualism (Case, 1985). Commonly, colleges deploy instructors in classrooms that may be adjacent but rarely connect in the work of teaching and learning. In the words of Case: "Over the generations of the community college, there has been little in the ethics of teaching by way of vibrant and compelling norms and values to urge teachers to initiate and maintain colleague networks or support systems conducive to the sharing of knowledge and experience. Past efforts at innovation and experiment in curriculum, instructional procedures, integrated programs, or special subunits within the college have run up against the tendencies of isolation and individualization" (1985, p. 83).

This destructive isolation is not unfamiliar to community college instructors experiencing what Palmer (1992) calls the "pain of dislocation" from students, from colleagues, from community, and from the commitment that originally brought them to the institution. Palmer explains this growing detachment in terms of a "generational rift" between instructors and students—literally a division between people of different ages, statuses, and life circumstances (1992, p. 11). For example, can an instructor with a secure job, paid-up mortgage, and guaranteed salary, working in a

277

college with constantly growing enrollments and stable resources, easily relate to a laid-off, middle-aged production worker or an 18-year-old high school graduate with marginal academic skills and zero market potential. It is almost as if the unconscious mind is at work saying: "I have a secure job and a comfortable income. I am working in an institution that is successful using every indicator of growth, and the future is likely to be secure as more and more students come through our doors. I want to relate to students, but do I really want to relate to them? We are living in two different worlds."

McGrath and Spear describe this difference as the "disarticulation of nontraditional students from the practices of academic life" (1991). Open-access colleges and their instructors experience natural barriers in making a difference in the lives of nontraditional students through teaching because they hold academic values that are culturally strange and unintelligible.

ORGANIZATIONAL ESSENTIALS FOR EFFECTIVE TEACHING

Clearly, faculty commitment and effectiveness in teaching are affected by important features of the institutions in which they work. Early in the development of community colleges, there were many innovations in teaching and many hours spent trying to tailor course content and delivery to customer preferences. Most instructors were concerned with the design of new courses or with incorporating student needs into current courses. Teaching was guided by a "performance standard" under which instructors worked closely with external and internal customers to develop course content and teaching techniques that would meet specific needs (Alfred and Linder, 1990).

As community colleges matured and curricula and instructors became older and more stable, teaching focused on efficiency and improving faculty performance, thus encouraging creative effort in workload definition and faculty evaluation. "Design standards" for instruction appeared, emphasizing process and adherence to published guidelines, and not so much to student and customer needs. To an alarming extent teaching and learning takes place in a context progressively more isolated from external markets, thereby undermining effectiveness. Look at the time spent by community college instructors with teachers and guidance counselors in high schools, with business and industry employers on the plant floor, and with professors and administrators on four-year college campuses. With the exception of recent tech-prep initiatives, the hours spent by full-time instructors with external customers in designing courses have steadily diminished since the 1960s. And now that community colleges face stiffer competition from external customers choosing to institute their own courses or turning to other providers for training, they must improve teaching to establish a new competitive advantage.

Changes in organizational culture and management that encourage innovation in teaching constitute an important undertaking for community colleges in lean times. A variety of organizational changes are essential if faculty are to renew their commitment to teaching.

1. Getting Faculty Involved with Information About Students as Customers. Provide faculty with improved student profile data at entry and exit and undertake an in-service faculty development program to familiarize them with the uses of student profile data for identifying desired learning outcomes in students. Engage faculty in systematic and ongoing student outcomes research (long and short term) as a method to demonstrate the relationship between student aptitudes, teaching strategies, and student learning outcomes. Focus the research effort on the principle of "value-addedness" in learners through exposure to different teaching and learning strategies.

2. Involving Faculty as Partners in Strategic Management. Increase faculty involvement in planning, scanning, and evaluating at the department level to encourage the development of "stakeholder values" among individual instructors. Faculty should be encouraged to participate in the development of strategic plans for academic programs, including information about trends and conditions in the external environment, program performance, competitor behavior, and customer needs and satisfaction.

3. Developing a Consistent and Relevant Reward System.
Improve the faculty reward system to ensure congruency between faculty expectations and the performance criteria used to make reward decisions. Focus faculty and administrative attention on the development of consensual goals related to teaching effectiveness: students' abilities and learning outcomes, instructional productivity measured in student enrollment and course retention rates, internal and external customer expectations, and the relationship of expectations to student outcomes.

4. Engaging Faculty in Decision Making Related to Issues and Policies that Affect Their Work Life. Increase the level of faculty involvement in decisions related to student flow through courses and curricula. Focus on consensus building among groups with different values related to the following dimensions of student flow: student mix and entry-level competencies; academic performance and progression standards; retention and graduation rates; and academic competencies at graduation.

5. Encouraging and Providing Opportunities for Faculty to Remain Abreast of Changing External Customer Needs. Maximize opportunities for faculty exposure to the changing requirements of external customers in areas such as general education knowledge, technology, and educational delivery methods.

6. Merging Values Held by Faculty and Administrators Regarding Important Dimensions of Teaching and Learning. Perform a "values audit" using small groups of faculty and administrators to identify common and differing values related to teaching and learning that can be reinforced in the reward system. Faculty need to obtain primary satisfaction from teaching. To accomplish this they need to relate teaching to outcomes valued by different groups.

The act of teaching does not by itself engender effective teaching. We need to create conditions, even inside large institutions, that empower instructors to experiment, to create, develop, and test—to innovate with teaching. Whereas short-term improvement in teaching effectiveness can be affected by assessment and incremental resources, long-term improvement requires collaboration and changes in organizational culture; that in turn means all customers connected to the enterprise of teaching. Customers working with faculty can improve teaching if the power to do this is available, and if decision makers know how to take advantage of their enterprise and skills. Those "ifs" constitute an important challenge for community colleges—a challenge that will not go away.

REFERENCES

Aleamoni, L.M. "Developing a Comprehensive System to Improve and Reward Instructional Effectiveness." Paper presented at the National Faculty Evaluation Project Workshops for Community Colleges, Gainesville, Fla., July 31, 1980.

Alfred, R.L. "Social Change and Community College Faculty: Is Effective Teaching Becoming Obsolete?" *Community College Review*, 1985, *14* (1), p. 9.

Alfred, R.L. and V.P. Linder. *Rhetoric to Reality: Effectiveness in Community Colleges*. Ann Arbor: Community College Consortium, 1990.

Alfred, R.L., R.O. Peterson, and T.H. White. *Making Community Colleges More Effective*. Ann Arbor: Community College Consortium, 1992.

Altieri, G. and others. *Faculty Planning, Development, and Evaluation System: Washtenaw Community College*. Ann Arbor: Washtenaw Community College, 1991.

Altschuler, T.C. and S.L. Richter. *Maintaining Faculty Vitality*. New Directions for Community Colleges, vol. 13, no. 4. San Francisco: Jossey-Bass, 1985.

Andrews, H.A. *Evaluating for Excellence: Addressing the Need for Responsible and Effective Faculty Evaluation*. Stillwater, Okla.: New Forums Press, 1985.

Andrews, H.A. and C.M. Licata. *The State of Faculty Evaluation in Community, Technical, and Junior Colleges Within the North Central Region, 1988–1989*. Chicago: Council of North Central Community and Junior Colleges, 1989.

Baldwin, R.G. and M.V. Krotseng. *Incentives in the Academy: Issues and Options*. New Directions for Community Colleges, vol. 13, no. 3. San Francisco: Jossey-Bass, 1985.

Boggs, G. *Evaluating and Developing Community College Faculty*. Sacramento: ACCCA Management Report, 1984.

Bradford, L.P. "The Teaching-Learning Transaction." *Adult Education*, 1958, 8 (3).

Cameron, K.S. "The Relationship Between Faculty Unionism and Organizational Effectiveness." *Academy of Management Journal*, 1982, 25 (1).

Case, C.H. "Supporting Faculty Leadership for Change." *Reviewing the American Community College*, San Francisco: Jossey-Bass, 1985.

Cross, K.P. "Improving Learning in Community Colleges." Paper presented at the National Conference of the League for Innovation in the Community College, Miami, Fla., October 1986.

Eggers, P. "Part-Time, Off-Campus Instructors: A Support Program for Improving Teaching Effectiveness." Paper presented at the Convention of the American Association of Community and Junior Colleges, Seattle, April 1990.

Johnson, P.E. *Creative Teaching in the Community College: Guidelines for Associate Faculty.* Tucson, Ariz.: Pima Community College, 1988.

Kocher, E.D. and C. Houston. "How Do You Rate?" Paper presented at the Conference of the Southeastern Association for Community College Research, "Community Colleges in the Information Society," Myrtle Beach, S.C., August 1983.

McGrath, D. and M.B. Spear. *The Academic Crisis of the Community College.* Albany: SUNY Press, 1991.

Olp, M. and others. *Appraisal of Faculty: Encouragement and Improvement in the Classroom.* Yuma, Ariz.: Arizona Western College, 1991.

Palmer, P.J. "Good Teaching: A Matter of Living the Mystery." *Change*, 1990, January/February, p. 11.

Peterson, M.W., K.S. Cameron, L.A. Mets, P. Jones, and D. Ettington. *The Organizational Context for Teaching and Learning.* Ann Arbor: The National Center for Research to Improve Postsecondary Teaching and Learning, 1986.

Ratcliff, J.L. "Faculty Evaluation as a Measure of Organizational Productivity." Southern Association of Community and Junior Colleges Occasional Paper, 1984, 2 (1).

Richards, B. "Characteristics of an Effective Teacher." Paper presented at the American Vocational Association Convention, St. Louis, Mo., December 1982.

Romanik, D. *Staff Evaluation: Commitment to Excellence.* Miami, Fla.: Miami-Dade Community College, 1986.

Saunders, D.S. *Faculty Evaluation: Process and Procedure.* Memphis: Shelby State Community College, 1981.

Smick, R.A. and J.R. Crunkilton. "Enabling Behaviors Exhibited by Selected Virginia Postsecondary Vocational Technical Instructors." Paper presented at the American Vocational Association Convention, Orlando, Fla., December 1989.

Tobias, E. and others. *Faculty Performance Management System: The Faculty Development/Evaluation System at Beaufort Technical College.* Beaufort, S.C.: Beaufort Technical College, 1986.

Walker, J.W. *A Successful Revision of a Faculty Evaluation Procedure.* Torrance, Calif.: El Camino College, 1982.

Watkins, K. (Ed.). *Innovation Abstracts,* 1981, 3 (33).

Whitman, N.A., D.C. Spendlove, and C.H. Clark. *Increasing Students' Learning: A Faculty Guide to Reducing Stress Among Students.* ASHE-ERIC Higher Education Report, Washington, D.C.: ASHE-ERIC, 1986.

Richard L. Alfred is associate professor of higher education, University of Michigan.

Chapter 15

Rewarding and Recognizing Community College Faculty

Breaking Set to Support Teaching and Learning

By Nancy Armes LeCroy

Students of creativity use the words "breaking set" to describe those episodes during complex problem solving when an individual or group breaks away from preconceptions to experience a significant new insight. At these times, problem solvers speak of seeing the familiar in a new way and of sensing a pleasant blend of two somewhat contradictory feelings: "Why did I not see that before?" and "Oh, what a wonderful surprise!" Generally, these episodes occur when problem solvers have been encouraged to look at their situation with a certain openness, even playfulness, after a period of incubation—mulling over pertinent information on the subject for some period of time.

This chapter will revisit the familiar topic of rewarding and recognizing community college faculty so as to make it possible for practitioners who want to support teaching and learning through reward and recognition to see fresh possibilities—to "break set."

This desire to see new possibilities amid familiar terrain does not suggest that many current programs of reward and recognition for faculty are not effective. Certainly they are. But it is equally true that as fundamental motivational tools in college communities, these programs have sometimes grown stale or episodic, with some becoming detached from a more comprehensive program of professional development. It is also true in some settings that standard features of reward and recognition programs that may consume substantial organizational resources are no longer effective motivators of faculty. That is, teaching professionals do not always perceive routine reward mechanisms such as an automatic cost-of-living adjustment or an oft-repeated award ceremony as either reward or recognition. When poorly conceived or haphazardly offered, these intended rewards may at best be taken for granted, or at worst be perceived negatively—as merely pro forma measures that in no way reflect faculty effort or communicate genuine appreciation.

There are at least two reasons why community colleges have an excellent opportunity to creatively expand their thinking about the reward and recognition of faculty. First, they have not codified their efforts—as universities have, especially through tenure and review—to minimize the importance of teaching and learning. Currently in four-year circles a great deal of energy is being expended to redefine scholarship to give teaching and learning a more rightful place in the reward structure. But even though prominent educators such as Ernest Boyer in *Scholarship Reconsidered* (1990) and prestigious professional groups such as the American Association for Higher Education are struggling to reinvent these mechanisms, the going is painfully difficult. In the meantime, community colleges continue to benefit from a rich tradition of rewarding teaching and learning. When formal tenure and review processes are in place, the lion's share of emphasis is focused on teaching-related activity; when not, the academic culture finds ways to consistently reinforce the fundamental value of teaching. In 1988 the Commission on the Future of Community Colleges pointed to these institutions' unapologetic celebration of teaching as an enormous advantage over four-year institutions, one that ensures connection to students and makes it possible to appropriately reward classroom-related functions.

A second reason community colleges have an excellent opportunity to expand their reward horizons is their long-demonstrated willingness to link these processes to professional development. Such a joining creates a context for a program capable of motivating faculty over entire careers. It honors a well-documented pattern of career longevity among teaching professionals. This is no small advantage.

AN OVERVIEW AND A DEFINITION

In trying to break through preconceptions, this chapter looks at reward and recognition from three vantages. In the first section, seven themes stressed in research are summarized, with most of the material garnered from various fields of psychology. Although the seven elements offer concrete guidance for building reward and recognition in any organizational setting, they clearly have application for community colleges. The second section looks at reward and recognition from the more focused vantage of community college faculty by suggesting four areas of high concern and value to them. In effect, these interest areas are excellent guideposts for reconfiguring, expanding, or creating new reward and recognition programs. The third section then presents a possible framework for implementation that incorporates many principles highlighted in the first two sections. It is offered as only one among many options for reframing and/or renewing reward and recognition in the community college culture—as one framework for breaking set.

In general, reward and recognition are efforts to motivate and reinforce positive behavior. Although creativity can broaden current definitions of reward and recognition, the two terms will be used here in interchangeable ways to include the following categories:

- *Professional Acknowledgment*—awards, celebration, the conferral of greater responsibility, etc.

287

- *Professional Support*—staff, technical help, time to do the job, supervisory encouragement, etc.
- *Resource Enhancement*—pay, promotion, benefits, incentives

SEVEN REINFORCERS OF REWARD AND RECOGNITION

It is important to note that these seven reinforcers need careful choreography by those involved in designing reward and recognition. If all were applied at the same time with equal intensity to the same initiative, these guidelines might well confuse results. Rather they are an arsenal of tools in a comprehensive program of reward and recognition. It is equally important to remember that this information has been selected, simplified, and summarized from more detailed and technical commentary. Thus these principles are best seen as a general rather than definitive road map.

Effort-Contingent

There is much research suggesting that effective reward is contingent on effort and may be structured in at least two ways. Effort-related reward may be conferred when a standard has been achieved (performance-contingent), or it may be awarded for progress toward or achievement of a goal (success-contingent). Although both approaches may be effective, success-contingent reward is preferred because it does more to increase interest and goal orientation.

Managing contingent relationships between effort and recognition is a ticklish business worth much careful thought. For example, it is self-defeating to create too difficult a performance standard or to applaud the wrong performance indicator. Surely most professional groups, community college faculty included, are fairly sophisticated at sorting through the implicit messages sent by various reward contingencies. They know that to attain the rewards they will have to teach to the test, provide special favors, or follow arbitrary rules. If placed in positions they view as compromising, many professionals are likely to express hostility, withdraw, or even sabotage the reward process.

According to this line of research, however, the surest way to kill motivation is to give reward without regard to performance. If all receive the same pin or banner or certificate or award—without regard to effort and accomplishment—the motivational impact is minimal. It is somewhat unsettling to consider that many community colleges have sought to keep reward and recognition programs completely separate from formal evaluation. Such a linkage, at least in carefully selected circumstances, would seem to present clear opportunities for rewarding effort.

A Combination of Intrinsic and Extrinsic Motivation

Intrinsic motivation is the desire to complete a task for its own sake because it is interesting, enjoyable, and challenging. Extrinsic motivation is the desire to complete a task for a reason outside the activity itself, such as pay, promotion, and approval. When it can be developed, intrinsic motivation is almost universally regarded to be more positive and powerful. It stimulates creativity. It promotes enthusiasm. In fact, intrinsic rewards actually teach; when you perform an act successfully because you are interested in it, you then know how to solve similar problems. By definition, knowledge, understanding, and pleasure in the activity are intrinsic rewards highly valued by faculty.

But the reality is, from early school days and before, that human beings are also reinforced through extrinsic reward. An individual is motivated to please the parent, teacher, or boss in order to receive the best possible grade, the special assignment, the salary increase, or the glowing letter of recommendation. Because educators typically made good grades, conform with skill to institutional bureaucracies, and are adept at pleasing authority figures, they have clearly learned to value and respond to extrinsic motivation.

Thus, any well-designed reward and recognition program must honor both patterns of reinforcement. Special emphasis should be placed on intrinsic motivation because of its correlation to high-quality performance and because it is often less consciously tended in the extrinsically oriented academic world.

Appropriate and Varied

Reward and recognition need to fit the person and the situation. Researchers suggest that establishing this fit requires much more than casual or general knowledge of those to be recognized and is usually determined by asking many questions, listening attentively, and then discussing options, not just once, but many times. A number of case studies show that reward programs fail because of a fundamental misunderstanding of the client. They suggest that such gaffes can be avoided by involving recipients in the design and management of any reinforcement plan.

Not only do adults have different needs, but they have more than one need at any given time. Employees simultaneously seek many kinds of satisfaction in the work environment, including economic gain, social relationship, and personal and professional growth. Thus a varied program of reward and recognition is required.

Discovering appropriateness and creating varied options for reward and recognition are often described as key roles of supervision. These management roles provide an ideal opportunity to ask individuals and groups what rewards they value. Supervisors must then be prepared to deal with the virtual certainty of variance. Whether responding to differences in race, ethnicity, or gender; accommodating the career stage and/or developmental phase; or choreographing logistics, they face a complex set of tasks. Even so, for community college professionals, designing appropriate and varied rewards differs little from tailoring teaching and learning strategies to a diverse student body—one approach simply will not be appropriate for all, and the greater the variety, the greater the likelihood of serving the full contingent.

Relational

A work environment that fosters community-building relationships provides the best context for developing and administering reward and recognition. Here research conforms to common sense. If the individuals honored know and trust those rewarding and recognizing them, they are much more likely to value the results. In other words, recipients need to feel they are recognized because colleagues have some genuine sense of who they are.

This leads to several possible strategies. It suggests that reward from closer to home means more. It stresses the importance that groups of colleagues can play in structuring reward and recognition and suggests that in a community college setting a department or discipline group may well come together to design a program based on this sense of relation.

One innovation that may encourage camaraderie and motivation within employee groups is the strategy of providing incentives (extrinsic motivators) to departments or work units rather than to individuals. As a framework for reward, it minimizes the sometimes debilitating effects of competition among individuals working closely together and instead fosters collaboration.

Immediate

The power of reward and recognition is strengthened when the reinforcement is offered as close to the act as possible. As Ross Perot said in an election infomercial, "Pat employees on the back while they are still sweating from the work!" This is not an unexpected guideline for educators. It follows the same path as the waves of research on student learning that find extraordinary value in providing the learner immediate feedback. It suggests that as human beings find learning easier with immediate feedback, they are also positively motivated when the reward is immediate. It may even suggest that the two processes are sometimes virtually interchangeable.

This reinforcement principle makes an implicit case for including informal reward and recognition processes in a comprehensive program. An impromptu celebration, a note fast on the heels of a job well done, a personal face-to-face encounter expressing gratitude, an unexpected opportunity to try a new assignment—

the informality of such reinforcements encourages immediacy and vice versa.

Spontaneous

Spontaneity also increases positive motivation. When the honor is unexpected, it keeps the reinforcement from seeming routine, which can unconsciously decrease a reward's value. Surprise not only increases immediate pleasure, but it carries more power than a predictable reinforcer. It is a bit like fishing: you keep casting because you believe you will get a strike every so often, but you do not know exactly when.

Spontaneity is also not as easy a process to encourage or manage as it might seem. For reward and recognition processes to be truly spontaneous, there must be a willingness to be self-revealing, take risks, and trust colleagues. Those involved must be comfortable enough with each other to enjoy the surprise. Most importantly, those who provide the rewards must constantly be alert to opportunities for recognizing good service and performance.

Growth-Reinforcing

At its best, reward and recognition stimulates growth when it presumes that a professional is making a career journey and will meet challenges along the way. As a principle, it suggests that an appropriately orchestrated reward program has the potential to move a professional from one career stage to the next, and from one developmental challenge to the next.

Psychologists at the Center for Creative Leadership have spent a decade studying growth-reinforcing behavior in organizations. Their first book-length report, *The Lessons of Experience* (McCall, Lombardi, and Morrison, 1988), documents the importance not only of completing challenging assignments, but of receiving appropriate reward for this achievement in order to increase the willingness to take up the next career challenge.

A subsequent book building on the same body of research, Ann Morrison's *The New Leaders* (1992), describes the critical role that reward and recognition play for women and minorities. It seems that without effective recognition and support, the higher expectations often placed on these new leaders are more likely to deplete and derail them. These books are particularly interesting examples of a larger body of research that demonstrates the merit of linking professional development with reward and recognition.

FOUR CONCEPTS VALUED BY FACULTY

After considering the general reinforcement principles helpful in effective reward design, the next step is to look closely at concepts that community college faculty claim to value. Studying their needs and preferences expands possibilities for reward and recognition and helps build a direct link to teaching and learning.

It also confirms many of the general principles already delineated here. Examining faculty preferences better ensures that reward will be appropriate to needs and interests. This strategy makes variety more likely because it places a broader array of possibilities for renewal on the discussion table. It increases the likelihood that additional intrinsic motivators of faculty can be discovered—motivators based on love of teaching, love of discipline, and desire to make a difference. Asking faculty what they value facilitates a developmental approach to their growth and renewal and builds a meaningful framework for relationships with colleagues.

Community

Faculty's desire for community was articulated by K. Patricia Cross in her watershed article, "Community Colleges on the Plateau" (1981), in which she analyzed research data drawn from the Community College Goals Inventory. It has continued as a major theme through *Building Communities* (Commission on the Future of Community Colleges, 1988) and in quite recent assessments such as the Carnegie Foundation for the Advancement of Teaching's 1990 report, *Campus Life: In Search of Community*. Over and over, faculty have stressed a fundamental desire to be meaningfully connected to one another in their work. It may seem ironic, but in spite of teeming hordes of students and multiple, proliferating tasks, faculty often feel isolated.

When faculty are queried about what creates a sense of community, their remedies are simple. They express a hunger for conversations with their colleagues, carried on in an atmosphere of informality, comfort, and respect. They also want their leaders to align them to a larger sense of vision and purpose. Intuitively they know that when aligned to a greater shared cause, they are much more likely to feel part of a community of learning.

The value that faculty place on becoming part of a learning community suggests a number of possibilities for reward and recognition. They include offering mechanisms and resources that promote working with colleagues in new and different ways; creating comfortable, informal conversation opportunities, often without specific agendas; finding innovative ways to connect new and part-time faculty to college life; encouraging mentoring in ways that support both mentors and proteges; and redesigning discipline meetings to encourage the growth of relationships, not just the completion of tasks. These and many more possibilities can counter feelings of isolation and disconnection.

Balance

The most recurrent theme the Futures Commission heard in faculty hearings was that community college teaching professionals are overextended—with classes too large, time too short, too many essays to grade, too many "problem students," too many committee meetings, too many bureaucratic trappings, and too little time to renew. Faculty depicted for the commission the balancing act required to teach a typical five-course load (with a three-course overload not uncommon) and manage an array of outside leadership assignments. Their concerns caused the commission to look for ways to focus the teaching and learning environment. "The Future of the Community College: Premises, Prior Questions, and Implications for Innovation" (Armes, 1989) describes these deliberations, and the *Building Communities* report spells out the resulting recommendations.

But this professional tug of war is only part of the problem. Faculty not only balance responsibilities within their professional lives, but they also balance competing personal and professional demands. Finding equilibrium is particularly arduous for new faculty. Not only are they often given more course preparations and committee assignments than veterans, but as Robert Boice reports in *The New Faculty Member* (1992), novices have not yet learned efficient ways to balance college expectations with personal needs. They need help and guidance if they are to avoid spreading themselves too thin.

The strong desire for greater equilibrium among faculty offers obvious opportunities for reward and recognition. It suggests that any program will be welcome if it provides time to work on projects of high interest, or that there may be real merit in pursuing benefit packages with options such as flexible scheduling, job sharing, or new options for professional and personal leave. It suggests that helping faculty learn to better apportion their time and set priorities is a way to demonstrate appreciation and support, and that using technology to streamline and make routine the more mechanistic components of work may be quite a boon. It even suggests that honestly assessing and remediating organizational tendencies toward "workaholism," unreasonable expectations, or burnout can become a powerful way to encourage faculty.

Challenge

At all stages of their career journeys, faculty value professional challenge. They wish to be intellectually stimulated, and they dread the specter of becoming stale or disengaged. Certainly they face enormous ongoing challenges in the classroom as they teach a clientele so diverse that the dominant theme it represents is variety. But not all parts of teaching provide intellectual stimulation. Community college faculty are not unreasonable in fearing the deadening effect of teaching the same preparation for years or grading an unending stream of papers in which students make remarkably repetitive errors.

This need for challenge and stimulation is why George Vaughan has made an ongoing case, most recently in the article "Faculty and Administrative Renewal" (1991), for the importance of scholarly research in community colleges. He sees research as intrinsically renewing, a stimulus to keep faculty intellectually engaged in their subject matter. It is also why Boice (1992) strongly recommends mentoring programs that link new and experienced faculty. The ongoing exchange stimulates both to become more analytical and try new things.

There are several ways that challenge can become grist for reward and recognition. First, since it is not uncommon for success stories to go generally unregarded and unreinforced in community colleges, the obvious strategy is to reward activity already under way. Surely those tasks faculty members take up at their own initiative provide wonderful opportunities for reinforcement. Rewarding self-challenge also encourages faculty to undertake new, risky tasks. A cursory listing of intellectually stimulating assignments that could become part of a reward program includes acquiring new expertise, assuming leadership of a major new initiative, assuming administrative duties, and working on interdisciplinary projects with other faculty.

Reflection on Teaching and Learning

Again and again community college faculty report a visceral understanding of the demanding, highly gratifying nature of teaching. Most work hard enough and interact with students often enough to experience the magic that occurs when teaching and learning processes are working. But many of these same faculty have little or no contact, either in preservice or in-service training, with educational practices designed to improve their teaching.

For these faculty, understanding the relationship between their own teaching and student learning is predictably superficial. As the Futures Commission noted, they often have little opportunity to consider how their teaching approach matches the needs of underprepared students or to share with and learn from colleagues regarding these matters. Even more perplexing, as they become more reflective on issues of teaching and learning and begin to apply research, their first discovery is that theory is not always easy to apply in a community college setting. They discover that what works in ideal circumstances—with students who are residential, full-time, young, well-prepared, and free from responsibility—will not be as likely to work with adult, commuting, part-time community college students who have family and work responsibilities.

For these reasons, faculty place high value on processes that enable them to become more reflective about teaching and learning. They look for and are positively reinforced by the opportunity to become more astute in these matters. One breakthrough concept is classroom research. Developed by K. Patricia Cross and Tom Angelo (1993), it envisions a process in which faculty members collect classroom feedback on student learning in order to make a clearer connection between how they teach and what students learn. Although this innovation is discussed in some detail in another chapter, its relevance here is as a complex, well-orchestrated mechanism that encourages ongoing reflection about teaching and learning. It is only one of several innovations that, by fostering this introspection, has the potential to be greatly valued by faculty. Others include learning communities, team teaching, and across-the-curriculum initiatives.

A PROPOSED FRAMEWORK FOR FACULTY REWARD AND RECOGNITION

A final task is to suggest what the general guidelines on reward and recognition, combined with the elements of high value to faculty, have to say about the overall structure of a reward program. Although there are many ways to reconfigure existing reward structures—a topic ripe for a brainstorming "break set" session—the following tenets might reasonably become part of a comprehensive framework. An effective, comprehensive reward and recognition program:

- Assumes that reward and recognition will not meet their desired goal nor appropriately motivate faculty if they are not given careful, ongoing consideration

- Becomes part of a larger comprehensive program of professional development, one that takes faculty career needs and developmental stages into account
- Seeks to develop long-lived mechanisms for conversations among faculty and between faculty and administrators about reward and recognition
- Organizes many of these conversations at the department or discipline level, where trust can be built, colleague relationships are often strong, and regular contact is possible
- Keeps these conversations informal, somewhat open-ended affairs that invite faculty to respond to questions such as:
  - What do you enjoy about the work you do?
  - What excites you most about teaching at this point?
  - What happens when you try to work especially hard and productively on this job?
  - What would increase your productivity?
  - Are there critical passages in a faculty career that need to be recognized?
  - What forms of recognition mean the most to you now? Have they changed?
- Asks faculty to discuss how to build community, offer balance, provide challenge, and/or encourage reflection on teaching and learning through a program of reward and recognition
- Involves supervisors in a number of these conversations, asking them to participate in but not typically lead these informal sessions
- Builds this feedback into a program that balances reinforcement principles in the following ways:
  - Combines formal and informal elements
  - Includes spontaneous as well as carefully orchestrated events
  - Provides both intrinsic and extrinsic motivation
  - Functions at the discipline or department level as well as at the institutional level
  - Develops activities that are both supervisor-led and colleague-led

- Plans a minimum of three to five years into the future to more realistically consider evolving faculty needs
- Expects the immediate supervisor of faculty to assume many logistical responsibilities to expedite reward and recognition—to run interference, scout resources, and interpret needs and desires to the broader college family
- Links to and supports collegewide reward and recognition as they now exists in all feasible ways
- Works to modify collegewide programs when they are not meeting needs and motivating appropriately
- Keeps clearly in focus that some of the most important forms of reward and recognition may occur informally and spontaneously—in impromptu fashion, among colleagues, between faculty members and their supervisors—often passing unnoticed by the college as a whole, but creating a culture in which offering support is a comfortable and comforting process

Of course, the success of any such framework depends on the willingness within the college to create a new culture for rewarding and recognizing faculty, one capable of supporting the central teaching and learning thrust. Commitment is required—a tenacious impulse to renew the core mission. Only then is it possible to break set.

REFERENCES

Angelo, Thomas and K. Patricia Cross. *Classroom Assessment Techniques: A Handbook for College Teachers, Second Edition*. San Francisco: Jossey-Bass, 1993.

Armes, Nancy. "The Future of the Community College: Premises, Prior Questions, and Implications for Innovation." In Terry O'Banion (Ed.), *Innovation in the Community College*. New York: ACE/Macmillan, 1989.

Boice, Robert. *The New Faculty Member*. San Francisco: Jossey-Bass, 1992.

Boyer, Ernest L. *Scholarship Reconsidered: Priorities of the Professoriate*. Princeton, N.J.: Carnegie Foundation for the Advancement of Teaching, 1990.

Commission on the Future of Community Colleges. *Building Communities: A Vision for a New Century.* Washington, D.C.: American Association of Community Colleges, 1988.

Campus Life: In Search of Community. A Special Report of The Carnegie Foundation for the Advancement of Teaching. Princeton, N.J.: Princeton University Press, 1990.

Cross, K. Patricia. "Community Colleges on the Plateau." *Journal of Higher Education,* 1981, 52 (2), 1981.

McCall, Morgan W., Jr., Michael M. Lombardi, and Ann M. Morrison. *The Lessons of Experience: How Successful Executives Develop on the Job.* Lexington, Mass.: Lexington Books, 1988.

Morrison, Ann M. *The New Leaders: Guidelines on Leadership Diversity in America.* San Francisco: Jossey-Bass, 1992.

Vaughan, George B. "Faculty and Administrative Renewal." In Dan Angel and Mike DeVault (Eds.), *Conceptualizing 2000: Proactive Planning.* Washington, D.C.: Community College Press, 1991.

Nancy Armes LeCroy is consultant to the chancellor, Dallas County Community College District, Texas.

Chapter 16

Guidelines for Auditing the Effectiveness of Teaching and Learning

By Terry O'Banion

"The community college should be the nation's premier teaching institution" (Commission on the Future of Community Colleges, 1988, p. 25)—*but is it?* When community college faculty's perceptions of teaching are compared to those of faculty in public four-year institutions, there are no significant differences in several key attitudes and activities. In the most comprehensive survey of its kind (HERI, 1991), involving more than 35,000 faculty members in 392 public institutions of higher education, 99 percent of the community college faculty said they considered "being a good teacher" an essential or very important professional goal; so did 98 percent of the faculty from four-year colleges and 98 percent of the faculty from universities. In the same survey, faculty were also asked to rate selected attributes as "very descriptive" of their own institutions. Only 6.2 percent of the university faculty rated the attribute "faculty are rewarded for being good teachers" as very descriptive. Interestingly, only 8 percent of the four-year faculty and 8 percent of the community college faculty rated it as very descriptive. In terms of their perceptions of the importance of being a good teacher and the importance institutions give to rewarding good teaching, there are no significant differences among faculty members in public community colleges, four-year colleges, and universities.

There is a major dislocation in the culture of higher education when faculty place such high value on good teaching, but believe that their institutions place extremely low value on rewarding it. This disparity reveals the unresolved tensions within higher education that make it difficult to explain education to our constituents outside the academy. Former Harvard President Derek Bok contends that "notwithstanding the improvements that may have taken place in the quality of undergraduate education in this country, the public has finally come to believe quite strongly that our institutions...are not making the education of students a top priority" (p. 15).

Public trust in education has eroded in part because of the reduced value institutions place on teaching and learning as the heart of the educational enterprise. The reform reports of the last decade outlined some of the factors contributing to this erosion, but more importantly, they have also pointed the way to a renewed emphasis on making the education of students a top priority. Ernest Boyer has suggested that "The 1990s may well come to be remembered as the decade of the undergraduate in American higher education" (1990, p. xi).

The authors of this book certainly believe that the 1990s hold great promise for improving and expanding teaching and learning in American higher education, especially in community colleges. Community college faculty may not differ from four-year college and university faculty in their perceptions of several key factors related to good teaching, but they do differ on many significant factors that make it possible for the community college to become "the nation's premier teaching institution."

Although many educators support the notion that conducting research contributes to teaching effectiveness, a sizable number of public four-year college and university faculty believe that conducting research interferes with their effectiveness in teaching

(HERI, 1992). Forty-four percent of university faculty and 32 percent of four-year college faculty reported that they somewhat agree or strongly agree that institutional demands for doing research interferes with their effectiveness as teachers. Only 6 percent of community college faculty expressed this view, probably because there is no institutional demand for research.

According to this same study, community college faculty also respect and enjoy each other more than their counterparts at four-year colleges and universities, contributing to a better climate for collaboration on improvements in teaching and learning. When asked to rate aspects of their jobs as satisfactory or very satisfactory, 80 percent of community college faculty checked "relationships with other faculty" while 74 percent of four-year college faculty and 69 percent of university faculty did so. "Faculty here respect each other" was checked by 38 percent of community college faculty and by only 24 percent of four-year college faculty and 23 percent of university faculty. Community college faculty also are more satisfied with the "competency of their colleagues," with 71 percent for community college faculty compared with 65 percent for university faculty and 63 percent for four-year faculty.

Community college faculty also give themselves higher marks on activities that support students, values that hold important clues for making teaching and learning effective. Almost twice the number (38 percent) of community college faculty indicated that "it is easy for students to see faculty outside of regular office hours at this institution," compared with 21 percent of university faculty and 31 percent of four-year college faculty.

Reflecting the community college's commitment to student-centeredness, 85 percent of community college faculty somewhat or strongly agreed that "faculty here are interested in students' personal problems." Seventy-three percent of four-year faculty agreed with the statement, but only 58 percent of university faculty did so. Interestingly enough, community college faculty do not place lower value on the intellectual development of students, as is sometimes suggested by critics. Seventy-six percent of community college faculty members said that "promoting the intellectual development of students" was the highest or a high priority of their institutions. Seventy-two percent of four-year college faculty and 71 percent of university faculty made this claim.

Community college faculty appear to be genuinely satisfied with their jobs and genuinely committed to the welfare of their institutions, creating an excellent climate to support teaching and learning initiatives. Eighty-two percent of community college faculty agreed strongly or somewhat that "faculty are committed to the welfare of the institution," while only 72 percent of four-year faculty and 68 percent of university faculty expressed this view. In terms of "overall job satisfaction," 74 percent of community college faculty gave a satisfactory or very satisfactory rating, compared with 65 percent of the four-year college faculty and 68 percent of the university faculty.

Community college faculty rated themselves higher than did four-year college and university faculty on such indices of institutional climate as respect for colleagues and relationships with each other; their interest in students' personal problems and intellectual development; the time they make available to students outside of class; their commitment to the welfare of the institution; and their overall job satisfaction. These perceptions, which reflect individual values of community college faculty, lay the groundwork for initiatives in teaching and learning that can make the community college the "nation's premier teaching institution." The opportunity to achieve that laudable goal awaits action by that institution's key leaders.

AUDITING TEACHING AND LEARNING PRACTICES

To paraphrase Richardson and Elliott earlier in this book, the teaching and learning climate is the visible product of a particular institution's invisible values. What faculty, administrators, board members, and staff truly believe about students and their abilities to learn and about teachers and their abilities to teach is reflected in the climate of teaching and learning. It is a case of yin and yang in which values influence climate, and climate in turn influences values. The values and climate are made most visible in the written policies and statements, practices, and related behaviors of the stake holders in the institution.

An audit of these policies and statements, practices, and related behaviors is an important first step for leaders who wish to make teaching and learning the highest priority of the community college. Drawing on the chapters in this book, which have been prepared by some of the leading community college educators, the following section is an attempt to develop guidelines that can be used to conduct an institutional audit of current teaching and learning policies and practices. The audit should be tailored to the special needs of an institution, but the guidelines are fairly generic and should apply to most any community college that wishes to improve and expand on its current commitment to teaching and learning. For those that find their policies and practices lacking in effectiveness, the chapters in this book offer some helpful solutions.

Institutional Policies and Statements

Every community college has a mission statement. In every mission statement there is some reference to ideals of good teaching and to interest in and support of students to ensure learning. Mission statements, however, are not usually living documents that stimulate creative response. At a minimum, they meet legal requirements and are trotted out and sometimes updated for representatives of accrediting associations and institutional committees responsible for launching yet another long-range plan.

For community colleges wishing to make teaching and learning the institution's top priority, the mission statement is a good place to begin. It is likely in need of an update reflecting a special emphasis on teaching and learning as the heart of the educational enterprise. This updating may occur after institutional leaders have prepared more specific institutionwide statements that document values related to teaching and learning.

- Does the mission statement make clearly visible the college's commitment to core values related to teaching and learning?

- Has the college prepared special statements of values, goals, and practices indicating commitments to teaching and learning as a high priority of the institution?
- To what extent does the governing board demonstrate understanding and commitment to good practices in teaching and learning?
- Is the president committed to making teaching and learning an institutional priority? How does he or she express that commitment?
- To what extent have faculty and staff been involved in developing the various institutional statements, and how do they support a continuing climate of commitment to teaching and learning?
- Could outside consultants and visitors recognize the institution's commitment to teaching and learning by observing practice rather than being told about the commitment? Is practice aligned with mission?
- Are the various statements living documents that are used continually to guide leaders and revised to reflect new goals and new practices?

Student Success Policies

Academic policies should ensure student success and reflect values derived from the mission and other institutionwide statements on teaching and learning. These policies are among the most important indices in the institution for auditing how institutional stake holders really feel about students and their abilities to learn. Unfortunately, many academic policies reflect values and practices designed for a different time, different place, and different students. If community colleges are to provide opportunities for students to be successful in some of the ways described in this book, they need to review and analyze current academic policies related to students and revise them according to their value statements to make them student success policies.

- Does the college have a required student assessment program designed to identify specific areas in need of remediation, counseling, or experience prior to undertaking more challenging activities?

- Does the college have a mandatory placement program, developed in tandem with the assessment program, designed to remediate, counsel, or provide experiences that will ensure success in more challenging activities?
- As the most important prelude to success in class, are all students in every term required to explore with a highly competent academic adviser their educational, vocational, and life goals, and their program and course choices to achieve those goals?
- Are new students required to participate in a series of well-designed orientation activities to acquaint them with the values and challenges of a college education, the social responsibilities of educated citizens, the culture and norms of college in general, and this college in particular?
- Has the college made it clear that students must register before the first day of class to ensure the benefits of attendance on the first day and during the first week? In other words, has the college abandoned late registration policies that interfere with sound teaching and learning practices for late registrants, on-time registrants, and faculty?
- Has the college established an early academic alert system designed to initiate special interventions of counseling, remediation, reduced course- and workloads, and special support services for students whose assessments indicate a proclivity for failure and for students who show early signs of failure?
- Are students required to attend classes with very few exceptions, and are these exceptions and procedures for their approval carefully spelled out?
- Are exceptions to these student success policies extremely limited, carefully spelled out, and strictly enforced by all college staff?
- Do faculty and staff members who are assigned responsibility for implementing the student success policies participate in developing and approving the policies?

Curriculum Review and Development

The curriculum is the expression of the collective faculty wisdom regarding what is worth learning. Three hundred years ago what was worth learning in formal schooling was fixed in the *trivium* and *quadrivium*, and every student took the same curriculum. Today the world is a bit more complex, and that is reflected in the comprehensive curriculum of the modern community college, which supports five different curricula in one organization: transfer/liberal arts, vocational/technical education, remedial/developmental studies, general education, and continuing education/community services. Distinct faculty groups serve the transfer and technical curricula, and some of these faculty are also advocates of and participants in the other curricula.

This is a complex arrangement, a bane and a blessing of the community college and one of its distinct characteristics. The arrangement is made more complex since these curricula are not fixed and are, or should be, in a constant state of flux as they are revised to reflect changing social and economic needs. Technical programs must be constantly updated, new programs initiated, and programs no longer relevant deleted to keep up with rapid changes in technology and economic conditions. Transfer programs must be updated to reflect such social changes as an emphasis on multiculturalism and women's studies and new knowledge constantly emerging in the established disciplines. New immigrants and underprepared high school students require curriculum changes in developmental education. Pressure to serve communities in new and deeper ways and to expand services to business and industry call for revisions in the continuing education/community services curriculum. The development of a sound program of general education has been a continuing quest of community colleges for decades.

It is the curriculum in the community college to which faculty apply their best expertise in making teaching and learning an institutional priority. In universities course content often represents the research interests of faculty or scholarly trends in a discipline. In community colleges faculty usually tailor course content to community and student interests, addressing the needs of hetero-geneous populations (Mellander and Robertson, 1992, p. 12). To ensure that the current curricula are designed to best meet the needs of current students and to ensure that they will be con-stantly updated to reflect changing needs, faculty must be ener-getic activists in curriculum review and development.

- Does the college have an established process, such as DACUM, to ensure the continuing review and develop-ment of the curriculum? Are all curricula in the college on a rotating schedule for review every three to five years, with allowances made for early review in areas of rapid change?
- How many programs and courses have been revised, added, and deleted in the last five years?
- Has the college established a general education program required of all students as recommended by the Commis-sion on the Future of Community Colleges? Is the general education program the usual political compromise of distri-bution requirements, or is it specially designed with its own internal integrity?
- Is there a well-developed special curriculum for underpre-pared and ESL students sequentially linked to other appro-priate curricula?
- Does the transfer curriculum meet the needs of the major-ity of transfer students, and does it prepare them to com-pete on an equal basis at the universities and four-year col-leges to which they transfer?
- Does the transfer curriculum articulate efficiently with the developmental studies program and the vocational-techni-cal program so that students can easily access the transfer program?
- Do minority students in the transfer program complete at the same rate as nonminority students?
- Is the vocational-technical program designed to meet com-munity and regional work force needs, and are these pro-grams articulated with training needs and opportunities in the community and region?

Instructional Innovation

A major hallmark of a college dedicated to making teaching and learning its highest priority is the extent to which faculty search out and create innovations in instructional processes. Some colleges have developed a climate in which innovation in general is highly prized as a characteristic of each institution's culture. Such climates often have their genesis in the visions of innovative presidents, but when a critical core of faculty engage in innovation they can survive changes in presidents and maintain an innovative spirit that undergirds teaching and learning effectiveness.

Sadly, some colleges that were highly innovative in the '60s and '70s have lost the innovative spirit. In some cases, faculty in these institutions are still riding on past reputations and reject any new ideas under the assumption that they have already tried everything. Constrained by limited travel funds and a general malaise that pervades many community colleges in difficult economic times, colleges and their faculties turn inward and disconnect from the community of innovators that show up regularly at the annual conferences of the National Institute for Staff and Organizational Development, the National Council for Staff, Program, and Organizational Development, and the League for Innovation.

Once lost, it takes considerable thought and a great deal of action to renew a college's innovative spirit. A first step is to audit current instructional innovations and related activities. When this is part of an institutionwide audit regarding effective teaching and learning policies and practices, there is great potential for a renaissance of instructional innovation.

- How many and which faculty are currently experimenting with instructional innovations they have borrowed or designed?
- Is there a program or focal point of interest that initiates and encourages instructional innovation at the college? If so, are faculty connected and responsive?

- Does the college have formal policies and programs of incentives, rewards, and recognition to stimulate instructional innovation?
- How many faculty members are experimenting with the following current instructional innovations:
  - Classroom assessment
  - Learning communities
  - Electronic journals and forums
  - Instructional skills programs
  - Campus Compact
  - Multimedia and interactive media
  - TQM in the classroom

Information Technology

The use of information technology in improving teaching and learning could be subsumed under the section on instructional innovation, except that it is becoming so pervasive and has so much potential for creating change that it is best treated separately. There are a number of leaders, such as EDUCOM President Robert Heterick, who believe that technology is "the primary vehicle by which institutions of higher education are going to re-engineer the teaching-and-learning process" (DeLoughry, 1992, p. A17).

As noted in Chapters 1 and 11 of this book, community colleges are rapidly expanding their use of the computer to improve teaching and learning. Whereas in universities computers are used primarily by professors for research and writing, in community colleges computers are used primarily by students to increase and expand learning. And community college faculty members are the driving force behind the use of computers by students as they adapt new information technology to extend and expand their own teaching.

When computers first appeared in community colleges, they were used almost exclusively for administrative purposes: registration, financial management, personnel, data collection, etc. Most community colleges now have information technology systems in place for managing their administrative functions, and in the last decade creative faculty have used computers in a variety of ways to improve teaching and learning.

- Has the college made a distinction between administrative and instructional computing? Has the college provided resources and appropriate organizational support to ensure the expansion of instructional computing?
- Is there a long-range scheme for developing, planning, managing, and updating information technology to support effective teaching and learning?
- Does the college participate in national and international networks for users of information technology and regularly support faculty participation in conferences and workshops on information technology?
- Does the college evaluate the effectiveness of information technology in improving teaching and learning compared to other instructional approaches?
- Is the college experimenting with instructional programs using information technology that will increase teaching productivity?
- To what extent is information technology used to build community among administrators, faculty, and students?

Faculty Selection and Development

The faculty make the college. They are the conjunction that connects the teaching *and* learning processes. In institutions that wish to make teaching and learning the highest priority, most activities focus on the faculty in terms of trying to influence them or in terms of serving their needs. This observation is not to be misconstrued in terms of meeting faculty needs identified by unions and other special groups, although these needs are quite often related to improving teaching and learning even when not couched within that framework.

The overarching goal of the community college—the goal that transcends power conflicts, special interests, and key personalities—is to provide opportunities for students to succeed. And that goal is impossible to achieve without the full support and involvement of the faculty—a simple truth but one sometimes lost in the complex issues of the day. Faculty are too often seen as the enemy or as sluggards by some trustees, presidents, and administrators. Some administrators and trustees seem to care more about the maintenance of buildings than they do about faculty members.

Leaders who understand the key role of faculty in making the institution work—that is, in fully realizing the changes possible at an institution totally dedicated to teaching and learning as its highest priority—will make the selection, development, and evaluation of faculty an ongoing and strongly supported activity throughout the institution. In addition there will be systems of reward and recognition in place that make the climate of the college attractive and challenging.

Not since the 1960s have college leaders had a better opportunity to revitalize the faculty as the key factor in making teaching and learning the heart of the educational enterprise. Over half the faculty in community colleges are currently in the process of retiring. The faculty hired in the next five years will determine the real nature of community colleges for decades to come. In this brief window of opportunity, visionary leaders must move quickly and carefully to develop value statements and processes for selecting, evaluating, developing, and rewarding the faculty who will determine whether a college will become an institution easily recognized as being dedicated to teaching and learning.

- Has the college assessed the retirement patterns of current faculty over the next ten years and determined replacement needs both in number and in kind?
- Has the college developed a statement of values regarding teaching and learning and derived characteristics of replacement teachers needed to achieve these values? Is there a clearly determined procedure for selecting new faculty that involves demonstrated effectiveness in teaching and ensures a cadre of teachers who will implement the values in the teaching and learning statement?

- Has the college created a mandatory staff development program for these new faculty—and for continuing faculty and part-time faculty as well—that will assist them in achieving personal and professional goals derived from the values statement on teaching and learning and the desirable characteristics of teachers? Is the staff development program coordinated by a highly qualified staff member on a continuing basis and integrated into the real-life activities of the college?
- Does the faculty evaluation system reflect the statement on values and characteristics of teachers and provide opportunities for faculty to take advantage of perspectives on their work from colleagues, supervisors, and students? Does the self-evaluation process provide opportunities to organize portfolios and other nontraditional resources for demonstrating effective teaching and improved student learning? Is assistance provided to teachers from the staff development program in preparing evaluations and in developing new competencies or upgrading skills?
- Has the college established a culture in which the most effective teachers are recognized and rewarded in ways appropriate to their achievement and that ensures respect and a sense of fair play from those not recognized and rewarded? Is good teaching genuinely celebrated at the college?
- Has the development of statements and systems regarding selecting, developing, evaluating, and rewarding faculty involved all institutional stake holders to the point that they feel ownership of the products?

Institutional Effectiveness

All things considered, if an institution and its consultants could give highly positive responses to most of the questions framed here for an audit of teaching and learning, such a college would be a model of institutional effectiveness. The core indices for measuring overall institutional effectiveness are related to teaching and learning activities. Certainly other factors, such as facilities, governance structures, community relationships, alliances with public schools and universities, and financial arrangements, need to be considered, but these factors for the most part are the peripheral structures that support teaching and learning.

The core indices for measuring overall institutional effectiveness related to teaching and learning are illuminated in the question, "Are the students at this college learning what they came to learn and what the faculty feel they need to learn, and is the community satisfied with the outcome?" An audit of the following questions will provide more specific information regarding answers to this key question.

- Have the retention rates increased at this college because of activities initiated in making teaching and learning one of the highest priorities of the institution? Are stake holders satisfied with these improved retention rates as the best students can achieve?
- Have grade point averages, course success rates, and program completion rates increased at this college because of activities initiated in making teaching and learning one of the highest priorities of the institution? Are stake holders satisfied with these improved averages and rates?
- Do students express more satisfaction in a variety of areas with their experience at the college, and are they more involved at the college because of activities initiated in making teaching and learning one of the highest priorities of the institution?
- Do faculty, staff, and administrators express more satisfaction in a variety of areas with their experiences at the college, and are they more involved in the college because of activities initiated in making teaching and learning one of the highest priorities of the institution?
- Does the community express more satisfaction with the college because of activities initiated in making teaching and learning one of the highest priorities of the institution?

Although measures are difficult to determine for the questions related to satisfaction, one can infer satisfaction if most of the other questions throughout the audit can be answered positively. If that holds true, satisfaction on the part of students, faculty, and the community is likely to be evident in a number of ways: laudatory editorials in the student and community newspapers; more cordial contract negotiations; more volunteered time; greater commitment to experimentation; increased interaction between students and faculty and among faculty; and more referendums passed by the community in support of the college. These measures of satisfaction may appear idealistic at a time in which higher education has lost the public trust, but they suggest a vision worth pursuing and not impossible to achieve.

In the opening section of this chapter, former Harvard President Derek Bok (1992) was quoted thus: "The public has finally come to believe quite strongly that our institutions...are not making the education of students a high priority." If community colleges have lost the public trust, they can regain it by making the education of students—by making teaching and learning—their highest priority. When teaching and learning become the highest priority of community colleges, these extraordinary institutions can lay proper claim to being the "nation's premier teaching institutions."

REFERENCES

Bok, Derek. "Reclaiming the Public Trust." *Change*, 1992, July/August, pp. 13-19.

Boyer, Ernest. *Scholarship Reconsidered: Priorities of the Professoriate.* Princeton, N.J.: Carnegie Foundation for the Advancement of Teaching, 1990.

Commission on the Future of Community Colleges. *Building Communities: A Vision for a New Century.* Washington, D.C.: American Association of Community Colleges, 1988.

DeLoughry, Thomas J. "EDUCOM's New Leaders Expected to Play a Key Role in Promoting Technology." *The Chronicle of Higher Education*, October 7, 1992, pp. A17-A18.

Higher Education Research Institute. "The American College Teacher: National Norms for the 1989-90 HERI Faculty Survey." Los Angeles: University of California at Los Angeles. In *The Chronicle of Higher Education*, August 26, 1992, p. 30.

Mellander, Gustavo A. and Bruce Robertson. "Tradition and Transformation: Academic Roots and the Community College Future." In B.W. Deziech and W.R. Vitter (Eds.), *Prisoners of Elitism: The Community College's Struggle for Stature.* New Directions for Community Colleges, no. 78. San Francisco: Jossey-Bass, 1992, pp. 9-21.

Terry O'Banion is executive director of the League for Innovation in the Community College.

Index

Terry O'Banion is executive director of the League for Innovation in the Community College, an educational consortium of leading community colleges in the United States and Canada dedicated to experimentation and innovation.

In his 33 years in community college education, O'Banion has served as dean of students in two Florida community colleges and as a professor of community college education at the University of Illinois in Urbana, where he was selected "Outstanding Teacher" seven years in a row. He has also been the vice chancellor of education for the Dallas County Community College District and a visiting professor at universities across the United States and Canada, including a Distinguished Visiting Professor at the University of Texas at Austin.

He is the author of ten books and more than ninety articles, chapters, and monographs dealing with various aspects of community college education, including the award-winning book, *Teachers for Tomorrow: Staff Development in the Community Junior College.*

The recipient of the 1994 Leadership Award from the American Association of Community Colleges, O'Banion was a member of the Association's blue-ribbon Commission on the Future of Community Colleges. He has been a consultant to more than 500 community colleges and universities in 45 states and Canada. He has received Distinguished Service and Leadership awards from five AACC-affiliated councils and the International Leadership Award from the National Institute for Staff and Organizational Development.

O'Banion holds a B.A. degree (*cum laude*) in English and speech and an M.Ed. in guidance and counseling from the University of Florida. He earned a Ph.D. in higher education administration from Florida State University.